PLAY AND THE
POLITICS OF READING

PLAY AND THE
POLITICS OF READING

THE SOCIAL USES OF MODERNIST FORM

Paul B. Armstrong

CORNELL UNIVERSITY PRESS

ITHACA AND LONDON

First published 2005 by Cornell University Press

Printed in the United States of America

Library of Congress Cataloging-in-Publication Data

Armstrong, Paul B., 1949–
    Play and the politics of reading : the social uses of modernist form / Paul B. Armstrong.
        p. cm.
    Includes bibliographical references and index.
    ISBN 0-8014-4325-3 (cloth : alk. paper)
    1. English fiction—20th century—History and criticism. 2. Literature and society—Great Britain—History—20th century. 3. Books and reading—Great Britain—History—20th century. 4. Literary form—History—20th century. 5. Modernism (Literature)—Great Britain. I. Title.
    PR888.M63A89 2005
    820.9'355—dc22
                                                          2004018217

Cornell University Press strives to use environmentally responsible suppliers and materials to the fullest extent possible in the publishing of its books. Such materials include vegetable-based, low-VOC inks and acid-free papers that are recycled, totally chlorine-free, or partly composed of nonwood fibers. For further information, visit our website at www.cornellpress.cornell.edu.

Cloth printing   10 9 8 7 6 5 4 3 2 1

For Beverly

CONTENTS

PREFACE

Reading is an important but neglected site of the political work done by literature. To some socially minded critics of literature, the idea that reading could be a political activity is no doubt implausible and contradictory. After all, reading might seem to be a solitary experience, private to the individual, and an orientation toward political matters in criticism would seem almost by definition to imply a turning away from a focus on consciousness and subjectivity. These are overly simplistic assumptions, however, that ignore some important social and political work that can only (or best) happen in the activity of reading, which is a social and historical experience through and through. To begin with, reading has a social, political dimension because we make sense of texts by forming hypotheses about meaning that emerge from the assumptions and conventions we bring from our other experiences with literature and life. Those presuppositions, expectations, and habits of understanding are defining aspects of our existence as social beings. Reading is a social experience in which we find our beliefs and conventions engaged and challenged by other ways of seeing, judging, and behaving. Reading consequently has a political dimension inasmuch as politics has to do with the exercise of power and the negotiation of differences. Reading is a paradoxical experience in which we grant a text power over ourselves in various ways by lending it our powers. This is especially evident, for example, in the ways narrators may seek to direct our attention, persuade us to see things in a particular manner, and otherwise manipulate our thinking—something they cannot do without our active involvement and cooperation, but with the result that we subject ourselves to another's intentions and desires and may find ourselves resisting or rejecting a text's explicit directions or implicit maneuvers.

The results of such engagements can be as various as there are texts and readers, but the point is that these aspects of reading are all social and historical experiences. These experiences can shape and change our character as social, political agents. They can have consequences for the habits, assumptions, and aims that we bring to other social engagements in our worlds. They can raise questions about such political matters as our sense of justice and responsibility. They can challenge and change our practices of relating to others, including others with conventions and beliefs different from our own. Indeed, for many people, reading is the social sphere where we are most engaged with perspectives and desires that are alien, foreign, unfamiliar—and it is therefore an experience where learning about the challenges and opportunities of negotiating differences is most likely to occur.

To think about reading in these ways has consequences for how we view the work of literary criticism. It is customary to think that the job of social and political criticism is to explicate the representational content of a text—to ask what it says about social issues or political questions. If reading itself is a site of important social and political activity, then the *how* of that experience is as important as the *what* of a text's mimetic commentary, and maybe more so. Asking questions about how formal textual strategies seek to engage a reader's assumptions and conventions is a specifically literary way to do the work of social, political criticism. This kind of close attention to the pressures and designs of the reading experience is something that we literary critics are (or should be) particularly skilled at. It gives us something special to contribute to the understanding of social and political matters, which is less likely to be provided by sociologists, political scientists, and historians. Even when social scientists are good interpreters, they are typically clumsy in discussing the formal qualities of texts (when they are not blind to them altogether). To ask about the political implications of the activity of reading, with special concern for how the forms of texts engage and challenge a reader's habits and expectations, is to conduct social criticism from a position of genuine professional expertise—and to avoid falling into the trap of writing literary criticism that sounds like naive social science.

This book is an attempt to explicate some of the political implications of the act of reading and to propose a particular approach to reading that I think has important social uses in the contemporary world. Reading can be a paradoxically reciprocal but nonconsensual activity, in the sense that it requires mutual recognition (the text depends on the reader's powers to bring its meanings into existence) but does not have to culminate in agreement (indeed, the disjunctive tension between the worlds of the text and the reader is a typical, important value of the experience of reading). Nonconsensual reciprocity of the sort that reading can model and teach is an important practical and theoretical need in politics today. I return repeatedly in the chapters that follow to the debate between Jürgen Habermas and Jean-François Lyotard about consensus and legitimation in order to suggest an alternative to the notion that interactions that are "rational" or otherwise socially productive and useful must have agreement as their goal. Reading as an exercise in nonconsensual reciprocity can provide a valuable model for a practice of democratic interaction that is not constrained by a conception of community as agreement but that avoids the dangers of violence, irrationality, and anarchy.

Reading in this way is, I argue, a particular kind of play. This argument draws on the description of play by Hans-Georg Gadamer and Wolfgang Iser as a potentially open-ended and to-and-fro activity. Such play differs from that of instrumental games, which aim to establish a winner and a loser and set play in motion only in order to close it off by the establishment of a hierarchy of meaning and value. Reading for nonconsensual reciprocity has more in common with the kind of play that Iser describes as endlessly expansive and resistant to closure. This kind of "free play" (as he calls it) entails an exchange of differences in a back-and-forth doubling of positions that is potentially unpredictable and open-ended, subversive and creative, unsettling and joyful. One political value of such doubling is that it can model a mutually beneficial interaction of differences that does not seek to compel agreement or secure the dominance of one particular side. Doubling of this kind also has the capacity to expose both sides to an ironic recognition of the contingency of their assumptions and aims in a manner akin to Richard Rorty's thinking about "liberal irony." Another of its uses is to allow the performance of different identities and social roles in the sort of emancipatory manner that Edward Said celebrates as being perpetually "out of place." As this book attempts to show, these are among the reasons why the seemingly apolitical activity of play has important political value. In ways that are perhaps surprising, Iser's notion of play offers a response to problems that concern contemporary social thinkers as diverse as Habermas, Rorty, and Said.

To argue theoretically that reading has political significance without demonstrating as much through practical criticism would be incomplete, unsatisfying, and probably unconvincing. The second part of this book shows how the experience of reading does political work, with examples from Henry James to James Joyce, and attempts to illustrate what it might mean to take the *how* of a text's engagement with a reader's assumptions and attitudes as a site of political activity that is just as significant as the *what* of its representational content. Although I could have chosen any texts as illustrations, I have picked a genre (the English novel) and a period (the transition from realism to modernism) that I know well, and I have selected texts that have a considerable range of political concerns. This set of texts recommends itself for historical reasons that are both literary and political. This moment in the history of the novel is especially interesting for the politics of reading because the late realists are beginning to push the conventions of representation in ways that introduce the more radical narrative experiments of modernism (see my *Challenge of Bewilderment*). James, Conrad, Forster, and Joyce are all still committed to the project of mimesis, and their narratives dramatize conflicts and concerns that are demonstrably a continuation of the great tradition of the novel as a medium of social representation. Increasingly from James to Joyce, however, the novel questions the epistemological standing of the conventions of realism in ways that eventually undermine and transform it. With growing daring, complexity, and ambiguity, the narrative strategies of these texts seek simultaneously to represent the world and to question the means through which representation occurs. This doubleness makes for texts in which it is particularly interesting and important to ask how the issues raised by the events dramatized in the narrative (and often strategically left unanswered) are addressed by the formal structures of the narrative.

The political moment of these texts is a turning point in the history of liberalism. Throughout the nineteenth century, British liberalism sought to broaden the franchise and bring reform to democratic institutions by making them more inclusive. The epistemological assumption of this reform, stated most eloquently and influentially by John Stuart Mill in *On Liberty,* was that expanding the community of debate and discourse would, through the free and open conflict of disparate opinions, ultimately create social harmony by fostering conditions in which a consensus about the truth could emerge. This model of truth and community came under serious challenge at the beginning of the twentieth century, as can be seen in the way these texts all worry about models of society that assume that conflicting assumptions, conventions, and desires will ultimately harmonize. Such anxiety is evident, for example, in the irony of the adverb and the ellipses in the epigraph of *Howards End,* Forster's classic text of modern liberalism in crisis: "Only connect . . ."

This challenge to a tradition of liberalism defined by inclusion and aiming for consensus has become even more acute in recent years, with the debates about the social and epistemological implications of multiculturalism. The need for a different model of community, not aiming for consensus or agreement, but based on reciprocity and the exchange of differences, emerges in powerful and pressing ways from James through Joyce, whose narratives explore conflicts that resist resolution and contradictions that refuse to dissolve into synthesis. Repeatedly for these writers, the way out of such impasses is to transform them into challenges for the reader. Studying these transformations is an opportunity, therefore, both to explore how reading can do political work and to think with these texts about the values and implications of nonconsensual reciprocity as a model for democratic community.

Such a conception of reading and community has important educational implications, and the postscript begins to lay those out. How we teach students to read—including our assumptions about how language works, how differences can be negotiated, and how understanding can be reached—has considerable social and pedagogical significance. That is one of the reasons why the culture wars of the eighties became so heated. Those battles are no longer in the headlines, but they are still being fought in the trenches (in board rooms, funding agencies, and department meetings), and the issues at stake matter as much now as ever. Informed by a pluralistic conception of language and literacy, the language arts curriculum can be a powerful instrument for educating students for democracy. Reading as an exercise in experimenting with exchanges based on nonconsensual reciprocity, and learning through such experiences about the challenges and opportunities of negotiating differences, are ways in which a curriculum in literary studies can do valuable social and political work—not by forgetting its primary concerns with language and literature, but by addressing these directly, and not by confusing education with advocacy, but by teaching the habits and skills necessary to make conflicts creative and productive. Thinking about the politics of reading as a playful incitement to negotiate differences in the spirit of nonconsensual reciprocity is connected to the important work of higher education today: making the classroom come alive as a place where students learn to become citizens in the community of communities that a genuine democracy should be.

I am glad to acknowledge the assistance I have received from the friends, colleagues, students, and audiences whose responses to my ideas have helped shape the arguments in this book. I am also grateful to the various institutions that have supported my work. The shortcomings of this project are, of course, no one's responsibility but my own.

The book began during time away from teaching and administration that was provided by the University of Oregon's sabbatical program and by a fellowship from the Oregon Humanities Center. A renewal of a research fellowship from the Alexander von Humboldt Foundation allowed me to return to the University of Constance to try out my ideas at an early stage among colleagues and friends there. An invitation to join the faculty of the Stuttgart Seminar in Cultural Studies provided the occasion to draft the book's opening chapter and gave me the benefit of criticism and suggestions from my students at the seminar, many of whom came from the new democracies of

Eastern Europe and whose perspectives on the workings of power and the possibilities of noncoercive exchange were especially revealing. I am thankful to Dr. Heide Ziegler for creating this opportunity for engaged collaborative exploration.

I am similarly grateful to the audiences in the Republic of South Africa with whom I was able to discuss the contribution that literary theory and humanistic inquiry might make to shaping a multicultural democracy—exchanges that had a practical urgency that was both compelling and illuminating. I am indebted to my hosts in Soweto, Potchefstroom, Zululand, and Pretoria and at UNISA, Rhodes, and Witswatersrand, but most of all to my friend and fellow Conradian Attie de Lange, who organized my visit.

A fellowship from the Royal Danish Academy allowed me to spend a productive, enlightening, and thoroughly enjoyable semester among the comparative literature faculty at the University of Copenhagen. Courses I offered there on the politics of interpretation, multiculturalism, and the theory of narrative provided an important testing ground for the ideas in this book. My thanks to Fredrik Tygstrup and Peter Madsen for arranging this visit and for making possible many lively conversations and productive disagreements.

Each of my books has grown out of my teaching, and this project is no exception. I am grateful to my graduate students at the University of Oregon for thinking with me about these issues in seminars on the politics of modernism and the theory of narrative. I owe a special debt to Margaret Johnson, Kasia Marciniak, and Amy Novak for forcing me out of the dean's office and into a seminar that they actually ran, where I learned as much as any other student.

Early drafts of various chapters appeared in *The Kenyon Review, New Literary History, Modern Language Quarterly, The Henry James Review, Conradiana, Modern Fiction Studies, Twentieth-Century Literature, Profession, The ADE Bulletin*, and *Liberal Education*. All have been rewritten for this book. I am grateful to the editors for permission to use this work and for their criticisms, advice, and suggestions.

The two readers to whom Cornell sent the manuscript offered suggestions for revisions that greatly improved the book. I am grateful to John Paul Riquelme and James Buzard for their candid criticisms and astute advice. I am also indebted to Bernie Kendler for his interest in and support for this project.

I have benefited for many years from the generous counsel and rigorous, probing, yet always playful conversation of my friend and mentor Wolfgang Iser. Others who have provided much-appreciated encouragement, criticism, and assistance over the years include Evelyne Keitel, Winfried Fluck, Patrick O'Donnell, Stephen Mailloux, John Carlos Rowe, Marshall Brown, E. Ann Kaplan, Keith Carabine, Jeremy Hawthorn, Molly Westling, George Wickes, Ed Casey, and the late Michael Sprinker.

My friends in the dean's office at Stony Brook—especially Gene Katz, Mary Rawlinson, and Nancy Tomes—contributed indirectly but importantly to this project by reminding me that university administrators lose their ability to exercise intellectual leadership if they cease to do intellectual work. My colleagues in the deanery at Brown have enlivened my sense of the theoretical, social, and ethical implications of curricular and pedagogical issues, and I am grateful to them for their example of how to bring theory and practice into mutually illuminating dialogue.

What I owe to my children Tim, Maggie, and Jack is harder to describe but no less real and genuine. I have learned much from each of them, although not always things that appear in this book. To Beverly, my favorite interlocutor and much else, I am grateful for more than I can say here, not least for reminding me that in a relation of true reciprocity no one ever has the last word (I hear her now wanting to interject, "But . . . !").

P. B. A.

Providence, Rhode Island

PART ONE

THEORY

1. THE POLITICS OF READING

Nonconsensual Reciprocity and the Negotiation of Differences

In our irreducibly multifarious world, we need to create forms of community that allow us to negotiate our differences without assuming a prior common ground or an ultimately attainable consensus. A particular conception of the reading process might help, I think, to address that need. In order to have mutually beneficial relations between incompatible cultural conventions and incommensurable beliefs, we need conditions and practices conducive to what Habermas calls "communicative rationality," where no force operates other than "the unforced force of the better argument" (*Modernity* 107). But this needs to be a genuinely heterogeneous rationality that does not assume, as Habermas does, that communication will or should result in agreement.[1] A nonconsensual form of communicative rationality would have at least two requirements that reading can help to stage, model, and habituate: (1) reciprocal, nonreified acknowledgment of the meaning-creating capacities of others who have perhaps radically different assumptions, experiences, desires, and interests; and (2) ironic recognition of the contingency and contestability of the conventions and beliefs on the basis of which one must nevertheless act, despite their unjustifiability.

I want to explore the first point by inserting a pioneering political theorist of reading, Jean-Paul Sartre, into the debate between Habermas and Lyotard

---

[1] On the notion of "communicative rationality," see also Habermas, *Communicative Action* esp. 10–42.

over the politics of legitimation.[2] I will then develop the second point by analyzing the implications for a politics of reading of the arguments of some important neoliberal thinkers (especially Richard Rorty but also Judith Shklar). What I hope will emerge is a view of reading as a paradoxical, democratic practice—a form of life that might make possible the reciprocally enhancing interaction of incompatible forms of life.

Reading and Nonconsensual Reciprocity

In the pivotal chapter "Why Write?" of his deservedly classic text *What Is Literature?* Sartre attempts to derive a political imperative from a description of the reading process through a bold if finally flawed argument, which is illuminating, I think, precisely because of the difficulties that undermine it. His memorable, controversial conclusion—that it is not "possible to write a good novel in praise of anti-Semitism" (58)—is less interesting than the reasoning through which he reaches it. His crucial claim is both political and epistemological: "the writer appeals to the reader's freedom to collaborate in the production of his work" (40). According to Sartre, the literary object is like a top, the child's toy, though a peculiar one because it exists only while spinning (see 34). Not reducible to the words on the page, the work comes into being only through the reader's active participation, which is "free" in at least two senses: It depends on choices and decisions that cannot be entirely determined in advance, and it consequently involves acts of transcendence, "a continual exceeding of the written thing" as the reader fills in gaps and makes connections that are not always prescribed (39). Because reading requires freedom for the very production of meaning, Sartre concludes that writers subvert the epistemological conditions necessary for their works to exist if they deny freedom either in their style (by seeking to overwhelm or coerce the reader) or in their themes: "It would be inconceivable that . . . the reader could enjoy his freedom while reading a work which approves or accepts or simply abstains from condemning the subjection of man by man" (57). Sartre concludes: "the writer, a free man addressing free men, has only one subject—freedom" (58).[3] In his view, the political essence of art follows from the essence of the reading process.

---

[2] On the debate between Habermas and Lyotard, see Wellmer esp. 105–9; Jay; Jameson, "Foreword"; Rorty, "Habermas and Lyotard"; McGowan 180–210; and Poster. My concern is less with the details of their debate, however, than with the issues it raises for the theory of reading.

[3] On Sartre's literary theory, see Goldthorpe 159–84; Hollier 83–103; and Howells 116–44.

One of the first things one wants to do now, more than fifty years after Sartre wrote, is to quietly revise his sexist word choice. This is not simply a change in what constitutes good manners, however. The question of who is left out by patriarchal language suggests that one man's appeal to freedom might be another person's (perhaps woman's) subjection. "Freedom" is not an absolute, then, but is a socially contestable value, and not all visions of freedom are mutually compatible. Sartre assumes that every appeal to freedom will be consistent with all others, but different communities may project antagonistic, incommensurable ideals of emancipation. The conflict of interpretations is in part a contest about what emancipation might look like (or whether it is possible at all). Sartre is blinded by what Lyotard calls the "grand narrative of emancipation," which tells the story of human history as a synthetic, teleological realization of liberty (see *Postmodern Condition* 31–37). A more radical conception of freedom would recognize itself in the diversity of language games and in their ongoing transformation and contestation through the invention of new moves—the heterogeneity that leads Lyotard to claim that "consensus is a horizon that is never reached" (61). The multiplicity of ways of reading is itself a sign of freedom, but the consequent contingency of "freedom" as a value makes reading and writing for freedom a contestable practice that will vary according to one's beliefs about human being and social life.

This flaw in Sartre's argument suggests that one cannot derive norms from experience through an impartial description, because how experience is interpreted depends on the norms one brings to bear on it. This circle also vitiates Habermas's attempt to define "communicative rationality" by appealing to "the suppositions of rationality inherent in ordinary communicative practice," standards implicit in "the normative content of action oriented to mutual understanding" (*Modernity* 76). Language, communication, and meaning are essentially contested categories, however, which are susceptible to widely diverging conceptions of what constitutes good practice. Habermas's twin assumptions that "participants . . . can act communicatively only under the presupposition of intersubjectively identical ascriptions of meaning" and that "reaching understanding is the inherent telos of human speech" are neither neutral nor self-evident (*Modernity* 198; *Communicative Action* 287). From Wittgenstein to Lyotard and Derrida, it is possible to see much more productive value in difference and disagreement, both in the means and the ends of linguistic exchange, than Habermas does. But this circle does not prevent one from arguing for a particular conception of communication—or of reading— and then trying to justify it as a value worth holding for various reasons, including its consequences for how it might shape our experience. Conceiving of reading as a heterogeneous, variable activity can make it desirable to argue for certain norms that the more monistic Sartre and Habermas also advocate (although they disguise their advocacy by claiming that their values are not contingent but inherent in the structure of communication).

One such norm is reciprocity. Because of the recognition a writer must extend to the reader's capacity for creating meaning, Sartre calls reading "an exercise in generosity": "each one trusts the other; each one counts on the other, demands of the other as much as he demands of himself" (*Literature* 45, 49). This description of writing and reading as acts of mutual recognition resonates with Habermas's sense of reasoned exchange as a nonobjectifying, noncoercive practice based on the assumption of equality. These visions of reciprocity are worth analyzing further precisely because the proper structure of reading and communication is less self-evidently derivable from experience than either Sartre or Habermas assumes.

Sartre's description of reading as a process of reciprocal recognition portrays an ideally noncoercive relation, but it also raises important questions about the role of power and constraint in the creation of meaning and in communicative interaction. Sartre describes reading as "a dialectical going-and-coming," an open-ended to-and-fro: "When I read, I make demands; if my demands are met, what I am then reading provokes me to demand more of the author, which means to demand of the author that he demand more of me. And, vice versa, the author's demand is that I carry my demands to the highest pitch. Thus, my freedom, by revealing itself, reveals the freedom of the other" (*Literature* 50).

This mutual disclosure of one another's meaning-creating powers suggests a sort of reciprocally enhancing meeting of subjectivities that runs counter to Sartre's analysis of the "look of the Other" in *Being and Nothingness*, where he argues that someone else's gaze threatens to objectify and take power over me because my self-for-myself is unrecognizable beneath my self-for-others (see 340–400). The rare gift of reading would thus seem to be its staging of a reciprocal exchange between subjectivities at the level of their being-for-themselves, which suspends the mutual objectification of gazes locked in a battle for power. The question would then be whether the kind of noncoercive, nonobjectifying interaction modeled in reading could be extended to other spheres of existence, including everyday communicative interaction.

Power is also at work in reading, however, as Sartre acknowledges in *Saint Genet*. There he describes how Genet fights back against others' objectifications of him by "set[ting] fascinating traps for other freedoms" through the rhetorical games he plays with the reader, who, in the experience of being manipulated, teased, enticed, and frustrated by the text, "recognizes Genet's freedom and knows that he is not recognized by Genet" (555, 552). This is a particular instance of the general problem of whether what Richard Poirier calls "the performing self" of the author in the text also facilitates the reader's powers or, vampirelike, seeks ascendancy at the reader's expense. The text's quest for power can also take less self-serving but no less problematic forms. For example, as Wayne Booth argues, "all narratives are 'didactic' " because "all works *do* teach or at least try to"—attempting to mold the reader's character or influence his or her beliefs (151–52).[4] The pedagogical and rhetorical ambitions of a text harbor a will to power in their very desire to change the recipient. Whether the text's intentions are benevolent or not, the reciprocity of reading would seem to stand in necessary conflict with the deployment of rhetorical power. Sartre recognizes this dilemma by describing reading as an exchange of "demands"—with the author's will to power parried and countered by the reader's reciprocal assertion of the right to set the terms of the encounter. Power is thereby not suspended in reading but made mutual in an endless to-and-fro of claims on the other, a dance in which both partners take turns leading.

The metaphor of the dance suggests a general paradox of power as it pertains to reading. As Foucault argues, power can be both repressive and productive (and is often both at once): "it doesn't only weigh on us as a force that says no, but . . . it traverses and produces things, it induces pleasure, forms knowledge, produces discourse" (119). If reading entails at least a partial submission to the rules of the games played by the text, these restrictions and constraints do not merely dominate and limit but also make possible the production of meaning. Or at least that is the reader's wager in accepting a text's offer to play. The reader, however, faces the dilemma posed by any discursive regime. How can one decide whether particular rules for "truth" are coercive or enabling, restrictive or constructive, objectifying or enhancing? Further, when one is in the middle of playing the game (or being played by it), does one even have the power to pose this question? These are issues that cannot be resolved absolutely or in the abstract, apart from a specific examination of concrete practices (and sometimes they cannot be raised at all).

The problem, as Habermas puts it, is how "to discriminate between a power that *deserves* to be esteemed and one that *deserves* to be devalued" (*Modernity* 125; original emphasis). This is a problem only because of the inherent duality of discursive rules as both coercive and creative, restrictive and productive. Such rules threaten the subject's meaning-making capacities but also make them possible. The very difficulty of deciding Habermas's question, however, gives value to reading as an arena in which this paradox of power can

---

[4] On the paradox of how a text might exert a kind of power that is emancipatory rather than coercive, see Chambers esp. 14–18.

be staged, played with, and explored. An advantage of reading is not only that readers can withdraw assent from textual regimes more easily than they often can in daily life, but also that the modeling capacities of reading allow them to examine and criticize dualities of repression and production that everyday communicative practices leave unquestioned.

One useful criterion for making the discrimination Habermas calls for is mutual recognition. Genet, whose games seem to subvert recognition, would therefore deserve the reader's suspicion and run the risk of the withdrawal of assent, even if his own experience of refused mutuality had set his rhetorical games in motion in the first place. Mutual recognition matters because reciprocity is not outside the realm of power. Lyotard suggests as much when he claims that "to speak is to fight, in the sense of playing"—a claim he qualifies in an important way: "This does not necessarily mean that one plays in order to win. A move can be made for the sheer pleasure of its invention" (*Postmodern Condition* 10). Wolfgang Iser distinguishes similarly between play "as achieving victory (establishing meaning) or as maintaining freeplay (keeping meaning open-ended)." The former kind of play mobilizes the rhetorical power that seeks to influence or change the reader. But power is also involved in play as the perpetual motion of differences—what Iser calls the "ever-decentering movement," the continual "oscillation, or to-and-fro movement, [which] is basic to play" (*Prospecting* 252, 255). According to Iser, this kind of play typically establishes boundaries in order to transgress them, setting up new oppositions that make possible new moves and that invite new border crossings, creating new worlds to be toppled and overturned so that yet other worlds can be constructed (see *Fictive* 69–86). The sort of decentering freeplay that seems more reciprocal and open-ended than attempts to achieve victory is itself an unsettled and unsettling process that can disrupt the relation between the players.

The creativity of transgression illustrates Nietzsche's contention that the construction of form requires both negation and affirmation—or, in his striking phrase: "If a temple is to be erected, a temple must be destroyed" (95). Destruction, assault, and violence seem inherent in the crossing of boundaries and the upsetting of existing structures that make possible new combinations of difference, new modes of play. Lyotard usefully distinguishes between "two different kinds of 'progress' in knowledge: one corresponds to a new move (a new argument) within the established rules; the other, to the invention of new rules, in other words, a change to a new game." This latter kind of innovation is necessarily disruptive, he argues: "The stronger the 'move,' the more likely it is to be denied the minimum consensus, precisely because it changes the rules of the game upon which consensus had been based" (*Postmodern Condition* 43, 63).

Lyotard criticizes Habermas's notion of "communicative rationality" not only because "consensus does violence to the heterogeneity of language games" but also because "invention is always born of dissension" (*Postmodern Condition* xxv; see also "Notes on Legitimation"). Lyotard's recognition of the violence and will to power of innovation, however, leads him to return to the question of "justice" after he has rejected the value of agreement. How, he asks, can we "arrive at an idea and practice of justice that is not linked to that of consensus"? Interestingly, despite his critique of communal assent as a repressive, monistic norm, his two requirements for "justice" both reinstate the principle of reciprocity: first, "a renunciation of terror," defined as "eliminating, or threatening to eliminate, a player from the language game one shares with him," and second, the stipulation that "any consensus on the rules defining a game and the 'moves' playable within it must be local, in other words, agreed on by its present players and subject to eventual cancellation" (*Postmodern Condition* 66, 63). Lyotard's very critique of consensus thus leads him to reaffirm the importance of reciprocity because mutual recognition is necessary to make possible the innovative, transgressive sorts of play he values.

Reciprocal acknowledgment and ever-renewed negotiation between the players are required to keep the space of play intact and to preserve the possibility of productive interaction between heterogeneous ways of playing. But the to-and-fro of reciprocity is not the same as agreement. As a norm for the heterogeneous, socially useful creation of meaning, nonconsensual reciprocity—mutuality without the assumption of prior or ultimate agreement—makes possible the ongoing generation and communication of differences, whether by obeying or transgressing the rules.

One value of reading is that it can be practiced in such a way as to stage this kind of interaction. This is a political value, I would argue, because the social bond staged in nonconsensual, nonobjectifying, mutually transformative exchanges with texts could model behaviors that would be useful in other social interactions. The sort of reading I have in mind would differ from either a conservative reverence of canonical authority or a radical unmasking of textual false consciousness. Reading guided by the norm of nonconsensual reciprocity would not assume that the outcome should be agreement with the values of the canonical text (nor would it assume that the values of worthwhile texts should be mutually compatible). Rather, an assumption of parity between the worlds of text and reader would mean that the authority of the conventions governing both are at play and at risk. Reading would thereby entail the ongoing staging of Habermas's question about which rules for the creation of meaning deserve credence without deciding in advance in favor of either the text or the reader—or without ever deciding once and for all, inasmuch as nonconsensual reciprocity grants all parties the ongoing authority to propose new rules and challenge existing ones. This kind of reading would thus enact Sartre's call for a "constant renewal of frameworks, and the continuous over-throwing of order once it tends to congeal" (*Literature* 153).

The perpetual questioning of authority implied by reading as a practice of nonconsensual reciprocity is not the same, however, as the hermeneutics of suspicion. Unmasking a text's deceptions can be an assertion of power that de-nies mutuality by refusing to hear the claim it would make on us. Similarly, lo-cating a work's primary worldly entanglements in its originating context can be a way of refusing to recognize its attempt to speak across historical or cul-tural distance, thereby preventing our different worlds from engaging one another. Nevertheless, the need to grant the work a hearing does not mean that one must assent to its claims or even, finally, take them at face value. As the example of Genet once again suggests, unmasking a text's strategies for asserting power over the reader can be a means of maintaining or creating rec-iprocity, especially (but not only) when it refuses us the recognition it de-mands. In reading, as in other social relations, it is not always clear when to believe or suspect one's interlocutor, if only because believing and doubting provide their own proofs. It is sometimes possible, however, to recognize what Gadamer calls a *Spielverderber* (or spoilsport), whose actions thwart rather than facilitate the playing of the game (92). Unmasking strategies that disad-vantage or marginalize other players, that exploit their good faith or restrict their capacities, would be a move not only authorized but indeed required by nonconsensual reciprocity. The ideal of nonconsensual reciprocity can there-fore provide a standard of justice against which to measure a text's—or any in-terlocutor's or fellow citizen's—claims, even if it cannot always tell us how to evaluate them.

Reading and the Negotiation of Differences

Nonconsensual reciprocity is not an end in itself but a means to facilitating the mutually beneficial exchange of differences. Creating and maintaining spaces in which different forms of life with incompatible values and beliefs can pro-ductively interact is a nontrivial challenge across a variety of social settings—from the classroom and academic department, where ideological battles are sometimes fought with alarming ferocity, to the national arena (not only in the United States), where ethnic and other kinds of diversity all too often lead to reciprocal demonization, and to the international scene, where in our fluid, post–Cold War, postcolonial situation the collapse of previously stabilizing oppositions has resulted in a proliferation of conflicts. Reading cannot, of course, solve all these problems. But a particular practice of reading could be

socially useful in the current climate by promoting the paradoxical and therefore precarious behaviors required for the ongoing negotiation of differences—a negotiation that is not only civil and nonviolent but mutually
worthwhile and potentially transformative.

A threat to the productive exchange of differences, as René Girard has observed, is the tendency of any epistemological community to demonize and
scapegoat the Other in a defensive refusal to acknowledge the contingency of
its own values and beliefs. This tendency is exacerbated by the mutually reinforcing dangers of habitualization and homogeneity. Habitualization is dangerous because assumptions acted on again and again become naturalized, and
homogeneity similarly promotes naturalization because unquestionably shared
values, conventions, and attitudes lose their sense of contingency. A practice
of reading as a nonconsensual engagement with differences can counteract
these kinds of normalization. The practice I have in mind would stress three
dimensions of the reading process: (1) how reading can stage the paradox,
constitutive of democracy, that there can be many forms of life with equal dignity and worth; (2) how reading can facilitate the imagination of change by
suggesting that the world could be otherwise; and (3) how reading can thereby
encourage the recognition of the contingency of the very beliefs one sets in
motion to make the text cohere.

What I am suggesting about reading does not have to happen. Reading does
not automatically make better citizens through its essential epistemological
processes (if it did, literature departments at colleges and universities would
be less politically self-destructive than they often are). Some interpretive
methods facilitate more than others do the playful openness to multiplicity
and the cultivation of contingency. But these attitudes are themselves compatible with a variety of hermeneutic strategies, not just one particular set of
presuppositions and procedures. They are democratically open to heterogeneity because they can be enacted in varying ways by readers with different assumptions, values, and conventions.

The reading practice I am proposing would stage the posture that Richard
Rorty calls "liberal irony" but would confront more fully and directly some
crucial difficulties that he tries to minimize or evade. According to Rorty, a liberal ironist "faces up to the contingency of his or her own most central beliefs
and desires." Liberal irony recognizes that "the idea that the world decides
which descriptions are true can no longer be given a clear sense," that a variety of not necessarily mutually compatible vocabularies or interpretive frameworks can therefore perform effectively, and that the most we can ever have is
"a circular justification of our practices, a justification which makes one
feature of our culture look good by citing still another." Liberal ironists therefore combine "commitment with a sense of the contingency of their own

commitment"—recognizing the lack of necessity of "their language of moral deliberation, and thus of their consciences, and thus of their community," but nevertheless "remain[ing] faithful to those consciences" (*Contingency* xv, 5, 57, 61, 46). The liberal ironist's combination of contingency and commitment is a contradictory practice that is easier to describe than to follow. Acting on one's beliefs tends to undercut professions of their contingency by habitualizing and naturalizing them. But keeping their lack of justification continually in view may inhibit action and engagement. The defining contradiction of liberal irony makes it precarious, susceptible to falling into either paralyzed skepticism or smug complacency if the tension lapses between doubting one's beliefs and nevertheless believing them.[5]

Reading can help to stage and model the paradoxical task of combining contingency and commitment because of the contradictory status of our beliefs when we read. In order to make the parts of a text cohere, we need to project hypotheses about the configurations they form, guesses that we generate from our more enduring, deeply held presuppositions about literature, language, and life.[6] The paradox of reading is that, by invoking our own beliefs in this way, we make another world take shape that may be based on assumptions and interests very different from and perhaps even antagonistic to the ones we hold. The very act of deploying our own beliefs and values may create a world that demonstrates their relativity and challenges their ascendancy. Again, this does not have to happen; it is very easy for the hermeneutic circle to remain closed, with our presuppositions confirming themselves by finding only what they seek. But if we read for nonconsensual reciprocity, directed by an ideal of dialogue as mutual recognition without the necessity of agreement, then the hypotheses about a work's configurations that we project can allow otherness to speak through beliefs it may question, at the very least by demonstrating their contingency. Reading would then entail precisely the characteristic paradox of "liberal irony," in that we concretize the different assumptions, values, and interests that make up the text's world by acting on conventions and commitments whose relativity the process of reading at the same time reveals. This contradiction of reading can make it an unsettling practice that can lead to the overturning of our beliefs or to their transformation as the possibility of new combinations of attitudes is disclosed.

Although Rorty values the invention of new modes of self-creation (he calls the poet "the vanguard of the species"), he tries to minimize the disruption caused when beliefs or vocabularies clash by "making a firm distinction

[5] On this dilemma, see West.

[6] See my *Conflicting Readings*, esp. 1–19, for a further explanation of the relation between these two levels of belief in understanding.

between the private and the public" (*Contingency* 20, 83). I want to examine
this problematic proposal in some detail because exposing the fallacies of the
"public-private" split as it pertains to reading and writing will allow me to explain how my model of reading offers a better solution to the problem of rival
conceptions of existence.[7] My conception of reading as an exercise in "liberal
irony" attempts to address the opposition of rival worlds, not as Rorty does by
trying to neutralize and contain it, but by transforming it into an opportunity
for socially useful interactions.

   Rorty is worried, and justifiably so, about the will to power of competing
vocabularies or visions of self-creation—about their desire to drive out rivals,
establish their ascendancy, and thus deny their contingency. "We should stop
trying to combine self-creation and politics," he advises; we should "equalize
opportunities for self-creation and then leave people alone to use, or neglect,
their opportunities" and "to work out their private salvations, create their private self-images, reweave their webs of belief and desire in the light of whatever new people and books they happen to encounter" (*Contingency* 120, 85).
A closer look at the reading process suggests, however, that the "private" and
the "public" are necessarily entangled and cannot be kept separate. The contradictions in Rorty's own account of reading confirm this. To begin with, to
"encounter new people and books" is obviously a social rather than purely private experience, even if it takes place in the mind of an individual reader. The
play of opposing beliefs that reading can set in motion is potentially transformative only because it is an intersubjective meeting of different presuppositions and values and not merely a purely personal, solipsistic communion
with oneself.

   Rorty's observations about reading and writing repeatedly call into question his separation of "public" and "private." For example, Rorty claims that
Proust "had no public ambitions"—"he managed to debunk authority without setting himself up as authority, to debunk the ambitions of the powerful
without sharing them" (*Contingency* 118, 103). But Proust can succeed as a
writer only by inculcating new ways of seeing in the reader, new attitudes toward "authority" that require changes in our beliefs that will themselves become authoritative if they win acceptance and become conventional, the kind
of attitude we recognize as "Proustian." Rorty acknowledges Proust's authority when he notes that, because of the adoption of *Remembrance of Things Past*
into the canon, "anyone who wants to write a bildungsroman has to come to
terms with Proust." Rorty also recognizes that "you cannot create a memorable character without thereby making a suggestion about how your reader

---

[7] Among the many critiques that Rorty's "public-private" split has deservedly received, see
Fraser; Bhaskar esp. 81–96.

should act" (136–37, 167). This is true, however, because the "private" experience of reading makes more of a "public" claim to mold our beliefs and values than he admits when he asserts that "novels are a safer medium than theory for expressing one's recognition of the relativity and contingency of authority figures" (107). Only a theorist could think this (ask Salman Rushdie or any of the many other writers whose fictions have seemed dangerous to the authorities).

These dilemmas arise because the beliefs about language, literature, and life that we encounter in texts seek to win assent and to displace the presuppositions and values of the reader. The rhetorical quest of texts to win over the reader's beliefs is a social, historical process. Reading may be a private act in some senses, but it is also a meeting of beliefs and values in the public space where conventions and attitudes compete for allegiance.

A more satisfactory response to this conflict is Rorty's argument that we should "call 'true' (or 'right' or 'just') whatever the outcome of undistorted communication happens to be, whatever view wins in a free and open encounter" (*Contingency* 67). But again the reading process suggests some necessary revisions in this formulation, first of all (as Rorty would I think agree) that perhaps no single view will prevail. In order to make sure that "persuasion" rather than "force" decides such encounters, Rorty places a premium on freedom: "If we take care of political freedom, truth and goodness will take care of themselves" (84).[8] As Lyotard's worries about "terror" suggest, however, freedom must be supplemented by mutual recognition to make such encounters "just." We cannot assume that rhetoric alone will create justice because persuasion entails a will to power, whether motivated by a Bloomian drive for ascendancy, the resentment of a Genet, or less complicated desires for dominance. "Undistorted communication" demands that we interrogate persuasion for violations of reciprocity. This dilemma is especially evident in the reading process, where the efforts of rhetorical power to move or shape the reader always threaten to disrupt the parity required for the to-and-fro exchange of mutual demands. The doubling of worlds that reading seeks to establish and maintain is a precarious achievement that requires vigilance as well as vulnerability from the reader.

If, however, nonconsensual reciprocity can make reading a playful exchange between the reader's beliefs and the text's, then this doubling may facilitate the "free and open encounter" Rorty calls for—perhaps, indeed, in a manner not so likely to occur in other areas of society where the power of shared, habitual frameworks may be less visible and thus more intractable.

---

[8] On this issue, see McCarthy, "Private Irony"; Rorty's response, "Truth and Freedom," and McCarthy's answer, "Ironist Theory." See also Rorty, "Priority."

One political value of reading is that its ability to reveal the contingency of the reader's customary commitments and conventions may open up possibilities of criticism and choice not available in everyday life under the normalizing pressure of prevailing epistemological regimes. Precisely because no standpoint outside of rival vocabularies is available for judging them, the conflict of beliefs that reading may set in motion can expose differences and distinctions that would not be evident within a single framework. The doubling of perhaps incompatible worlds in reading can disclose their comparative advantages and disadvantages not in relation to some neutral ground but diacritically, by delineating what they are not.

By staging the interaction of incommensurable conceptions of existence, the reading practice I am advocating implies something like what Ronald Dworkin calls the right to "equal concern and respect" necessary for democratic governance: "Government must treat those whom it governs with concern, that is, as human beings who are capable of suffering and frustration, and with respect, that is, as human beings who are capable of forming and acting on intelligent conceptions of how their lives should be lived" (272–73).[9] A call for equal concern and respect similarly informs Rorty's stipulation that liberal ironists "include among [their] ungroundable desires their own hope that suffering will be diminished, that the humiliation of human beings by other human beings may cease." Rorty's liberal ironist thinks "cruelty is the worst thing we do" (*Contingency* xv), and the cruelty of humiliation is particularly repugnant because it denies others their power of self-creation. "Humiliation" is not a stable value, however, because what counts as a worthwhile conception of existence is subject to dispute. The meaning of a worthy life— and thus of what might be considered shameful or wounding—is not a given but a variable susceptible to cultural contestation.

---

[9] Dworkin is unfortunately self-contradictory on the issue of whether this definition of democracy implies that consensus can be found to resolve disagreements about belief and value. He says, "There are hard cases, both in politics and at law, in which reasonable lawyers will disagree about rights, and neither will have available any argument that must necessarily convince the other" (xiv). But at the end of *Taking Rights Seriously* he contradicts his earlier pluralism about "hard cases" and claims they have one right solution (see 290). It may be, as he argues, a pragmatic necessity of the justice system that such cases must be resolved: "It remains the judge's duty, even in hard cases, to discover what the rights of the parties are, not to invent new rights retrospectively" (81). But Dworkin then adds: "Reasonable lawyers and judges will often disagree about legal rights, just as citizens and statesmen disagree about political rights" (81). Granted that sometimes (as in a court of law) conflicts must be settled by declaring a winner and a loser, leaving space for those differences to be negotiated without presupposing a unitary outcome when it is practical and possible to do so would seem an obligation entailed by Dworkin's insistence on the ultimate right to "equal concern and respect."

Judith Shklar consequently distinguishes between "injustice," a socially remediable wrong, and "misfortune," an accident or debility for which no one is responsible: "the line of separation between injustice and misfortune is a political choice" that can be questioned and revised, and "yesterday's rock solid rule is today's folly and bigotry." A society may wish to alleviate the suffering of misfortune, but it has a stronger obligation to redress the grievances of injustice. As Shklar points out, however, "it will always be easier to see misfortune rather than injustice in the afflictions of other people. Only the victims occasionally do not share the inclination to do so." But in a democracy "their sense of their rights . . . deserves a hearing," she argues, because to do otherwise would be to deny them the "minimum of human dignity" (*Injustice* 5, 8, 15, 35, 86).[10] In a democratic society the shape of justice is therefore constantly open to change because it is a differential product ever subject to contestation and redescription. The line between "misfortune" and "injustice" gets drawn and redrawn through protests in which aggrieved citizens present and dispute their opposing senses of what they are due. This process is necessarily conflictual and differential because, as Lyotard points out, "it is in the nature of a wrong not to be established by consensus" (*Differend* 56).

Rorty hopes that "cruelty" and "humiliation" can be defined less problematically. He calls on us "to separate the question 'Do you believe and desire what we believe and desire?' from the question 'Are you suffering?' " (*Contingency* 198). These cannot always be so cleanly separated, however. Some kinds of suffering seem easier to recognize than others regardless of the vocabulary employed (the anguish of a dying cancer victim, for example, as opposed to the suffering caused by sexual harassment, racial discrimination, homophobia, or religious bigotry). This greater visibility may simply reflect the greater agreement within the society about the applicable epistemological and moral categories. More is at stake here, however, than the notorious and perhaps undecidable question of whether another's pain can be recognized outside of a vocabulary. Shklar's distinction between "misfortune" and "injustice" shows that significant areas of dispute with practical consequences may still remain even if, following Rorty, each party recognizes the other's suffering. A victim of homophobia, for example, has weighty, nontrivial reasons for preferring to be recognized as a victim of social injustice instead of having

---

[10] Rorty borrows his injunction against cruelty from Shklar's earlier book, *Ordinary Vices* 7–44. He misrepresents her position, however, inasmuch as she argues that for "liberal and humane people" to "choose cruelty as the worst thing we do" is not to resolve or bypass the dilemmas of moral relativism but to encounter all sorts of "paradoxes and puzzles" about what to count as cruel and how to rank different evils (44). He also ignores her clear declaration that "it is not possible to think of vices as simply either private or public" (243).

his or her sexual orientation stigmatized as a misfortune. The status of some kinds of suffering can be controversial because it has yet to be settled through political negotiation between parties who hold different views about the wrongs that can humiliate or injure, views that go back to their different conceptions of what constitutes a worthy life. In such disputes, what the different parties "believe and desire" is integral to their sense of what is cruel and humiliating, and such conflicts are consequential rather than merely metaphysical because decisions about how to define injustice establish norms for individual and social behavior.

Conceiving of reading as a nonconsensual interaction between different worlds can make it an arena for playing out the question of injustice. For this to occur, construing texts needs to be seen as a double nonconsensual to-and-fro in which the values and beliefs of both players are at stake. By juxtaposing conventional norms with views that contest their inevitability, this doubling of worlds can challenge the naturalization of the prevailing notions of injustice and humiliation. By bringing opposing conceptions of existence into a dialogue that reveals and questions the defining limits of each, reading can enact the renegotiation of what counts as a correctable social wrong. By demonstrating the contingency of the beliefs the reader sets in motion and suggesting alternative assumptions, desires, and interests, the process of reading can stage an exchange of differences that may have the power to reconfigure social values.

This dialogue does not have to happen, however, either in reading or in other areas of social life, because the voice protesting injustice is very easy to squelch or ignore.[11] The reading practice I am advocating would try to keep alive the potentially transformative, often unsettling conversation through which the meaning of injustice can change. Reading in this way would keep in mind the lack of necessity of the conventions and commitments it puts in play

[11] Hence the legitimacy of Terry Eagleton's concern about Gadamer's description of tradition as "the conversation that we are": "It cannot . . . come to terms with the problem of ideology—with the fact that the unending 'dialogue' of human history is as often as not a monologue by the powerful to the powerless, or that if it is indeed a 'dialogue' then the partners—men and women, for example—hardly occupy equal positions" (*Theory* 73). Although my model of nonconsensual reciprocity derives in part from Gadamer's notion of "play" as a to-and-fro between interlocutors (see Gadamer 103), the conflictual dialogue about "injustice" I am describing is more open, wary, and self-critical than the deference to the authority of tradition that Eagleton criticizes. Nonconsensual reciprocity is not blind to the conflict between mutually exclusive ideologies with different degrees of power; this is, rather, one of the problems such a dialogue is meant to address by questioning the claims of opposing ideologies to ascendancy and attempting to transform their competition into mutually beneficial play. A level playing field cannot always be achieved by epistemological or hermeneutic means alone, but mutual recognition is nevertheless useful as a vehicle for making dialogue possible.

for the very reason that the conversation about injustice is precarious, ever in danger of being shut down by the self-protective force of prevailing norms or by the will to power of rival voices.

Readers who themselves have a sense of injustice may reply that they cannot afford to bracket their convictions because that may disadvantage them in their arguments against oppression. The necessary contradiction of such a position is that these readers require injustice to be a variable, so that its meaning can be changed, even as they need to act as if their own values were absolutes—self-evident rights whose violation is an intolerable outrage. If, however, they win their argument (perhaps by invoking the values of mutual recognition and equal concern that also inform my conception of reading), they must then relinquish their absolutism or else they will lapse into the same exclusionary essentialism against which they protested. My politics of reading should be their ultimate goal and their implicit norm, even if they must temporarily, for strategic reasons, act as if their beliefs and values were not contingent. Otherwise their refusal to compromise would be indistinguishable from a terroristic attempt to stop the play of reading by securing the permanent dominance of one particular conception of existence, and the correction of the injustice they seek would itself result in injustice. This is, of course, one of the reasons why liberation movements sometimes become tyrannical when they win.

Every kind of reading differs according to its practical aims, and my goal of creating a space of play where differences can freely and reciprocally interact will be more or less compatible with the aims of other politically engaged readers. What this problem suggests is that my politics of reading, although an attempt to facilitate the negotiation of differences between incommensurable forms of life, is itself based on beliefs and values that other ways of reading may contest. Although the doubling I advocate sets ideologies against one another to disclose their contingency, it is not without its own ideology and is itself a contingent, contestable practice. This paradox is also a constitutive contradiction of democracy. Democracy is one form of life among others, even as it offers itself as a mode of structuring the relations between different forms of life that would (or so it argues) allow them to thrive. This claim rests on values, assumptions, and aims that other conceptions of existence may not accept. But such contestation is not, as is sometimes thought, disabling proof of the false promise of pluralism (it isn't "neutral" after all). It is instead evidence of the contingencies and conflicts that make democracy possible and, in the view of its advocates (like myself), preferable to other modes of life that would stifle heterogeneity. Democracy is a contestable value, but that makes it worth advocating, indeed makes it necessary for those who believe in it to plead its case—to argue for the worthwhile consequences of the equitable exchange of differences that mutual recognition can facilitate.[12] There is no place outside of the contingencies of ideology, value, and belief. The practice of reading as a potentially transformative play of differences is an attempt not to transcend those contingencies but to discover ways of living with them that are mutually beneficial and just. Reading can, among its other pleasures and rewards, provide guidance for negotiating differences, and its injunction to us for doing so is "Play!"

Modernism and the Crisis of Liberalism

One could follow this injunction with any set of texts. I have chosen to test and explore its implications in the second part of this book with texts that I happen to know well because of a lifetime of professional engagement as a critic and teacher that has taken a particular, contingent shape. The novels of late realism and early modernism also recommend themselves, however, because they are frequently concerned with the ambiguities and challenges of "liberal irony" for reasons that go back to the literary and political situation in which they were written. Their engagement with their historical circumstances enables them to speak across historical distance to our own contemporary concerns because we are, I think, still living with the legacy of unresolved (and perhaps unresolvable) dilemmas that the early modernists confronted.

James, Conrad, Forster, and Joyce wrote at a moment of crisis in the history of liberalism that reverberates in philosophy and contemporary political life. The epistemological faith of English liberalism through the various reform measures of the nineteenth century, articulated most memorably by John Stuart Mill in *On Liberty,* assumed that a policy of inclusion of positions and points of view would result in the emergence of truth through a give-and-take of differing opinions. This was the conviction behind the Reform Bills of 1832 and 1867 and the progressive extension of the franchise. Broadened participation, it was hoped, would strengthen rather than jeopardize social cohesion (that this was a matter faith is suggested by the description of the 1867 Reform Bill as a "leap into the dark"). As the following representative passage from *On Liberty* suggests, the implicit notion of "truth" behind Mill's defense of the free exchange of opinions is ultimately monistic: "We have hitherto considered

---

[12] A further implication of the contingency of "democracy" is, of course, that it is not a unitary, self-evident state of affairs but is subject to conflicting interpretations even among its advocates (as, for example, among Habermas, Lyotard, Rorty, and myself). For a particularly illuminating example of such controversy, see Taylor, "The Politics of Recognition," and the comments by Wolf, Rockefeller, and Walzer in Taylor, *Multiculturalism and "The Politics of Recognition."*

only two possibilities: that the received opinion may be false, and some other opinion, consequently, true; or that, the received opinion being true, a conflict with the opposite error is essential to a clear apprehension and deep feeling of its truth. But there is a commoner case than either of these; when the conflicting doctrines, instead of being one true and the other false, share the truth between them; and the nonconforming opinion is needed to supply the remainder of the truth, of which the received doctrine embodies only a part" (45). This classification of opinions as either true, false, or partially true leaves out a fourth possibility that has defined the agenda of liberalism after Mill—namely, that equally legitimate "truths" may exclude one another and cannot therefore be viewed as incomplete, complementary parts of a whole.

What George Dangerfield strikingly calls "the strange death of liberal England" just before World War I resulted from the inability of liberal strategies of compromise and accommodation to respond to the absolutist, exclusionary demands of Irish separatism, women's suffrage, and the labor movement. The "truths" of each group were incommensurably at odds with the "truths" of other segments of society in ways that questioned the liberal faith that a grand narrative of progress and emancipation could be synthesized out of local narratives through gradual, increasingly inclusive reforms. The Ulster Protestants who refused assimilation to a Catholic Ireland, the suffragettes whose call for the franchise challenged the entire patriarchal order, the workers whose wage demands brought the country to the brink of class warfare—these were all cases where irreconcilable "truths" opposed each other without the possibility of compromise or consensus.[13] With these incommensurabilities, the faith that inclusion would strengthen the social bond was challenged in a fundamental way.

Mill's epistemology—his sense that differences between points of view are temporary stages on the way to disclosing "truth" agonistically, through competition between opposing opinions—was not an adequate model for dealing with these sorts of conflicts. The prewar battles that paralyzed liberalism were less like differences within a common world than battles between worlds. After a postponement brought about by the Great War, England's Liberal Party fell into insignificance because of the failure of the consensus model of truth. Part of the problem was that the violence of the protesting parties and the bad faith of the Liberal ministers undermined the conditions of Habermasian "communicative rationality." But the incommensurability of

---

[13] See Dangerfield 78–291 for an account of how "the Tory rebellion" (over Ireland), "the women's rebellion," and "the workers' rebellion" baffled and incapacitated the ruling Liberal Party. Although inspired by Dangerfield's narrative, the argument that this paralysis suggests a failure in the epistemology of liberalism is my own.

the perspectives in these disputes shows that even in ideal communicative conditions, where (as Habermas would say) the only force that matters is the persuasiveness of an argument, agreement is not always possible. Liberal politics needed a new epistemology to deal with unsurpassable differences of perspective that could not be reconciled or synthesized and that could not coexist in peaceful pluralism. Exploring the consequences of irreconcilable disagreement and imagining forms of justice not based on consensus have therefore defined the epistemological agenda of liberalism after Mill. That is why contemporary neoliberals (not only Rorty, Shklar, and Dworkin, but also Michael Walzer, John Rawls, and Charles Taylor) see democracy as fundamentally paradoxical—a form of life based on the recognition of the equal dignity and worth of perhaps irreconcilable forms of life.[14]

The role of irony in negotiating the complications and ambiguities of such a world is where liberalism meets modernism. Recognizing that the novel's traditional pursuit of mimetic verisimilitude reveals the contingency and contestability of different representations of reality, modern novelists from Henry James to James Joyce and beyond confront, in the medium of their art, various epistemological and social issues that parallel the crisis of liberalism in the politics of the period. Because of their self-consciousness as novelists about the variability and constructedness of realistic representations, they understand that staging relations between contraries with an ironic appreciation of their unsynthesizable heterogeneity is a necessary skill for orienting oneself in an irreducibly multifarious universe. How to negotiate irreconcilable differences between worlds is a defining issue not only for their experiments with narrative form but also for the stories they tell about the contingencies of belief and the conflict of interpretations.

The novelists I explore in part 2 reflect a variety of attitudes toward the possibilities and limits of irony as a formal instrument and a social attitude. Henry James finds irony productive because it allows him to play with indeterminacies that he imagines future generations of readers will find enlivening. The inability to forge consensus becomes for James the ironic foundation of a community engaged in a potentially never-ending play of differences. It is not at all obvious, however, that irony is a politically productive attitude. More pessimistic than James, Conrad turns over to his readers the challenge of resolving various contradictions that he cannot see his way past, although he believes that the possibility of community, commitment, and engagement depends on overcoming a skepticism he finds invincible. The play of Forster's irony is often more arch and defensive than James's expansiveness because he shares

---

[14] Appropriately, these thinkers are not all in agreement about the epistemology of the new liberalism, as my analysis of Rorty, Shklar, and Dworkin should suggest.

Conrad's view that an ironic recognition of the contingency and contestability of one's beliefs is necessary medicine against mystification in a world of conflicting interpretations. He nevertheless seeks connection and affirmation without believing that community and consensus are possible (or desirable, inasmuch as ideological solidarity can, he shows, turn even well-intentioned souls into bullies). Joyce shares James's sense of the creative potential of ironic indeterminacy, and he is as skeptical as Forster and Conrad of the contingencies of any declaration of faith, but he also worries that an ironic loosening of commitment to one's commitments can encourage passivity and disengagement, and he seeks self-contradictorily to use irony to advance his own claims to creative power by demonstrating its endless capacity for subversion.

Reading modern fiction has political consequences in large part because it enacts and explores the social uses of irony. What one does after gaining such an orientation is another question; and staging, taken as an end in itself, is open to the criticism that it is ultimately unproductive. Playing with contradictions ironically may be more epistemologically complex and illuminating than a unified consciousness, but single-minded purposiveness can be more powerful precisely because of its willful blindness to alternatives. The act of staging can seem like mere verbal play, where effective political practice demands choices between incommensurables. This is a danger of which much modern fiction is acutely aware. Novelists as different as James, Conrad, Forster, and Joyce—and to their names could be added Faulkner, Mann, Pynchon, and many others—depict not only the necessity of a doubled consciousness but also the danger that it could issue in empty indecisiveness or impractical self-contradiction. The question of whether or how irony can lead to productive social practice preoccupies many modern novelists for the very reason that it cannot be given a clear, unequivocal answer. Their recognition of the need for an ironic consciousness is typically matched by their sense that it can be a temptation and a trap.

Before I turn to the readings in part 2, I want to develop further my model of play as a vehicle for mediating epistemological, cultural, and social differences. My model of reading as an exercise in nonconsensual reciprocity is based on a belief in the productive capacity of dialogue between opposing positions, and so it seems appropriate to develop the model by bringing into conversation two theorists whose differences are so extreme that they might seem to have little to say to each other. As I hope to show in the next two chapters, however, Wolfgang Iser's aesthetic theory and Edward Said's cultural politics can do more useful social and epistemological work in dialogue with each other than either can in isolation. My goal in staging their conversation is not to create or discover consensus but, rather, to demonstrate how "play" as nonconsensual reciprocity can make differences interact productively.

2. PLAY, POWER, AND DIFFERENCE

The Social Implications of Iser's Aesthetic Theory

From the early days of reader-response criticism, Wolfgang Iser's literary theory has been accused of apolitical idealism, but this charge misrepresents his thinking about the social functions of literature.[1] *The Fictive and the Imaginary*, the culmination of his reflections about the art of representation, does not explicitly address the politics of literature, and its emphasis on the value of "play" and the "as if" might seem to disengage the aesthetic experience from worldly concerns. As I have begun to suggest, however, "play" can be a profoundly important social activity—for example, by facilitating productive uses of difference to create forms of community among decentered human beings whose dissonances and dislocations resist unification. The key point here is that Iser views fictions as vehicles for staging various kinds of open-ended exploratory interactions. In ways that are perhaps not immediately obvious,

[1] On this point, see also Fluck and Thomas in the *New Literary History* issue "On the Writings of Wolfgang Iser," in which an earlier version of parts of this chapter appeared. According to Fluck, "By dismissing his literary theory as 'liberal' or 'liberal humanist,' oppositional critics have dismissed an account of aesthetic experience that could enrich their own work" if they were to recognize the power, complexity, and subtlety of "the idea of negation" that informs Iser's thinking about literature (199–200). Fluck offers a perceptive, wide-ranging explanation of how Iser sought a theory of the social and aesthetic functions of literature that would provide the critical distance lacking in totalitarianism without retreating into the false promise of art as an ideal, transcendent realm, which the Nazi regime and the Holocaust had discredited. Thomas shows in insightful detail how Iser's Anglo-American critics (especially Stanley Fish and Terry Eagleton) have systematically oversimplified and misunderstood a theory that does not fit their categories.

his aesthetic theory thereby offers a model of the emancipatory uses of power in the service of communicative democracy.

Iser reads the literary as evidence of culture-forming processes. The apparently boundless variety of the fictional, which would seem to thwart any general theory, has enormous value, in his view, as evidence of the capacity of human beings to generate versions of themselves: "Literature . . . has a substratum . . . of a rather featureless plasticity that manifests itself in a continual repatterning of the culturally conditioned shapes human beings have assumed. . . . [L]iterature reveals that human plasticity is propelled by the drive to gain shape, without ever imprisoning itself in any of the shapes obtained" (*Fictive* xi). For Iser, fictions are attempts by human beings to give form to themselves, attempts that reveal in the process that human beings have no definitive form. Without a shape to present itself as, human being would be nothing, but since we can only grasp ourselves as a form that is not what we are, there is no limit to the shapes human beings can try on. The plasticity of human being that gives rise to the multiplicity of fictions also makes possible cultural differences. Accounting for fictional multiplicity can consequently help explain how different cultures are constructed, and the manner in which fictional worlds interact may then also offer a model for how cultural differences can be mediated.

In these ways, Iser's theory can help to answer some practical, not merely aesthetic, questions that are often asked about the epistemological consequences of cultural differences: If the modes of seeing in different communities are at least in some respects irreconcilable because they reflect incommensurable presuppositions about the human situation, how can such communities understand one another? Or are cultures windowless monads—communally solipsistic entities in which only those who share the same conventions can make sense to and of one another, with everything outside the culture's walls either ignored or relegated to the status of error? Can one culture use its own terms to say something about another culture without engaging in a hostile act of appropriation or simply reflecting itself and not encountering the otherness of the Other? Or is any attempt to theorize about the field of cultural differences doomed because it will invariably remain captive of one position within it?

If only as an ethical ideal—that is, as a goal to orient our actions as interpreters—we need a model of transcultural understanding that respects alterity without rendering it inaccessible and allows worlds to communicate without sacrificing their integrity, their defining difference. I think this ideal can be provided by Iser's notion of "play"—especially his claim that, although some games are aimed at establishing a winner and a loser in a hierarchical, closed manner, play also includes (even in such games) an opposing movement that resists closure and seeks to continue and renew itself (see *Prospecting* 252–55; *Fictive* 247–80). According to Iser, as we have seen, the fundamental, defining action of play is a "to-and-fro movement" that, he argues, "permits the coexistence of the mutually exclusive" (*Prospecting* 255). In his view, unsynthesizable difference is what makes the back-and-forth movement of play possible, unpredictable, and potentially self-renewing. Iser proposes that the act of representation be understood as a form of play because it typically stages interactions between values, conventions, and ways of seeing that otherwise might not encounter one another. The outcome of such staging is not necessarily a resolution of differences but can be, instead, an open-ended, back-and-forth movement between them. This sort of interaction between mutually exclusive positions "allows us to conceive what is withheld from us," Iser argues, without collapsing the differences that constitute the play-space (*Prospecting* 261). What we need in order to allow cultural differences to engage each other in a mutually revealing manner is this kind of reciprocal, nonconsensual play.[2]

The need for such a model of cross-cultural interaction is suggested, I think, by a well-known critique of the failure to achieve it—Edward Said's *Orientalism*, his deservedly influential unmasking of the cultural prejudices of the West. Said's argument about how knowing other cultures can participate in the imperialist domination of them is a powerful indictment of the dangers of ethnocentric epistemological self-enclosure. It is not at all clear, however, whether Said's critique demonstrates the inevitability of transcultural opacity or implicitly projects an ideal that is the reverse of the mistakes it discloses. Not only Said's critics but also his allies and friends have pointed out that the epistemology of *Orientalism* is contradictory. On the one hand, he argues that all knowledge is imbued with social and political assumptions, whether recognized or not. On the other hand, he often implies that truthful representations could have been achieved if the Orientalists had simply looked at "reality" or had acknowledged the undeniable "humanity" of their subjects, without explaining how such acts of understanding could have avoided cultural bias. "Orientalism" has the status of error because it does not capture the "truth" it is after, but the reasons for this failing call into question the very possibility of a "true" representation. As one of Said's critics concludes: "If one attempts to discover whether alternatives to Orientalism are possible, . . . Said is of no

---

[2] Gabriele Schwab also finds in Iser tools for mediating differences. See her discussion of how "negativity and indeterminacy facilitate a productive interaction" of differences—what she calls "cultural contact"—in her essay "Iser's Aesthetics of Negativity" (77, 81). For evidence of Iser's interest in the problem of cultural differences, see Iser and Budick (especially his own essay "The Emergence of a Cross-Cultural Discourse: Thomas Carlyle's *Sartor Resartus*") and his Wellek Lectures, *The Range of Interpretation*.

help in spite of the acknowledgment that such alternatives are a pressing need" (Porter 151).[3] One way to address this need would be to ask whether an alternative to Orientalism can be constructed from Said's critique of its errors—an alternative that avoids ethnocentric self-enclosure without presuming the possibility of a knowledge unmediated by culturally specific conventions and categories. I think that it can, and this alternative turns out to have much in common with Iserian play.

Orientalism and Cultural Solipsism

Said defines "Orientalism" as the systematic, persistent claim of Western scholarship to such an authoritative knowledge of the mysteries and customs of the Near East that it does not listen to the Other and refuses it the right to speak for itself. Instead of recognizing the Other as an equal and irreducible partner in an unpredictable encounter, the Orientalist projects interpretations based on an established set of assumptions, which thus develops "the self-containing, self-reinforcing character of a closed system" (*Orientalism* 70). To summarize, the four "principal dogmas of Orientalism" are, according to Said: the assertion of an "absolute and systematic difference between the West, which is rational, developed, humane, superior, and the Orient, which is aberrant, undeveloped, inferior"; the methodological assumption that "abstractions about the Orient, particularly those based on texts representing a 'classical' Oriental civilization, are always preferable to direct evidence drawn from modern Oriental realities"; the belief that "the Orient is eternal, uniform, and incapable of defining itself"; and the feeling that "the Orient is at bottom something either to be feared (the Yellow Peril, the Mongol hordes, the brown dominions) or to be controlled (by pacification, research and development, outright occupation whenever possible)" (300–301).

Said's summary indictment of Orientalism is important not only for what it says about a failed tradition of transcultural scholarship but also for its argument about the relation between knowledge and power: "To have such knowledge of such a thing is to dominate it, to have authority over it. And authority here means for 'us' to deny autonomy to 'it'—the Oriental country—since we know it and it exists, in a sense, as we know it" (32). The point here is not only that a scholarly enterprise can be complicit with imperialism (although that too, of course, is Said's claim—that knowledge, as a form of

---

[3] Among the many commentaries on *Orientalism*, Brennan, Karatani, and Wang offer especially insightful critical perspectives that are fundamentally sympathetic to Said's project. For an example of the hostile criticism this text has received, see Windschuttle.

power, can be part of the apparatus of imperial domination). The more fundamental point is that knowledge, often conceived of as a quest for mastery and authority, can become invalid because of the very will to power that motivates it. If knowing the Other becomes mastery and domination, then the epistemological authority of the expert closes off the exchange between different worlds. The openness to alterity of dialogue is replaced by the repetition of an established meaning that cannot be challenged by an Other whose autonomy and authority it denies.

The closure of a culture upon itself is an example of vicious hermeneutic circularity. One way of phrasing the question posed by Orientalism is a classic paradox of hermeneutics: How can the unfamiliar be understood if the familiar provides our only access to it? How can one manage not "to cancel, or at least subdue and reduce, its strangeness" if a community can make sense of the new and anomalous only by grafting them onto what it already knows (87)? Said charges generations of Oriental scholars with prejudice, and that claim in itself would not be so interesting if it did not also call attention to the epistemological dilemma that without presuppositions and expectations an interpreter cannot understand anything at all.[4] If, as Gadamer argues, prejudgments (*Vor-urteile*) are necessary to understanding because "truth" is not simply a given waiting for reason to reflect it accurately (see Gadamer 265–307), then how can we know without the self-fulfilling preconceptions Said condemns? Can one distinguish clearly and unequivocally between a legitimate presupposition and a blinding bias? According to Said, Orientalism let its set of available types run roughshod over the particularities of individuals: "We must imagine the Orientalist at work in the role of a clerk putting together a very wide assortment of files in a large cabinet marked 'the Semites,' " and "the human being was significant principally as the occasion for a file" (*Orientalism* 234). But no individual can be understood without some reference to types—to kinds that explain its relations to other entities according to various classifications of similarity and difference. The power of the notion of "Orientalism" itself is indeed precisely its value as an explanatory type.

A major reason for the vicious circularity Said rightly complains about is that Orientalism's presuppositions are never put at risk by its encounter with the Other. Said notes that "it is perfectly natural for the human mind to resist the assault on it of untreated strangeness" (67). Orientalism is an example of the tendency of cultures "to impose . . . transformations on other cultures, receiving these other cultures not as they are but as, for the benefit of the

---

[4] See my *Conflicting Readings,* especially the chapter "Interpretive Conflict and Validity," 1–19. The tests for validity that I discuss in subsequent paragraphs (efficacy, inclusiveness, and intersubjectivity) are analyzed in more detail there.

receiver, they ought to be": "what the Orientalist does is to *confirm* the Orient in his readers' eyes; he neither tries nor wants to unsettle already firm convictions" (67, 65). Disorienting and bewildering the interpreter by frustrating preset convictions is, however, a way to expose the beliefs as deficient and persuade their holder of the need to abandon or revise them. Only if Occidental prejudgments about the Orient are invoked and then *not* validated can they be altered or overturned. Holding oneself open to bewilderment is an ethical imperative if one would avoid being a captive of one's beliefs.

This is more easily said than done, however, because power can easily undermine various tests for validity that interpreters commonly invoke to check and revise their hypotheses. One such test is the pragmatic question: Does an interpretation work? Said's critique of the complicity of Orientalism with imperial administration suggests, however, that the instrumental bias of the pragmatic test may make it more a gauge of power than of knowledge. "The vindication of Orientalism" was, he says, "its later effectiveness, its usefulness, its authority" as a tool for colonial bureaucracies (123), but this very political efficacy casts doubt on its epistemological value. The effectiveness of a hypothesis may be a sign of its ability to manage a situation rather than of its adequacy as a recognition of otherness if it works by silencing and suppressing rather than disclosing the other world.

The test of inclusiveness—the ability of a hypothesis to organize evidence without anomaly—is similarly liable to being corrupted by power. Said complains about the self-validating tendencies of "discursive consistency" (273). A set of assumptions may generate mutually reinforcing statements whose coherence is a result of the homogeneity of the beliefs behind them, and the internal consistency of an interpretation may blind an interpreter to the possibility that his or her reading is a mere projection. The problem, however, is that the coherence of an interpretation is also a signal that it is successfully fitting parts together into a meaningful pattern. The hermeneutic dilemma here is that the internal consistency of a discourse may be evidence of the ability of one's presuppositions to make reliable (because coherent) sense, but it may also be an engine for assimilating otherness to one's own beliefs and categories and insulating them from criticism or challenge.

The test of intersubjectivity may similarly become undecidable because of political subversion. Said's indictment of Orientalism as a discipline, a tradition, and an enduring and influential scholarly institution suggests that consensus can be blinding and coercive. Although interpreters frequently judge a hypothesis by its ability to win adherents and to withstand attacks, intersubjective agreement may not be proof against solipsism. The very force of agreement between like-minded interpreters may lock them into a self-reinforcing blindness to another community's way of seeing. The oxymoron "communal solipsism" may sound like an impossible self-contradiction, but it is one of the main obstacles to transcultural understanding.

Power can undermine all of these tests for validity because the dominance of the knower over the known may prevent the interpreter from experiencing a potentially enlightening disorientation. Said wonders "how one can study other cultures and peoples from a libertarian, or a nonrepressive and nonmanipulative, perspective" (24). The tests for validity go wrong in the ways I have described because what Said calls "the principle of inequality" (151) between knower and known prevents otherness from challenging the hypotheses that claim to have mastered it. Equality between knower and known is hermeneutically necessary because it acts as a check on the powers of an interpreter's beliefs and encourages a posture of vulnerability, of openness to reorienting experiences of surprise and frustration.

The philologist Leo Spitzer describes the hermeneutic circle as a "to-and-fro movement" (19–20, 25) between guesses about the overall configuration of a text and the details they attempt to fit together. Such an endless, reciprocal, back-and-forth motion is implicit in the paradox that one can understand the parts of any text only by projecting a sense of the whole, even though one can grasp the whole only by working through the parts. The resonances between Spitzer's formulation of the hermeneutic act and Iser's notion of play are not accidental, I think, because only a playful interaction between hypotheses and evidence can allow them to be mutually formative while preventing the power of the interpreter's beliefs from forcing otherness into preset patterns. Interpretation must be playful to move beyond simple self-replication of the assumptions with which one begins. As Spitzer and Iser describe it, a playful relation between interpreter and text implies a principle of equality that allows revisions and reversals to occur. Respect for the integrity and the unpredictable alterity of the partner in play is necessary for the interaction to be potentially self-changing, for it to generate something new that neither participant could predict or produce alone.

Equality is not the same as identity, however. The difference between a community's self-understanding and another culture's interpretation of it is not only what makes possible battles for epistemological power; it is also a precondition for exchanges based on mutual recognition. Said is correct to complain about the "sense of the irreducible distance separating white from colored, or Occidental from Oriental" that "kept the Oriental-colored to his position of object studied by the Occidental-white, instead of vice-versa" (228). Reversing roles by investigating the investigator asserts the principle of equality (what is an object can also be a subject, and vice versa), and such reversals keep play open. But collapsing the distance by attempting to replace difference with identity would prevent any exchange at all.

That is one of the problems with the seemingly unobjectionable proposal to let the other culture speak for itself. Said complains that "from the beginning of Western speculation about the Orient, the one thing the Orient could not do was to represent itself" (283). The ability to author descriptions of oneself is certainly an important assertion of a culture's dignity and worth and a crucial counter to the domination inherent in being taken as another's object. To privilege self-representation, however, is to confirm boundaries instead of allowing them to be crossed. In what language should self-representation occur, for example, if the lack of equivalence between the terms and conventions of cultures is responsible in the first place for their mutual misunderstandings? And what if a community's own language is not adequate to describe its situation? Indeed, how could the question of the adequacy of a language be asked at all if there weren't alternative languages contesting its claims? Disagreement about what counts as an "adequate" representation is, after all, a central issue in cross-cultural conflicts, and the difficulty of resolving these disputes comes about in large part because there is no ground outside of language to which the combatants can appeal.

Self-representation may also not be sufficient for liberation. One reason a culture is oppressed may be that it lacks a language capable of exposing and protesting its conditions of domination. When Gayatri Spivak warns against "the first-world intellectual masquerading as the absent nonrepresenter who lets the oppressed speak for themselves," she has in mind two dangers: not only that "the benevolent Western intellectual" may be yet another version of "the ethnocentric Subject . . . establishing itself by selectively defining an Other," but also that the oppressed people may not possess a sufficiently powerful understanding of themselves to diagnose their oppression or a satisfactory means of expressing their concerns ("Subaltern" 292). The traditional goal of hermeneutics—understanding others better than they understand themselves—may mask a potentially blinding will to power, but it also anticipates the insight of the various modern "hermeneutics of suspicion" (to borrow Paul Ricoeur's term) that a claim of privilege for self-understanding may be a mask or a delusion. One culture may find in the languages and ways of seeing of another culture the means it would not otherwise have at its disposal for resolving its own problems and realizing its possibilities. To pursue its own interests and aims, one community may need to borrow hermeneutic and linguistic resources from another. Transcultural learning of this kind requires a back-and-forth movement between different worlds that questions rather than assumes the self-sufficiency of self-representation.

Said blames the blindness of Orientalism on its "binary" structure: " 'We' are this, 'they' are that" (*Orientalism* 237). "The result" of such differentiation, he warns, "is usually to polarize the distinction—the Oriental becomes more Oriental, the Westerner more Western—and limit the human encounter between different cultures" (46). In Said's view, Orientalism cannot see similarity because it is blinded by difference: "Orientalism failed to identify with human experience, failed also to see it as human experience" (328). As René Girard has argued, demonizing and scapegoating the Other by insisting on its radical alterity is a dangerous and all-too-easy way for a community to achieve solidarity (see 1–67). No doubt cultures often resemble and overlap one another in ways that a claim of complete incommensurability overlooks, and such commonalities allow different worlds to recognize one another as potential partners in a game of give-and-take. But play requires difference as well as similarity. As Spivak argues, "knowledge is made possible and is sustained by irreducible difference, not identity" (*Worlds* 254). Asserting the common humanity of the players is a move that could put an end to their interaction because binarism is inherent in the to-and-fro movement of play. The goal of the play between cultures should not be the eradication of differences, a move that would stop the game just as surely as would the insistence on the primacy of a single opposition.

If there is a "common humanity" that play discloses, it is the lack of an essential nature to human being, a lack that allows a diverse array of forms of life to emerge. This lack makes possible a "doubling" that in turn can be a powerful means for staging interactions of difference. With Helmuth Plessner, Iser finds that "division is characteristic of human beings": "Being oneself . . . means being able to double oneself" (*Fictive* 80, 81). Iser cites with approval Plessner's argument that human being has a "*doppelgänger*" structure: "Human being as a being . . . is generally related to its social role but cannot be defined by a particular role. The role-player or bearer of the social figure is not the same as that figure, and yet cannot be thought of separately from it without being deprived of its humanity. . . . Only by means of the other of itself does it have—itself" (Plessner 10:235; quoted in *Fictive* 80). Iser describes this duality as evidence of "our decentered position—our existence is incontestable, but at the same time is inaccessible to us" (81). We are, but we do not have a being that absolutely and essentially defines us, and we can be and know ourselves only through roles that we both are and are not. As Iser explains, "the fact that we cannot capture ourselves in any absolute role lifts all limits on the number of roles that can be played" (82).[5]

---

[5] This is, of course, a theoretical statement of an idealized state of affairs and not a material description of any particular individual's conditions of existence. Marx similarly distinguishes between our capacity for self-creation and the roles through which we create ourselves, and he laments how the fixity of the roles determined by capitalist conditions of production and exchange limit human plasticity. See the well-known passage in *The German Ideology* where he crit-

He consequently regards "the constitutive dividedness of human beings as the source of possible worlds within the world" (84). "Doubling," as a manifestation of human decenteredness, is the anthropological source of cultural differences.

Doubling is also (at least potentially) a way of bringing these differences into creative, mutually illuminating interaction. Play involves "doubling" because its basic structure is oscillation. As such, it has the power to bring differences into relation through the very movement of their opposition. When two opposing communities of belief try to communicate with or interpret one another, the asymmetry between the explanations they offer need not simply result in pointless talk at cross-purposes (although that can and often does happen). If mutual recognition can prolong the encounter, their asymmetry can bring about a play of differences, a back-and-forth movement, that can usefully inform and change both parties (and perhaps give them pleasure, not merely the aggravation of misunderstanding and conflict). Doubling perspectives in this manner will not necessarily unify them, although it can disclose potential alliances or common ground between opposing cultures that neither side had previously suspected. Nor will doubling generate a transcendental position from which the entire play-space can be understood. In lieu of an indubitable, unitary foundation for knowledge and being, doubling describes how encounters between different worlds can occur, without claiming to provide a logic that restricts or governs such meetings. Because a transcendental observation point and a universal logic are not available, acts of doubling opposing perspectives within a field of play are the most we can hope for—and all we need—in our effort to get outside ourselves.

The obvious objection to this model of cross-cultural understanding is that "play" itself is a Western, ethnocentric concept. And, indeed, especially in aesthetic theory, the idea of "play" has a long and rich tradition in Western thought (see Spariosu). One could argue, further, that the whole question of whether cultures can communicate is ethnocentric, the result of Western

---

icizes the "fixation of social activity" caused by the division of labor and speculates about different social relations that would "make it possible for me to do one thing today and another tomorrow, to hunt in the morning, fish in the afternoon, rear cattle in the evening, criticise after dinner, just as I have a mind, without ever becoming hunter, fisherman, shepherd or critic" (53). Marx's notion that people produce themselves through their labor shares with Plessner and Iser a conception of existence as a doubled relation between who we are and how we create, express, and discover ourselves through roles that both are us and are not. This doubleness can be an emancipatory resource that evinces and expresses human plasticity, but it also informs the tragedy and the paradox of alienated labor, as Marx describes it, through which we create roles and products that in turn control and coerce us.

preoccupations with individuality and consciousness, a legacy of Cartesianism that haunts even contemporary language philosophies through their very efforts to get beyond it. David Hall and Roger Ames point out, for example, that "in Confucian social theory, a person is irreducibly communal," with the consequence that solipsism is never a problem for Confucius because "experience is, ab initio, intersubjective" (160). But they also note that "one always begins to think where one is" (12): "We have no choice but to attempt to articulate the other tradition by seeking out categories and language found in our own tradition that . . . can be reshaped and extended to accommodate novel ideas" (14). This is true of their book, *Thinking through Confucius,* which acknowledges the irreducibility of ancient Chinese philosophy to Western categories of thought even as it uses those categories to make an unfamiliar culture's ways of thinking accessible. Their project is interestingly paradoxical in its insistence on difference and its desire to overcome it, and the paradox here is that of "doubling" and "play"—setting in motion a to-and-fro exchange between familiar categories and unfamiliar ways of thinking in the hope that the encounter will transform both.

The notion of "play" as a way of engaging cultural difference may be Western, but proposals for mediating between different worlds can only come from within those worlds. There is no transcendental ground from which the conflict of interpretations can be described and negotiated because any representation of such a ground is itself an interpretation subject to conflict (see my *Conflicting Readings* 151–57). What must mark proposals for interworldly mediation is not universality but respect for alterity and openness to further negotiation and change through the encounter. Although I would not want to rule out in advance that varieties of "play" might be found in many different cultures, what recommends it as a mediator is not that it can claim universality but rather that it embodies a principle of equality between the partners in the exchange and that it is open to transformation. Built into the openness of play is the possibility that the encounter may change the terms of engagement. "Let's play" is a beginning gambit that one culture can offer another, and the response may be "What do you mean by that?" or "Let's do something else instead," and "play" as "doubling" and "to-and-fro movement" would allow the legitimacy of those responses and enable a reciprocal negotiation and exploration of possible modes of relationship that neither side alone could anticipate. Although the proposal to play may be a beginning move, the terms of play do not dictate that it be where the game ends. The possibility of self-transformation is inherent in play itself, and that open-endedness makes play a Western notion of relatedness that can disclose the Occident and the Orient to each other because it does not insist that the encounter proceed or end on Western terms.

Power and the Ethics of Play

Play can be extraordinarily emancipatory, but its ambiguities raise important questions about the ethical uses (and abuses) of power. The central contradiction here has to do with the opposition between "free" and "instrumental" play. Difference can generate ever-new versions of itself because the doubleness of play is potentially endless, but play is also a way of deploying power for particular ends. Keeping the to-and-fro going ("free play," as Iser calls it) and aiming to establish a result ("instrumental play") are aspects of play that may contradict each other but also depend on each other. There is an instrumental quality to free play itself to the extent that each move back and forth is an attempt to establish meaning and decide the outcome. But no game can be purely instrumental without ceasing to be playful and becoming merely a means to an end. Even in instrumental games, no move has a meaning intrinsic to itself. Each move depends on a reply and a result it cannot entirely control: "every game begins with a move whose consequences can never be totally foreseen" (*Fictive* 261). The element of free play in all games is that every move is incomplete and depends on what it is not, a future it has not yet reached.

"Free play" and "instrumental play" are opposites that are deeply and profoundly linked. This can be seen, for example, in the games texts play, games that range between open-endedness and closure.[6] On the one hand, as Iser points out, "because of their forms, games must inevitably be limited; in contrast with play, they are designed for endings. The result ends play." Even with the most anarchic, disruptive, open-ended text, "the endlessness of play cannot be maintained, since the text itself is limited" (*Fictive* 265, 257). On the other hand, in contrast to "result-oriented games, especially mathematical, strategic, and economic ones, as well as those of chance and skill, all of

---

[6] The four categories of games that Iser borrows from Roger Caillois—*agōn, alea, mimicry,* and *ilinx*—show how free and instrumental play may combine to make games more open-ended or more directed toward finality (see Caillois). Although *agōn* (games of contest or struggle) and alea (where chance rules) are both defined by the ends of winning and losing, their valence may change in textual games. Strategies where conflict seeks resolution in the triumph of one position may be countered by moves aimed at opening up the possibility of unforeseeable, uncontainable consequences. Iser describes *mimicry* as a game tending toward closure because it promotes "the forgetting of difference" (*Fictive* 262) between the copy and the original and opposes disruptions that might undermine the illusion of reality. But the element of free play in imitation's pursuit of verisimilitude is exposed by *ilinx*, the game of subverting all fixed positions in order to induce vertigo. This "carnivalization of all the positions assembled in the text" (262) exposes the boundlessness and multiplicity of possible illusions given the ultimately ineradicable difference between the fictive and the real. Even the subversion of roles in the interests of opening up meaning depends, however, on instrumentally directed ends for it to undermine. Its liberating aims are significant only against the backdrop of the games of finality it undercuts.

which are designed to remove existing play spaces," a text can take as its game the multiplication of opportunities for play, whether by "play[ing] against each other" the various games it includes or by demonstrating that they can be played without end, so that the "game is not ended by itself but by its player" (265, 266). Although some determinate or didactic texts may aim to close off play in the interests of the results they desire, it is possible to play the games of even these texts in ways that keep open and expand their potentiality for meaning. Even the most instrumental text can, because it is a text, be read in ways that open it up to meanings and purposes it cannot limit (by taking its games for observation as games, for example, rather than submitting to their ends, or engaging its strategies with other modes of instrumental play governed by different notions of finality). Paradoxically, although all texts have limits because they are finite ways of playing particular games, the only ultimate limit on their capacity to mean is the resourcefulness and energy of the player (or the history of readers) in keeping their play in motion.

Because of these contradictions, textual games are especially illuminating models of the social functions of play. Iser's explanation of the paradoxes of play is important not only as a clarification of the games of texts but also as an exploration of the usefulness of play as a particular way of using power. The opposition of free and instrumental play distinguishes helpfully between ways power may be employed. In contrast to the widespread assumption that power aims only and always for dominance, the aim of instrumental play to achieve victory and end the game by determining the result contrasts with the uses of power for expanding the potential for meaning that the to-and-fro motion of free play makes possible. The element of potential open-endedness in instrumental play suggests that even the use of power for masterful ends is not monolithic but contains a countermovement onto which the subversive counterflow of free play can cathect. The need that free play has for limits and aims offers a critique of the dream of innocence of open-ended play without finality, but the disclosure of the playful element of instrumental games opens up the possibility that power can be used without the inevitability of coercion or violence.

The interaction of free and instrumental play in textual games provides a model for the ethical use of power. Guided by such an ethics, instrumental play would become ironic about its ends by recognizing their contingency. Such an ethics would instruct instrumental uses of force that the achievement of their aims can be self-defeating by ending the game that had defined them. But such an ethics would also inform free play that its subversive, anarchic dynamic is powerless without the forms and aims that give play meaning. The will to infinite expansion of free play would be countered by an ironic awareness of its inability to sustain itself without the other it opposes.

The counterflow of free and instrumental play informing such an ethics would have the aim of preventing any one game from dominating all the others in the interests of keeping the space of play open. It would seek to have rival games engage each other with the recognition that their conflicts do not merely frustrate the will to dominance of each but can be mutually enhancing because opposing modes of play typically depend on and benefit from each other. The play-space opened up by such an ethics would be a democratic community of often incommensurable games whose principle of interaction is not indifferent tolerance but ironic and energetic engagement with difference.

One move that such an ethics of play would exclude is terror. Defined, following Lyotard, as the elimination or threat of elimination of a player from a language game, "terror" is a radical violation of the mutual recognition on which reciprocal exchange between worlds depends. There is an element of terror in Orientalism inasmuch as "the muteness imposed upon the Orient" as Europe's "silent Other" precluded an exchange between them (Said, "Reconsidered" 93). Terror cannot easily be exorcised, however, because power is involved even in decentered play. The to-and-fro movement between positions can easily turn into combat that seeks to close off the encounter by a masterstroke or a devious stratagem that would secure dominance for one side. The role of power in the back-and-forth motion of play poises it ambiguously between decentered, open-ended reciprocity and the quest for victory that would terminate the exchange and, much like terror, refuse equal recognition to the losing side (the violent overtones of a term like "sudden-death elimination" are all to the point). Something like "terror" is always present as a possible move that play itself may tempt the parties to try.

This ambiguity is intensified when the parties to the exchange seek to decide through it whether some games are more worth playing than others. Such evaluations are often what participants in cross-cultural encounters seek. Said argues that there is something "combative" in the Arnoldian notion of "culture" as the best that has been thought and said because "the assertively achieved and won hegemony of an identifiable set of ideas . . . over all other ideas in society" eliminates or at least threatens the right of alternatives to assert their claims (*World* 10). The problem here is that being convinced of one's convictions includes believing that they are worth being believed. It is this belief that is usefully tested and held in check by cross-cultural encounters, but those exchanges must then be governed by an ethics of play based on a principle of equality that opposes the inherent tendency of either side to think most highly of its own presuppositions and conventions. Play as an ethical norm requires that the participants agree not only to use power but also to limit it, and nothing can guarantee that such mutual consent will not give way to one party's decision that its interests (for example, the vindication of its own assumptions and values) will be best served by resorting to overpowering tactics. The interests of knowing otherness will be violated by such refusals to accept mutual constraints on power, but those are not the only or the most pressing aims that a group may have.

In yet another ambiguity of the kind that ethics welcomes, however, some acts of violence or disruption and some quests for power may be justified by the ideal of decentered, reciprocal play itself. When mutual recognition or equal power do not exist, then a struggle to redefine the terms of the encounter may be more important than "play" and may even be required to clear the ground for it. In order to construct a play-space, various power struggles may be necessary to break down obstacles to reciprocity and to allow a hitherto silenced Other the right to speak on equal terms. In such instances, "play" provides a norm against which to measure deficiencies that could justify political action, including fights that are not playful but seek to make play possible. Said's "determination not to allow the segregation and confinement of the Orient to go on without challenge" ("Reconsidered" 95), for example, is an act of moral courage that is justified in terms of an ethics of play.

Criticism defined as the unmasking of oppression and domination should not be an end in itself, however, but should be practiced as a preliminary battle for power that aims to allow play to emerge. The necessary contradiction of such criticism is that it seeks a victory that, if achieved, could very well replicate the structure of domination and subordination it originally sought to overcome. A victory of this sort would mean replacing the occupants of the dominant position—not a trivial matter if you are the oppressed party—but not putting an end to oppression. The way out of this contradiction is to regard winning the game not as an end but as a beginning that would open up for the first time the kind of play that resists hierarchies and ends.[7]

Another important objection to an ethics of play is that it is implicitly co-optive and conservative. To some leftist critics, my plea for mutual recognition

---

[7] This is a utopian vision, to be sure, and as such it has much in common with other imaginings of social liberation. Marx was engaged in an analogous kind of thinking when he described the emancipation of the proletariat as the fight against the oppressing class that, when victorious, would end class oppression and emancipate everyone. I am similarly imagining that the win-or-lose game might be played in such a way as to transcend that very kind of game altogether in a victory that would create a play space where winning and losing would not be desiderata. This is of course contradictory—fighting a fight to end fighting—but that does not make it illogical, let alone undesirable. The dangers of utopian thinking are well known and should not be underestimated or ignored. The value of such thought experiments nevertheless is their normative power to postulate ethical and social ideals that project a goal worth seeking despite the difficulty, perhaps impossibility, of attaining it.

and reciprocity might seem like the "repressive tolerance" of liberalism, which, in the guise of accepting difference, actually constitutes "an appeal for cohesion" that would stifle dissent and prevent "basic change" (Bercovitch 644, 645). My condemnation of terror might seem like yet another "form of exclusion which . . . denies its own exclusivity" (Weber 45). According to this criticism, it is a typical liberal tactic to gesture toward an all-encompassing inclusion in order to disallow any radical opposition to the existing order: "The only things that can be excluded are things that would exclude"—that is, any fundamental alternatives to the way things are (Wills 318; see Rooney 1–63).

"Doubling," where both parties put their assumptions at risk, is not simply repressive tolerance. A to-and-fro exchange in which the presuppositions of both communities are tested and can be overturned, and through which their conventions can be denaturalized and exposed for critical examination, is the opposite of a self-preserving defense against otherness. Because of the challenges and transformations play makes possible, such an encounter can be subversive—an engine for change, not a means of preserving the status quo by assimilating and denying difference. Play is not occurring if the Other is merely tolerated and is not taken seriously as a coequal whose differences call into question the naturalness and legitimacy of one's own categories and conventions. An ethics of play requires that differences not only recognize but also engage one another, and it is therefore not the same as indifferent acceptance, which can be a strategy for prolonging suppression of the Other.

The charge of disallowing exclusion is similarly unfounded. Play as a way of staging encounters between incommensurable worlds does not deny exclusion but presupposes it. I have proposed "play" as a way of mediating (but not transcending) cultural differences precisely because worlds can exclude each other and because no generally persuasive version of truth can be found that would be acceptable to all communities of belief. Exclusion as the irreducibility of difference is what makes play possible and necessary. But exclusion as the violent refusal of recognition of otherness is something I do reject (along with Said and Spivak and many other critics on the left), and my reason is both ethical and epistemological: only a principle of equality and reciprocity between cultures can allow pursuit of the ideal of noncoercive understanding that escapes the self-enclosure of hermeneutic circularity. The mutual exclusiveness of communities with incommensurable beliefs makes it imperative that we seek modes of interaction that avoid the dangers of communal solipsism and suppression of otherness. The question that the charge of excluding exclusion begs is how interpreters from different, mutually exclusive communities can find ways of relating to one another that avoid solipsistic self-replication or a destructive battle for power. A desirable alternative to solipsism and violence is, I think, play.

A more fundamental objection to my hermeneutics of play might be that it ignores the real cultural conflicts, which are not epistemological but economic and political. Said points out, for example, "the almost insuperable discrepancy between a political actuality based on force, and a scientific and humane desire to understand the Other hermeneutically and sympathetically in modes not always circumscribed and defined by force," and he argues that "an interlocutor in the colonial situation is . . . by definition either someone who is compliant . . . or someone who . . . simply refuses to talk, deciding that only a radically antagonistic, perhaps violent riposte is the only interlocution that is possible with colonial power" ("Representing" 217, 209–10). As I have argued, there are situations where play is not possible because of structural inequalities between the parties—structures of domination that are not ultimately epistemological in origin and that will not be eliminated by an ethical decision to undertake different hermeneutic practices. An epistemology of play is not a substitute for other kinds of political engagement aimed at contesting the rule of force.

However, to the extent that structures of knowledge are instruments of domination, play as a regulative ideal for negotiating differences can provide a standard on which to base critiques of the complicity of interpretive practices with various forms of hegemony. It provides norms that justify Said's critique of Orientalism, for example. It can also suggest alternative practices through which knowledge might not simply replicate the prevailing structures of domination. The premise of much postcolonial criticism, after all, is that the hegemonic solipsism of Orientalism and related modes of epistemological domination might be avoided even though the political and economic structures of imperialism still exist. If we are not doomed to be victims of Orientalism but nevertheless cannot rise above its snares to a realm of transparent representation, then our starting point must be the choice to interpret otherwise—an ethical decision based on enlightened self-consciousness about alternative epistemological models. That is where an epistemology of play can provide guidance and perhaps hope.

Furthermore, epistemological conflicts are not always reducible to economic and political causes. Knowledge is not only a subsidiary partner to other forms of domination. The will to know is also a specific instance of the will to power with its own problems and possibilities. Even if we lived in a world in which all other forms of inequality had been eliminated, epistemological differences would still give rise to irreconcilable conflicts that could become occasions for battles for power. One characteristic of the current global situation is that incommensurable cultural differences—irreconcilable practices of understanding based on opposing beliefs—are a site of contestation in and of themselves, regardless of how these differences are embedded in other political contexts. Aspirations for ascendancy can be epistemological as well as economic or political. To resist a Hobbesian world of epistemological warfare pitting each against all, and to pursue instead a vision of the productive, even playful interaction of differences, would require a commitment to follow norms that will not exist unless they are practiced. An epistemology of play as a response to the challenges and dilemmas posed by cultural differences imagines another world than the one we currently inhabit. But imagining that the world might be otherwise is a precondition for changing it.

Let me summarize my argument about the social uses of play by returning briefly to the Habermas-Lyotard debate discussed in chapter 1. An ideal of play based on nonconsensual reciprocity opposes Habermas's notion that cultural oppositions constitute a condition of fragmentation that should be overcome by noncoercive, cooperative negotiation guided by the goal of agreement. Differences may not be the result of a splitting off of faculties in the interests of specialization, as Habermas's critique of modernity argues (see "Incomplete Project"), but may instead reflect irreconcilable oppositions between games based on mutually incompatible rules, assumptions, and aims. There may be some value in Habermas's goal of establishing conditions of undistorted communication where no force rules other than the force of the better argument, but not because agreement about the "better argument" will result from uncoerced exchanges or even because power can ever be banished from such interactions (as the contradiction in the formula "no force other than . . ." implicitly recognizes). Rather, as an attempt to establish conditions of reciprocity that rule out violent intervention, Habermas's model of uncoerced negotiation would facilitate play in Iser's sense of a potentially ever-renewing doubling of positions. The counterflow of various forms of play that Iser describes would help to establish and maintain such exchanges, not by banishing force—an impossible dream—but by setting up interactions between opposing assertions of power that would counter each other's will to dominance. A play-space of reciprocally interacting positions offers an alternative to the consensus model of how cultural differences might communicate nonviolently.

Such a play-space also opposes the notion that the only alternative to the coerciveness of consensus must be advocacy of the sublime powers of rule breaking. Iser shares Lyotard's concern that privileging harmony and agreement in a world of heterogeneous language games limits play and inhibits semantic innovation and the creation of new games. But Lyotard's endorsement of the "sublime"—the pursuit of the "unpresentable" by rebelling against restrictions, defying norms, and smashing the limits of existing paradigms—is undermined by contradictions that Iser's explication of play recognizes and addresses. The paradox of the unpresentable, as Lyotard acknowledges, is that it can be manifested only through a game of representation (see "What Is Postmodernism?"). The sublime is, consequently, in Iser's sense, an instance of doubling. If violating norms creates new games, this crossing of boundaries depends on and carries in its wake the conventions and structures it oversteps. The sublime may be uncompromising, asocial, and unwilling to be bound by limits, but its pursuit of what is *not* contained in any order or system makes it dependent on the forms it opposes.

The radical presumption of the sublime is not only terroristic in refusing to recognize opposing games and their rules. It is also naive and self-destructive in imagining that it can possibly do without them. As a structure of doubling, the sublime pursuit of the unpresentable requires a play-space that includes other, less radical games with which it can interact. Such conditions of exchange would be provided by the nonconsensual reciprocity of play.

Iser's notion of play offers a way of conceptualizing power that acknowledges the necessity and force of disciplinary constraints without seeing them as unequivocally coercive and determining. The contradictory combination of restriction and openness in how play deploys power is evident in Iser's analysis of "regulatory" and "aleatory" rules. Even the regulatory rules that set down the conditions to which participants submit in order to play a game "permit a certain range of combinations while also establishing a code of possible play. . . . Since these rules limit the text game without producing it, they are regulatory but not prescriptive. They do no more than set the aleatory in motion, and the aleatory rule differs from the regulatory in that it has no code of its own" (*Fictive* 273). Submitting to the discipline of regulatory restrictions is both constraining and enabling because it makes possible certain kinds of interaction that the rules cannot completely predict or prescribe in advance. Hence the existence of aleatory rules that are not codified as part of the game itself but are the variable customs, procedures, and practices for playing it. Expert facility with aleatory rules marks the difference, for example, between someone who just knows the rules of a game and another who really knows how to play it. Aleatory rules are more flexible and open-ended and more susceptible to variation than regulatory rules, but they too are characterized by a contradictory combination of constraint and possibility, limitation and unpredictability, discipline and spontaneity.

As a rule-governed but open-ended activity, play provides a model for deploying power in a nonrepressive manner that makes creativity and innovation possible not in spite of disciplinary constraints but because of them. Not all power is playful, of course, and some restrictions are more coercive than enabling. But thinking about the power of constraints on the model of rules governing play helps to explain the paradox that restrictions can be productive rather than merely repressive. Seeing constraints as structures for establishing a play-space and as guides for practices of exchange within it envisions power, not as a force to be resisted in the interests of freedom, but (at least potentially and sometimes) as constructive social energy that can animate games of to-and-fro exchange, in which the constraints placed on the participants' interaction enhance the possibility of self-discovery and self-expansion. Whether repression or emancipation prevails in any particular situation is not intrinsic to the structure of power; it depends, rather, on how games are played.

3. BEING "OUT OF PLACE"

Edward Said and the Contradictions of Cultural Differences

As an outspoken public intellectual who did not shy away from controversy, Edward W. Said was at times a polarizing figure. The controversy ignited by his memoir, *Out of Place*, illustrates this all too clearly.[1] What went largely unnoticed, however, in the arguments about whether this or that autobiographical claim happened to be true was the role of the memoir in Said's evolving thought about cultural differences. Interestingly, the contradictions defining his personal history suggest a more complicated and compelling model of the politics and epistemology of cultural difference than can be found in either of his most important theoretical books on the subject, *Orientalism* and *Culture and Imperialism*. Moreover, his memoir explains why these two books contradict one another, the latter criticizing and revising the earlier text's depiction of the epistemology of imperial domination and identity formation, even though Said's commentaries on *Orientalism* obscure this by rewriting the first book in the image of his later views. The persona Said constructs in his memoir can help us understand, even better than his theoretical writings, how personal identities and community affiliations are created and how cross-cultural

---

[1] The games of "gotcha" that the memoir provoked are exemplified by Weiner's notorious *Commentary* essay. See Emily Eakin for a balanced account of the *Commentary* controversy and a sympathetic interview with Said about its charges. See Buruma for a representative negative review of the memoir and Alcalay for a positive one.

conflicts thwart the hermeneutic and political ideal of reciprocity.[2] Said's memoir testifies to the value of "doubling" and "play" as vehicles for mediating cultural differences.

Out of Place describes a life that was more contradictory and complex than either his friends or critics acknowledge. For example, although Said was born in West Jerusalem and speaks in the preface of his immense sadness at returning there after a long exile, his memoir shows that during most of his childhood and youth he lived in Cairo, where his father, a self-made man and enormously talented entrepreneur, ran "by far the largest office equipment and stationery business in the Middle East" (91). The elder Said, who was the regional representative for Royal, an office machine company, pioneered the introduction of an Arabic typewriter. Edward was a tireless defender of the downtrodden and the oppressed, but his youth was privileged because of his father's wealth, which allowed for first-class ocean travel and long stays in suites in the world's best hotels. His father, furthermore, although Palestinian by heritage, happened to be an American citizen because he had spent ten years in the United States as a young man and had fought in the American army during World War I. Said reports that his father hated Jerusalem and that his odd, inordinate pride at being an American is the reason why his son attended English-speaking schools in Cairo and was then sent to America for preparatory school and college. The material advantages of an American passport and his father's Egyptian-based business success contributed in no small way to Said's ability to fashion himself as an exiled Palestinian intellectual.

When his detractors use these contradictions to dismiss his persona as a fabrication, however, they miss the point. The memoir reveals, interestingly, that although Said refers to himself as "the Oriental subject" (*Orientalism* 25), his position is much more heterogeneous, contradictory, and complex than this self-characterization suggests:

My own experiences of these matters are in part what made me write this book. The life of an Arab Palestinian in the West, particularly in America, is

---

[2] In this respect, I am interested in what Paul John Eakin would call the "narrative identity" that Said constructs in telling his life as a story. This is not his actual, lived experience, in all of its confusing immediacy, but rather an interpretation of that experience. My essay in turn offers a different interpretation of Said's history by analyzing the complexities and contradictions of the life story he tells in his memoir and by placing this narrative in relation to other texts he has written. Said's life story and my interpretation are alternative constructions of a history that transcends both versions even as, like all histories, it is only available through different renderings of it. For a useful discussion of the relation between "narrative" and "identity," see Eakin's chapter "Storied Selves: Identity through Self-Narration." For an analysis of some of the epistemological ambiguities of history and historical interpretation, see the chapter "History, Epistemology, and the Example of *The Turn of the Screw*" in my *Conflicting Readings*.

disheartening. There exists here an almost unanimous consensus that politically he does not exist, and when it is allowed that he does, it is either as a nuisance or as an Oriental. The web of racism, cultural stereotypes, political imperialism, dehumanizing ideology holding in the Arab or the Muslim is very strong indeed, and it is this web which every Palestinian has come to feel as his uniquely punishing destiny. (27)

The racism and prejudice afflicting Moslem Arabs are real and despicable. Nevertheless, Said's identification with the "Oriental" here is a simplistic self-representation that *Out of Place* complexly revises. Curiously, his name literally does bear the traces of empire inasmuch as "Edward" was suggested by the Prince of Wales; but "Said" is a pure invention by his father, who chose it to replace his original surname "Ibrahim" for reasons that are not clear to any of the surviving members of the family (although again empire may have had a role if this act of self-naming testified to his American drive to create himself). "The travails of bearing such a name were compounded by an equally unsettling quandary when it came to language," Said reports. "I have never known what language I spoke first, Arabic or English, or which one was mine beyond any doubt" (*Place* 4). An American Palestinian in Egypt with equal facility in Arabic and English (because both were spoken in his American-Egyptian home), Said is a hybrid from the very beginning—which is the very point of *Out of Place,* in contrast to the monolithic assertion of identification with "the Oriental subject" in *Orientalism.* Said's hybridity extends to religion. Although as an adult he frequently and eloquently defended Islam against the prejudices and misunderstanding of Americans, he was raised a Christian by parents who had been married in a Baptist church in Nazareth where his mother's father was the pastor (after holding a ministry in Texas, of all places).

The complexity of Said's background and the multiplicity of his identity are, he says, "a form both of freedom and of affliction" (*Place* 12). His lack of a straightforward, unitary national and cultural identity, and of a sense of belonging to a single community and a coherent heritage, left him with a profound and defining ambivalence:

I have retained this unsettled sense of many identities—mostly in conflict with each other—all of my life, together with an acute memory of the despairing feeling that I wish we could have been all-Arab, or all-European and American, or all-Orthodox Christian, or all-Muslim, or all-Egyptian, and so on. . . ."What are you?" [he remembers being asked]; "But Said is an Arab name"; "You're an American?"; "You're American without an American name, and you've never been to America"; "You don't look American!"; "How come you were born in Jerusalem and you live *here?*" [i.e., Cairo]; "You're an Arab after all, but what kind are you? A Protestant?" (5–6)

At an American junior high school in Cairo, he remembers that "the over-all sensation I had was of my troublesome identity as an American inside whom lurked another Arab identity from which I derived no strength, only embarrassment and discomfort. I saw in [American classmates] Stan Henry and Alex Miller the much more enviable, rocklike hardness of an identity at one with the reality" (90). At Mount Hermon, however, he finds that being "out of place in nearly every way, gave me the incentive to find my territory, not socially but intellectually" (231). Throughout his life a longing for the wholeness and harmony that others seem to have but he does not conflicts with a sense of the liberating values of dissonance and multiplicity:

> I occasionally experience myself as a cluster of flowing currents. I prefer this to the idea of a solid self, the identity to which so many attach so much signifi-cance. These currents, like the themes of one's life, flow along during the wak-ing hours, and at their best, they require no reconciling, no harmonizing. . . . A form of freedom, I'd like to think, even if I am far from being totally convinced that it is. That skepticism too is one of the themes I particularly want to hold on to. With so many dissonances in my life I have learned actually to prefer being not quite right and out of place. (295)

Said's defining contradiction is this doubled condition of desiring a unified, assimilated "rocklike" identity (all Arab, all European, or all *something,* what-ever that may be, rather than a heterogeneous ensemble of ill-fitting parts) and of enjoying the liberating, expansive pleasures of multiple identities that never fully cohere.

Similar contradictions defined the experience of Joseph Conrad, the Pol-ish-English sailor-writer about whom Said has written at length, for reasons that are no doubt at least partly autobiographical. According to Said, Conrad was "so many different people, each one living a life unconnected with the others. . . . He was a self-conscious foreigner writing of obscure experiences in an alien language, and he was only too aware of this" (*Conrad* viii, 4). Con-rad himself described his identity as double: "Both at sea and on land my point of view is English, from which the conclusion should not be drawn that I have become an Englishman. That is not the case. Homo duplex has in my case more than one meaning" (Najder 240). Conrad both is and is not Eng-lish, just as he both is and is not Polish. Said's cultural identity is similarly double and split, inasmuch as he too both is and is not American, just as he is and is not Palestinian. Conrad responds, similarly to Said, by alternately wish-ing passionately for solidarity with a community and skeptically asserting the inevitability of cultural differences and interpretive multiplicity. Solidarity and fidelity are absolute moral values for Conrad because, as his oft-employed narrator Marlow asserts, "We exist only in so far as we hang together" (*Lord*

Jim 223). Writing no doubt out of his experience of alienness, however, Conrad also repeatedly dramatizes a profound and insuperable loneliness as the bedrock of existence, because who we are to ourselves can never be identical with who we are for others. Conrad oscillates between advocating solidarity and demystifying its deceptions and dangers by showing that social cohesion can be a mechanism for scapegoating others who remind us uncomfortably of the doubleness of identity, a split existence that may be more marked in exiles and émigrés but that characterizes human being in general (that is the point, for example, of the panic unleashed by the shipwrecked foreigner in his early story "Amy Foster," or of the trial and Brierly's suicide in *Lord Jim*).

The doubleness of cultural identity that Edward Said and Joseph Conrad (the adopted name of Józef Teodor Konrad Nałęcz Korzeniowski) exemplify gives evidence of the fundamental decenteredness of human being that Helmuth Plessner captures in his telling phrase "Ich bin, aber ich habe mich nicht [I am, but I do not have myself]." According to Wolfgang Iser, as we saw in the preceding chapter, this paradox describes the plasticity of humanness, which does not have one essential form but stages itself in an ever-changing variety of modes of being. For Iser and Plessner, this doubleness is responsible for the heterogeneity of identity positions within any given culture and the even greater multiplicity of identities across different cultures with varying constellations of roles and conventions. Émigrés or exiles who have experienced conflict between the roles of their community of origin and the roles they must learn if they wish to assimilate to their adopted culture might be more attuned to the doubled relation between the role player and the role than a "native" for whom the role seems natural, a given, simply who one is. Such an assumption is a mystification that covers over the possibly unsettling but also potentially liberating decenteredness and negativity of identity.

The role of the negative in the formation of cultural subjects means that one's belonging to a nation or community is not simply a given, determined once and for all, but (in Homi Bhabha's terms) a "narration" dependent on both "pedagogy" and "performance." In teaching a people the lesson of their belonging, "the scraps, patches, and rags of daily life must be repeatedly turned into the signs of a national culture," Bhabha explains, "while the very act of the narrative performance interpellates a growing circle of national subjects. In the production of the nation as narration there is a split between . . . the pedagogical, and the . . . performative," and this split "becomes the site of *writing the nation*" (297; original emphasis). If a nation, culture, or community must be "written" to exist, the negative distance between individual identity and group belonging is the difference that makes pedagogy both possible and necessary. This negation means that performances of cultural or national identity will be double structures of staging "who one is" in narrations that necessarily do not represent who "we" are. Otherwise the narrations wouldn't need to be performed and learned in order to continue to define "us." As structures of difference, nations and cultures are therefore internally heterogeneous and open to variation despite the stories they may tell of their timeless homogeneity.

Said refers to similar phenomena in his distinction between "instinctual filiation and social affiliation," a distinction that also suggests the pedagogy through which he learned to perform his own Palestinian identity. According to Said, cultural belonging is a matter both of "filiation" (with the community into which one is born) and "affiliation" (with groups to which one becomes aligned by virtue of social, political, or professional practices). These modes of belonging can reinforce or oppose one another: "affiliation sometimes reproduces filiation, sometimes makes its own forms" (*World* 24). Although Said is Palestinian by filiation inasmuch as he was born in Jerusalem, his long sojourn in Egypt meant that he paradoxically became Palestinian only by affiliation—by learning from his parents and relatives what the diaspora of 1948 meant and by taking on the appropriate attitudes and identifications for this mode of cultural belonging. His family in fact spent the year of 1947 in Jerusalem, but Said describes his then twelve-year-old self as "a scarcely conscious, essentially unknowing witness" of the "dislocation our family and friends experienced," a tragedy that had to be explained to him because he did not immediately comprehend or feel it: "Only once in a typically sweeping way did my father elucidate the general Palestinian condition, when he remarked about [a friend's] family that 'they had lost everything'; a moment later he added, 'We lost everything too.' When I expressed my confusion as to what he meant, since his business, the house, our style of life in Cairo, seemed to have remained the same, 'Palestine' was all he said" (*Place* 114, 115).

After this one moment of solidarity with his community of filiation, however, Said's father attempted to go about his business in Egypt as if nothing had happened. Looking back, Said says, "It seems inexplicable to me now that having dominated our lives for generations, the problem of Palestine and its tragic loss, which affected virtually everyone we knew, deeply changing our world, should have been so relatively repressed, undiscussed, or even remarked on by my parents. . . . But the repression of Palestine in our lives occurred as part of a larger depoliticization on the part of my parents, who hated and distrusted politics, feeling too precarious in Egypt for participation or even open discussion." He reports that "it was mainly my aunt Nabiha who would not let us forget the misery of Palestine" through her charity work with refugee families in Cairo (117).

Although he was born Palestinian and witnessed the Palestinian diaspora, Said's identity as a Palestinian did not come naturally. He first had to learn it from his aunt despite his parents' efforts to educate him to a different set of identifications, and he then recommitted himself to it with the publication of *Orientalism* in 1978, an event that seemed surprising to many at the time, because his earlier books on Conrad and poststructural literary theory had not suggested the identity of the oppressed Oriental subject he affirms, discloses, and performs there. My point is not that this identity is false or misleading but, rather, as the distinction between filiation and affiliation suggests, that it, like all cultural identity, is double and split. Said both is and is not Palestinian, and he therefore must learn and perform this role, a role that he can identify with only because it is not simply who he is.

The negativity and doubleness of cultural identity can have a variety of outcomes and consequences, none of them prescribed in advance. National identity can feel like a trap or a prison, an alienation we experience by producing it, because we are not the roles we find ourselves in, even as we sustain their coercive authority by performing the patterns of belonging that define us. Or it may seem a haven and a refuge from the unsettledness of a decentered existence. Or, alternatively, the contingency of cultural belonging can allow the negative to be used for play, transformation, or protest—to create a space for self-assertion and self-expression out of the difference between who one is and who one is not. A culture may, however, seek to deny the contingency of its defining roles and its resulting heterogeneity by unifying against an Other whose difference is threatening because it suggests the decenteredness of identity. Such solidarity of the "us" versus "them" scapegoats the Other by branding it as "evil" or inferior, the goal being material or epistemological domination that will contain and control its threat (this is, of course, the epistemological mechanism and the moral and political purpose of "Orientalism"). Or the doubleness of existence may allow someone to cross boundaries and exchange differences with others in a process of cross-cultural negotiation—provided that the material conditions to make this possible are available (as they were to Said). This is easier said than done, however, because even when material or economic interests are not at stake (as of course they typically are), the negativity of cultural identity can unleash a fearsome will to power, motivated by a desire to overcome the anxieties of decenteredness and doubleness by mastering the threat of difference, and the fragility of expansive, playful cultural negotiation and exchange may hardly stand a chance.

Edward Said's memoir dramatizes these contradictions, and his various theoretical works are an attempt to formalize and understand them. His aim, he says, is to increase the unlikely possibility that being "out of place" can be creative and constructive rather than anguished and embattled. Hence his description of his vocation as a critic: "Criticism must think of itself as life-enhancing and constitutively opposed to every form of tyranny, domination, and abuse; its social goals are noncoercive knowledge produced in the interests of human freedom" (*World* 29). He explains: "The dictum 'solidarity before criticism' means the end of criticism. I take criticism so seriously as to believe that, even in the very midst of a battle in which one is unmistakably on one side against another, there should be criticism, because there must be critical consciousness if there are to be issues, problems, values, even lives to be fought for" (28). The doubleness and negativity of cultural identity make criticism possible because distance and detachment allow a perspective on oneself and one's world, a perspective that could not exist if we were simply unitary. But this negativity can also lead to battles for domination even in the realm of criticism: "All texts essentially dislodge other texts or, more frequently, take the place of something else. As Nietzsche had the perspicacity to see, texts are fundamentally facts of power, not of democratic exchange" (45). Said's life and intellectual career repeatedly show this tension between a desire for a utopian space where differences could be exchanged in noncoercive, mutually liberating relations and a hard-nosed recognition of the realities of power that seeks to control and contain difference by structuring it into a hierarchy of domination and subordination.[3]

In *Out of Place* Said reports a series of mutually reinforcing incidents in which he is branded "Other" in a manner that illustrates the role of negation in identity formation—the process of exclusionary differentiation that, he will later argue, is crucial to Orientalism in particular and culture in general. Creating itself in opposition to what it is not, culture is "a series of exclusions legislated from above, but enacted throughout its polity," "a differentially negative doctrine of all that is not best, . . . a constantly practiced differentiation of itself from what it believes to be not itself" (*World* 11, 12). This is the general rule, of which one particular instance is the construction of the "Orient" as the valorizing "Other" counterposed to the Anglo-European world: "The construction of identity—for identity, whether of Orient or Occident, France or Britain, while obviously a repository of distinct collective experiences, is finally a construction in my opinion—involves the construction of opposites and 'others' whose actuality is always subject to the continuous interpretation and re-interpretation of their differences from 'us.' Each age and society re-creates its 'Others' " ("Afterword" 322). Here again identity is a

---

[3] Jim Merod makes a similar point: "The overt celebration of the sentimental is not Said's project in the least, although an undercurrent within his writing suggests a desire to exert a utopic theme, a hope for the usefulness of intellect to increase cultural contestation at the expense of outright skirmishes, bloodshed, brutality, and carnage" (115). Rather than a mere "undercurrent," however, I see here a defining tension between a tough-minded skepticism and a reasoned belief in the possibility of critical, productive conflict that exists throughout his career but becomes especially marked in his two late works, *Culture and Imperialism* and *Out of Place*.

double structure that depends for its defining difference on the Other it negates, just as, in Foucault's classic analysis on which Said silently depends, "reason" constituted itself in the Enlightenment by constructing "madness" as what it was not.

Said first consciously experienced this negation when he was taking a shortcut home from school across the grounds of his father's club, and an Englishman who was secretary of the club and the father of one of his classmates challenged him: " 'Don't you know you're not supposed to be here?' he asked reprovingly. I started to say something about being a member, but he cut me off pitilessly. 'Don't answer back, boy. Just get out, and do it quickly. Arabs aren't allowed here, and you're an Arab!' If I hadn't thought of myself as an Arab before, I now directly grasped the significance of the designation as truly disabling" (*Place* 44). One moral of this story is that his identity is not simply a given but must be learned, here by being branded with a racist label that seems odd to young Edward because it assigns him to a group outside the community of the club he belonged to. The Englishman thinks he is pointing out a natural fact (the boy's presumed race), but instead he is exercising the oppositional power of negation. He creates an affiliation (club member) by excluding others, and the conflict for young Edward is that he thereby discovers an affiliation he hadn't felt (his Arab identity) by the refusal of one he had taken for granted.

This incident shows what Jean-Paul Sartre calls the power of the "look of the Other" to define and categorize the self, as when the playwright Jean Genet is caught stealing and is labeled "thief," a category he then rebels against by performing it with a vengeance: "All right then, call me a thief. I will be the thief!" (see *Genet* 17–22, 49–58). The Other's gaze fixes and controls, but redefining the label by playing it in one's own way creates room to maneuver and the possibility of answering back. On several other occasions the young Said experiences the power of the defining label that would fix and place him, and he struggles for ways to escape and protest. After a field trip to a sugar refinery on the Nile, his American teacher reprimands him for his bad behavior: "Miss Clark had purposely, deliberately, even fastidiously, defined me, caught me, as it were, from within, had seen me as I could or would not see myself. . . . 'Who is this person?' I imagined them saying, 'a little Arab boy, and what is he doing in a school for American children? Where did he come from?' " (*Place* 86). Or later, at a summer camp in Maine, when he takes an extra hot dog beyond his ration, a counselor named Murray calls him a "sneak": "It was only years later, when I read Stendhal, that I recognized much the same kind of deformation in Julien Sorel, who when he is suddenly confronted with a priest's direct gaze swoons away. I felt myself to be a shameful outsider to the world that Miss Clark and Murray wished to exclude me from" (137). Or again, at a British school where he plays the "bad boy" as "a form of resistance" and is then confronted by a teacher who expels him: "Isolated, pinpointed, transfixed, I had suddenly stepped outside every circle I had once inhabited" (186, 209). Here as before, an experience of exclusion defines him even as it solidifies the authority of the person who asserts the power to label him and cast him out.

There may be at least a little personal mythologization at work in Said's depiction of himself as a repeated victim of the Anglo-American imperial gaze who fights back by rebelling against his oppressors. Regardless of the truth or falsity of these self-representations, what is interesting is the epistemology of the response he describes. These incidents and others like them lead him over the course of his young life to construct two selves—the public Edward who is chastised, criticized, and categorized and "my inner, far less compliant and private self, who could read, think, and even write independent of 'Edward.' . . . It was something private and apart that gave me strength when 'Edward' seemed to be failing" (165). He speaks of "the almost absolute separation that existed between my surface life at school and the complicated but mostly inarticulate inner life I cherished and lived through the emotions and sensations I derived from music, books, and memories intertwined with fantasies. It was as if the integration and liberty I needed between my selves would have to be endlessly postponed, although I subliminally retained the belief that one day they would somehow be integrated" (202).

Once again contradictory, his split self is simultaneously a resource and a cause for anguish and regret. He desires an integral, unified self, but he finds refuge and strength in the contradiction between his self-for-others (the Edward others see and seek to discipline) and his self-for-himself (his interior world of aesthetic pleasure and rebellious thoughts). This doubleness allows him to distance himself from the authorities and criticize their power and defining categories. If he is not powerful enough to fight back and win, he can nevertheless create an alternative world for himself that allows escape from their reality and that exposes its inadequacy. (Books, film, and music grant him this space of protest, criticism, and solace. Interestingly, these are mainly Western texts, including especially European music and his beloved opera, but also, surprisingly, American films with heavy colonial overtones like Tarzan and the Arabian nights—which shows that the cultural resources of imperialism can be employed for other purposes than domination and hegemony even when they are also serving those ends.)

One frequent criticism of *Orientalism* is that it describes the defining gaze of the Orientalist as so powerful that the Oriental subject would seem to have no way of fighting back. Said asserts later, in *Culture and Imperialism,* that "never was it the case that the imperial encounter pitted an active Western intruder against a supine or inert non-Westerner; there was *always* some form of active resistance, and in the overwhelming majority of cases, the resistance finally won out" (xii). Given the power that *Orientalism* attributes to the categorizing projections of Western Orientalism in constructing its object of study, it is hard to theorize how such resistance would be possible. According to *Orientalism,* "the Orientalist attitude . . . shares with magic and with mythology the self-containing, self-reinforcing character of a closed system, in which objects are what they are *because* they are what they are, for once, for all time, for ontological reasons that no empirical material can either dislodge or alter" (70). One flaw of the epistemology of *Orientalism* is that it fails to explain how it could have come to be written as a powerful act of answering back. *Out of Place,* a more subtle and complex text, shows the possibility of resistance by demonstrating how the doubleness of identity formation allows a critical consciousness to develop in opposition to the definitions of the dominant authority. Because Edward Said both is and is not the Edward defined by the gaze of the authorities, his doubleness allows him to evade their control and, eventually, to turn their weapons (their texts, traditions, and interpretive procedures) into instruments for fighting back and asserting his own identity. Opposition of this kind would not be possible if identity were single and unitary.[4]

In an afterword written for the 1994 edition of *Orientalism* (one year after *Culture and Imperialism* was published), Said expresses bewilderment and disappointment that his book had been taken as "anti-Western" and had been embraced by Arab nationalists as "a systematic defense of Islam and the Arabs" (331). He especially regrets that the "us-them" constitution of the Other that he had criticized in the Orientalist has returned in the anti-hegemonic assertion of the Oriental subject's claims: "in all my works I have remained fundamentally critical of a gloating and uncritical nationalism" (337). Instead of overcoming polarizing oppositions, he laments that his attack on the strategy of exclusionary differentiation has inadvertently reinforced them.

In fact, *Orientalism* is contradictory on this score. His book does ask "whether there is any way of avoiding the hostility expressed by the division, say, of men into 'us' (Westerners) and 'them' (Orientals)," and he regrets that

---

[4] There are obvious parallels here to Hegel's classic analysis of the master-slave dialectic, which in turn thoroughly if silently informs Sartre's interpretation of Genet's transformation of authority's defining gaze into an opportunity for rebellious self-consciousness and self-fashioning. See also Said's brief but interesting discussion of Fanon's rereading of Hegel to illuminate the battle between colonizer and colonized (*Culture* 210). Said's point is that Fanon's appropriation of Hegel shows "the partial tragedy of resistance, that it must to a certain degree work to recover forms already established or at least influenced or infiltrated by the culture of empire" (210). I would only add that such a transformation of the dominant culture's instruments into tools for oppositional purposes is made possible by the doubling I have described.

"the result is usually to polarize the distinction—the Oriental becomes more Oriental, the Westerner more Western—and limit the human encounter between different cultures, traditions, and societies" (45, 46). But he also asserts that the power of Orientalism as a hegemonic "system of truths" was such "that *every* European, in what he could say about the Orient, was consequently a racist, an imperialist, and almost totally ethnocentric. . . . As a cultural apparatus Orientalism is *all* aggression, activity, judgment, will-to-truth, and knowledge" (204; emphasis added). In his afterword he claims that his book "stress[ed] the actualities of what was later to be called multiculturalism, rather than xenophobia and aggressive, race-oriented nationalism," and he calls it "a multicultural critique of power using knowledge to advance itself" in "the realization, almost universally acknowledged, that cultures are hybrid and heterogeneous and . . . so interrelated and interdependent as to beggar any unitary or simply delineated description of their individuality" (Afterword 335, 347). He is perhaps closer to the truth when he acknowledges that "*Orientalism* is a partisan book, not a theoretical machine" (339)—what Nietzsche calls a *Streitschrift* (or "battle text") that fights power with power, with the danger that it may reproduce the divisions Said claims later to want to transcend.

Said's ambivalence about *Orientalism*'s reception expresses the contradiction I have described between his longing for solidarity with a community (to be "all" something) and his appreciation of the values of multiplicity (the fluidity and freedom of not belonging). As a *Streitschrift, Orientalism* is an oppositional text that encourages a homogeneous identification with the oppressed alongside whose interests Said unequivocally aligns himself (calling himself "the Oriental subject"). He thereby achieves a moment of unitary, "rocklike" identity, turning the tables on the others who had labeled and displaced him by naming and subordinating them (through his powerful coinage "Orientalism," which was quickly accepted as a useful category for demystifying and condemning a wide sweep of people, texts, and cultural and epistemological practices). Instead of being cast out, he assumes the superior posture of knowing the authorities better than they know themselves—his act of polemical revenge on those who had fixed and labeled not only him but also those others with whom he now claims solidarity. This revenge is epistemologically justified to the extent that all texts are, as Nietzsche claims, combatants in a never-ending battle for power, always seeking to dislodge their rivals for political, cultural, and intellectual domination.

The problem, however, is that Said gains the unitary, superior identity he had long desired (to be "at home" in a homogeneous community) only by setting himself in antagonistic relations with other groups and conventions he also identifies with. The American-European traditions that were central to his education, became his personal refuge as a young man, and formed the foundation of his professional identity as an author and critic have the status for him of personally defining intellectual and cultural affiliations. The further problem, of course, is that such solidarity denies the internal heterogeneity and feeling of difference that give him a powerful sense of freedom (the pleasure of not fitting any of the homogenizing categories that are thrust upon him). As much as he desires solidarity, the singular self he thereby attains also betrays himself.

Said responds to this dilemma by proposing in *Culture and Imperialism* a heterogeneous model of cultural differences that claims to reject polarization (what he calls there "the rhetoric of blame"). Similarly, in his afterword to the second edition of *Orientalism,* he recasts this book as an argument for multiculturalism, rather than as a polemic against imperial domination that risks reproducing the "us–them" exclusionary structures of differentiation it unmasks. Said explains in his afterword that "most people resist the underlying notion that human identity is not only not natural and stable, but constructed and occasionally even invented outright," and he claims that his critique of Orientalism was aimed primarily at its failure to recognize the constructedness of its cultural categories: "as a system of thought Orientalism approaches a heterogeneous, dynamic, and complex human reality from an uncritically essentialist standpoint" (332, 333).

Although not entirely unfaithful to the original text, this argument fails to recognize that the Foucauldian notion that identity is created by "us–them" exclusionary negation and the Nietzschean claim that knowledge is all a battle for power provide him in *Orientalism* with little or no alternative to the epistemological structures whose polarizing effects he now laments. If the author of *Orientalism* wins this contest, he becomes the "us" who succeed in defining "them," and he thereby himself risks essentializing and homogenizing the others whom he has powerfully categorized and labeled. As he writes in *Culture and Imperialism,* "the world is a crowded place, and . . . if everyone were to insist on the radical purity or priority of one's own voice, all we would have would be the awful din of unending strife, and a bloody political mess" (xxi): "A new and in my opinion appalling tribalism is fracturing societies, separating peoples, promoting greed, bloody conflict, and uninteresting assertions of minor ethnic or group particularity" (20). In order to construct an alternative to "unending strife," however, one needs a notion of culture as more than simply a battle for dominance. One needs a model of semiotic and epistemological relations that recognizes the Nietzschean moment but then suggests how a victory might lead to different conditions of exchange (reciprocal, emancipatory, and noncoercive) instead of perpetuating the winner-loser dichotomy and the tit-for-tat of cultural and epistemological conflict.

Said gestures toward such a model in his advocacy of "contrapuntal criticism" in *Culture and Imperialism*. Attempting to move beyond the dualism of *Orientalism*, Said acknowledges that "the difficulty with theories of essentialism and exclusiveness, or with barriers and sides, is that they give rise to polarizations that absolve and forgive ignorance and demagogy more than they enable knowledge" (31). This is true not only of the institution that *Orientalism* attacks and unmasks but also of the reverse polarization that he laments in the way his book was received. The "contrapuntal perspective" Said proposes in *Culture and Imperialism* would seek "to think through and interpret together experiences that are discrepant" (32). As he argues, "partly because of empire, all cultures are involved in one another; none is single and pure, all are hybrid, heterogeneous, extraordinarily differentiated, and unmonolithic" (xxv). He consequently asks "how a post-imperial intellectual attitude might expand the overlapping community between metropolitan and formerly colonized societies. By looking at the different experiences contrapuntally, as making up a set of what I call intertwined and overlapping histories, I shall try to formulate an alternative both to a politics of blame and to the even more destructive politics of confrontation and hostility" (18).

This is an attractive ideal, and it is not surprising that Said would draw from the realm of music, always a space of expansive, noncoercive pleasure for him, for a metaphor of cross-cultural exchange that goes beyond battles for power. It is not clear, however, that the notion of "counterpoint" (the harmonious juxtaposition of different melodies) can accomplish this political and epistemological work, other than to point toward its desirability. As a metaphor for negotiating cultural differences, "counterpoint" assumes what needs to be established—the possibility of moving beyond perpetually divisive conflict to a productive, creative exchange of differences—without demonstrating systematically how this can be achieved.

The challenge, as Said himself describes it, is how to overcome the contradiction between the politics of force and the human desire to understand the Other undistorted by considerations of power (see *Culture* 56). In large part this is, of course, not an epistemological problem but a political one—how to replace structures of domination and subordination like imperialism with democratic relations based on equality and mutual respect. But the question then returns as to whether that political ideal is epistemologically possible. Is not the ideal of democratic equality helplessly naive about the ubiquitous interdependence of knowledge and power, which would remain problematic even if economic and material parity were created and inequities based on race or gender eradicated? Such sweeping changes are hardly likely, to be sure, but the point of this thought experiment is to suggest that even under otherwise ideal conditions, the will to know may always carry with it a will to power that would disrupt the democratic negotiation of differences by seeking to replace equality with dominance.

This is the difficult issue that Said both illuminates and obscures with his metaphor of "contrapuntal criticism":

> As we look back at the cultural archive, we begin to reread it not univocally but *contrapuntally*, with a simultaneous awareness both of the metropolitan history that is narrated and of those other histories against which (and together with which) the dominating discourse acts. In the counterpoint of Western classical music, various themes play off one another, with only a provisional privilege being given to any particular one; yet in the resulting polyphony there is concert and order, an organized interplay that derives from the themes, not from a rigorous melodic or formal principle outside the work. (51)

Polyphony is created out of the discordant concord of counterpoint because the will to dominance of any one melody is contained by a structure that orders all of the conflicting elements into a relationship that is nonsynthetic and nonunitary but nevertheless reciprocal. This feat depends both on the controlling force of the composer's intention and on the socially accepted conventions and rules of contrapuntal music.

The situation in cross-cultural interpretation is not exactly analogous. The contrapuntal interpreter may intend to achieve a similar discordant concord among heterogeneous cultural materials, but there is nothing like the conventions of counterpoint to govern the juxtapositions and conflicts with which the interpreter works. How to establish such a game—conditions of exchange governed by nonsynthetic, nonconsensual reciprocity aimed not at solidarity or dominance—is precisely the challenge, and it is the question that the metaphor of counterpoint begs.

A more adequate alternative may emerge if we examine Said's claims for exiles and émigrés, who in his view are more likely than others to understand and exemplify the contrapuntal ideal. He describes *Culture and Imperialism* as "an exile's book": "For objective reasons that I had no control over, I grew up as an Arab with a Western education. Ever since I can remember, I have felt that I belonged to both worlds, without being completely *of* either one or the other. . . . Yet when I say 'exile' I do not mean something sad or deprived. On the contrary belonging, as it were, to both sides of the imperial divide enables you to understand them more easily" (xxvi, xxvii; original emphasis). Said's claims for himself as an "exile" are once again contradictory, inasmuch as they simultaneously assert the ascendancy of the special identity he has long desired (as the exemplary exile, he is "all something" after all), even if this identity is not the integration he had sought but a recognition that doubling and difference are inescapable. The broader question, however, is whether an "exile" occupies a unique, privileged position or represents practices more generally available to others with different histories. I have argued that Said's status as an exile who finds himself always "out of place" stages our general destiny as beings whose identity is double and split. If so, then hybridity and heterogeneity would constitute a potential common ground for cross-cultural understanding rather than a basis for one individual's epistemological privilege.

What matters from this perspective, I would argue, is not whether some of us are "exiles" and others not, but rather how we engage in historical acts of doubling. These practices are necessarily both situated and open-ended and will vary according to the particular circumstances and horizons of the practitioners. The decisive distinction is whether such practices aim to be conflictual and divisive (differences used as instruments for exercising the will to power) or hermeneutically productive, noncoercive, and mutually liberating (differences employed as the enabling materials of "contrapuntal" exchanges). Here again the metaphor of "counterpoint" is too ahistorical—that is, too static, closed, and unsituated—to suggest adequately the open-ended work of constructing mutually enhancing exchanges with otherness. Although music is, like writing, a temporal art, the goal of establishing harmony or concord is too stable and insufficiently heterogeneous to figure adequately the movement of differences interacting across historical horizons and cultural boundaries. Furthermore, the aim of creating and sustaining noncoercive, emancipatory relations that are nonconsensual but reciprocal is not necessarily to establish harmony. Interactions that are lively, liberating, and mutually enhancing may be productively discordant without being violent or oppressive.

A more adequate metaphor for illuminating these complications is "play," in Iser's analysis of this double-sided term. Unlike "counterpoint," "play" does not decide in advance whether its aim will be conflict or reciprocity, discord or concord, domination or mutual enhancement. Iser's distinction between kinds of "play" is once again useful here—between "play" that entails an instrumental attempt to master and control (culture on the model of the will to power) and "play" as an open-ended, unpredictable to-and-fro movement (power used in a reciprocal exchange intended to multiply differences rather than to freeze them into the single hierarchical distinction between winner and loser). The second kind of play supplements the notion of culture as a battleground (the conflict characteristic of "instrumental play") with another model of culture as emancipatory interchange. The difference is between games that aim to end play with the victory of one side and open-ended interchanges that are playful precisely because they resist resolution. The two kinds of play are related, however, because noncoercive, nonmanipulative interactions can degenerate into gamesmanship (reciprocity being undermined

by instrumentality), even as the momentum of play in a game can seek to perpetuate itself and avoid the disappointment of closure. A more complex and
open-ended metaphor than "counterpoint," Iserian play can provide a way of
thinking about the reciprocally beneficial, nondemonizing interaction of differences that Said seeks as an alternative to the will to power of Orientalism or
the various "rhetorics of blame."

There are at least two other reasons for preferring "play" rather than
"counterpoint" as a metaphor for mediating cultural differences. First, unlike
contrapuntal music, the to-and-fro of noninstrumental, truly reciprocal cross-
cultural play will not be governed by the intentions and will of a single creating subject (constrained as he or she may be by rules of composition and other
generic conventions). The subject of play is not the individual participants, if
the exchange between parties is genuinely reciprocal and productive of meanings that neither fully controls. Rather, play that is truly playful simultaneously depends on their activities and transcends them. One paradox of play is
that the participants create an interaction that in turn steers and molds their
behavior so that it may seem to have a subjectivity of its own that is not reducible to either party.

Second, the conventions governing the exchange in nonconsensual but reciprocal interactions are not set by one party or determined in advance (as
they are in the case of a composer who accepts the conventions of counterpoint and produces music within their bounds, however much she or he may
playfully seek to extend them). The question of which conventions govern the
exchange is something that may be played with. The discovery that the conventions of neither party are fully adequate to facilitating a productive interaction between them may lead to the creation of new games and new rules that
do not quite match what either participant brings to the exchange but emerge
as unexpected consequences of their negotiation—a result of each disclosing
the limits of the other's assumptions and beliefs by virtue of their differences
from one's own position, even as unexpected possibilities for selecting and
combining elements from each world may open up new meanings and perspectives neither could generate independently.

The point of my attempt to set Iser and Said in dialogue with one another
in this chapter and the last has been to demonstrate the mutually beneficial
consequences of this kind of play. These are two thinkers who might seem to
have little to say to each other. Instead, their differences make them surprisingly interesting and reciprocally useful interlocutors. Each illuminates the
other and becomes transformed through the exchange in ways that neither
could accomplish on his own. Iser's notion of noninstrumental play as a means
of fostering interactions between mutually exclusive positions reveals and
speaks to gaps in Said's thinking about cross-cultural understanding that he

himself recognizes and tries to fill (less adequately, I think) in his speculations about "contrapuntal criticism." Conversely, Said's powerful demonstration of the dangers of the drive for ascendancy implicit in the will to know other peoples and cultures discloses darker implications and consequences of human plasticity than Iser sometimes seems to recognize in his celebration of literature's capacities for staging our potentiality for being. In turn, the need to develop alternatives to the oppression and blindness of cultural solipsism suggests social and political uses of Iser's aesthetic theory that he himself does not explicitly develop and that show powers of his thinking he may not be fully aware of.

As in any good conversation, the Iser-Said encounter takes directions that neither would have chosen independently, and the result of the exchange is something more than either party could have produced by himself. The idea that play has the political value of making possible a kind of nonconsensual reciprocity that allows cultural and other differences to interact creatively should not be seen, however, as a point of agreement that unifies these two disparate thinkers. Neither would probably recognize it as his own. It is, rather, an idea that emerges from their encounter and that in turn shows the usefulness of this kind of exchange.

PART TWO

CRITICISM

4. ART AND THE CONSTRUCTION OF COMMUNITY IN "THE DEATH OF THE LION"

What are the uses of art in constructing community? This is a central question for the politics of reading, and it is the main concern of Henry James's story "The Death of the Lion"—a short but complex and suggestive text that I would like to use to provide an initial model of the practical criticism that might follow from my theoretical arguments about power, play, and reading. In this story, the author's rapid rise to glory and equally sudden passing out of the limelight and into the grave leave the reader asking not only what care art deserves but also whether forms of social relation might be found that are reciprocal and mutually enhancing rather than conflictual, destructive, and violent. Contrary to traditional critical opinion, James does not view the private aesthetic realm as an authentic sphere of meaning and value that could provide a sanctuary from the fallen public world.[1] "The Death of the Lion" shows that similar battles for power, zero-sum games, and exclusionary structures occur in both domains. The communicative irrationalities of the public sphere are replicated in the realm of privacy. I echo Habermas's phrase "communicative rationality," however, because I share his belief (as does James, in

[1] An interesting twist on this argument is Seltzer's claim that to posit in James "an aesthetic outside the circuit of power . . . is itself the ruse of power," a deception that reinforces "modern technologies of social control" and "the dissemination of power throughout the most everyday social practices and institutions" by pretending that these realms are not political (147, 18). My contention is that James understands art as thoroughly implicated in questions of power and that he consequently wonders whether art can deploy power for emancipatory social ends.

my view) in the possibility of uses of power based on reciprocity and mutual recognition rather than on willful domination and control. How community might be constructed using power in this way is, I will argue, the challenge "The Death of the Lion" poses to its readers. In this tale as in his other ambiguous stories about authors and writing, James's criticism of the misuse of art implies an alternative mode of caring for the aesthetic and being with others, one that is nowhere dramatized in the text but is enacted as a challenge to the reader through the mediation of its form of narration.

Because identity and social forms are contingent structures of difference rather than intrinsic givens, they are open to a variety of uses and ends that are not predetermined. The question of how a community cares for art matters to James because the contingency of identity and social relations can lead to contradictory results. The instability of a world of differences can be invigorating and transformative, but the oppositions that make meaning possible can just as easily become the instruments and the stakes in conflicts between rival wills to power. The mutability of social forms can allow emancipatory acts of self-creation that fixed structures would prevent, but it can also inspire projects of personal apotheosis that use contingency as a tool to assert ascendancy. Fluid relations can make possible a playful reciprocity based on mutual recognition and engagement, or they can become a field of contest between opponents who would structure them for their own purposes.[2]

"The Death of the Lion" portrays art and artists as objects of a battle for power between rivals for ascendancy and as instruments for instituting exclusionary structures of domination and control. This negative picture raises the question of whether, in a thoroughly contingent world, art can be used socially as a mediator fostering mutual recognition and an emancipatory exchange of differences. The act of reading might be a place where that could start, but the dilemma for the reader is that such a beginning can be made only by reading against the narrator and becoming his rival in a struggle to control the meaning of his tale.

How the construction of the author may construct the community, and vice versa, is evident in how *The Empire* (a name that signals almost too

[2] Ross Posnock wrongly assumes that what he calls "a politics of nonidentity"—"a strategy dedicated to disrupting the compulsion to fix identity" and a "suspicion of the assimilating, homogenizing thrust of totalizing systems" (16)—is inherently emancipatory: "a fluidity of identification instills a capacity for a mutuality that is the basis of vital citizenship," he argues, and helps "create individuals possessing the maximum capacity for experimental, tolerant, communal activity" (23, 259). This healthy-minded affirmation of the liberating, communal implications of the contingency of identity and society ignores the darker side of its availability for power, conflict, and violence. A two-sided sense of the values and the dangers of a mutable world of differences is more adequate to the paradoxes of contingency and to James's complex appreciation of its contradictory potential.

blatantly that issues of power and community building are at stake) elevates
Neil Paraday:

> The big blundering newspaper had discovered him, and now he was proclaimed
> and anointed and crowned. His place was assigned him as publicly as if a fat
> usher with a wand had pointed to the topmost chair; he was to pass up and still
> up, higher and higher, between the watching faces and the envious sounds—
> away up to the dais and the throne. The article was "epoch-making," a landmark
> in his life; he had taken rank at a bound, waked up a national glory. A national
> glory was needed, and it was an immense convenience he was there. (110)

The functions of exclusion and regulation in establishing fields of difference
are on display here. If socially defining distinctions depend on the institution
of a negative (the identity of something defined by what it is not), then one can
inscribe differences by placing someone in a position others are *not* entitled to.
Similarly, regulatory acts of social control institute a field of distinctions by as-
signing each party a place that is *not* someone else's. In such differentiating
acts of establishment, power is not merely repressive but productive, as
James's metaphors suggest: "*The Empire* . . . fired, as if on the birth of a
prince, a salute of a whole column" (110), a militaristic display of annuncia-
tory force, while the "fat usher with a wand" directs everyone in the ceremony
to their proper places, a disciplinary role shortly ceded to a critic who appears
on Paraday's doorstep, "a stout man with a big black beard, who, save that he
wore spectacles, might have been a policeman" (112). Regulation by seeing
and defining constitutes the author through the use of a disciplinary power
that also creates a web of relations around him.

The whole process is curiously anonymous and artificial. Considerable
agency and force are at work here, but the agents seem inscrutable, arbitrary,
and unpredictable. Paraday's elevation grants him an ascendancy that he has
no control over and that oddly disempowers him. Although his glorification
seems to recognize his unique, irreplaceable talents and accomplishments, he
is substitutable, "an immense convenience"; if not him, someone else would
have been found. As a "lion," he is a symbol defined by what he stands for and
by the purposes these representational values serve, and his function as a
counter in a system of relations is again consistent with the anonymous, impersonal quality of his elevation. The recognition he receives does not recognize Paraday as he understands himself but only as he performs a role he is
not invited to help define.

Social bonds are established here through triangulation, by spectators gaz-
ing together on a shared object. They see Paraday ascend to a position of absolute visibility, like a sacrificial offering whose expenditure unites the
participants in the ceremony. The result may be to naturalize community—to

make the national glory of the imperium seem a manifest destiny—but this in turn represses and disguises the arbitrariness of the contingent materials and structures through which community is created. The contingency of identity and social roles makes possible a process of community formation that attempts to erase the evidence of contingency.

James's story calls attention to the artificiality of identity through what might otherwise seem like an extraneous detail—the pseudonymous gender switching of Paraday's two main rivals, Guy Walsingham (a woman) and Mrs. Dora Forbes ("It wouldn't be 'Miss,' " the narrator is told, because "there's a wife!" [116]). "In the age we live in," the narrator finds, "one gets lost among the genders and the pronouns" (144). He reports himself "bewildered: it sounded somehow as if there were three sexes" (115–16). Loosening the bonds between gender identity and sexual difference can open up identity to greater freedom of play, a less encumbered staging of roles, than a fixed system of referential correlation would allow. This semantic liberation can cause confusion, however, a blurring of distinctions that otherwise facilitate the cognitive mapping of the social scene. But this bewilderment can also be illuminating because it reveals the role of coded, contingent differences in constituting the social map (even sexual identity is recognizable only through metonymic markers: Dora Forbes is "an indubitable male" because "he had a big red moustache" [116]).

The gender switching in James's story does not serve emancipatory play and exploration but is instead an instrument in the participants' battles for gain, authority, and privilege. The blurring of boundaries contributes not to innovative self-creation but to the manipulation of differences to achieve distinction.[3] The male pseudonym is "convenient, you know, for a lady who goes in for the larger latitude" (114), and Mrs. Forbes practices "the slight mystification" of his female pen name "because the ladies are such popular favourites" (116). Rather than disrupting the gender categories of society, this manipulation of roles confirms and exploits them—the masculine pseudonym granting the male privilege of frank sexual exploration and comment, the feminine name reinforcing the conception of women as frivolous readers of domestic fiction. Again contingency can be deployed in opposing ways, either

---

[3] See Bourdieu. Posnock is once again blind to the negative possibilities of such confusion and sees only its positive implications: "both in American gender and culture a certain vertiginous blurring . . . would make the self and social arrangements more flexible and thus more tolerant of a range of behaviors beyond conventional norms" (22). On the contingency of gender differences as well as sexual identity, see Butler (especially 1–34), who recognizes that nothing is decided by the recognition that contingency extends all the way down—that this only sets the terms of the problem but does not resolve it.

enhancing an emancipatory mutability of identity or serving an instrumental will to power.[4]

Because identity is not a fixed quantity, it is established through a process of circulation that at the same time constructs the community through the very act of exchange. The narrator reports: "my glorified friend . . . was the king of the beasts of the year. No advancement was ever more rapid, no exaltation more complete, no bewilderment more teachable. His book sold but moderately, though the article in *The Empire* had done unwonted wonders for it; but he circulated in person to a measure that the libraries might well have envied" (122).

The construction of authorship serves purposes apart from aesthetic appreciation and occurs in other ways, through dinner invitations, sitting for one's portrait, or posing as a public intellectual ("contributing his views on vital topics and taking part in the periodical prattle about the future of fiction" [137]). Paraday opines: "No one has the faintest conception of what I'm trying for . . . and not many have read three pages that I've written; but I must dine with them first—they'll find out why when they've time" (122).

The flaw in his pragmatism is that the social construction of authorship is distinct from the act of reading and does not require it. The narrator says that "the uses I have seen him put to infuriate me" (142), and these uses eventually use him up. His death not only dramatizes the cost of instrumentalizing human relations, taking Paraday not as he is for himself but as a means to ends that he can at most attempt to bend to his own purposes. His mortality also signals that identity is a structure of substitution, with others always ready to replace the absent party (as Guy Walsingham and Dora Forbes vie for his position).

The death of the "king of beasts" thereby calls attention one last time to the contingency of identity that makes circulation possible. Existence is not necessary, and others will take our place when we go. The meaning of life is decided by the exchange of mutable actors through various roles that define who they are during their temporary occupancy of them. This circulation in turn constructs the differences that make up the community. Because a community comes into being and sustains itself through acts of substitution, the

---

[4] This doubleness is interestingly reflected in a dispute about how to read gender differences in the story. King sees "slippery genders" as a sign of James's "fear of collapsed male privilege" (23), whereas Person infers from James's representation of these gender-switching writers "a more expansive attitude toward sexuality, which their cross-gendered voices pluralize even further" (197). In King's reading the contingency of gender destabilizes power relations and prompts James's defensive reaction, but for Person the changeableness of identity promotes a liberating multiplicity. In my view James understands contingency here and elsewhere as double-faced because it can be both threatening and emancipatory.

exchanges that construct its meanings and values also define its identity—its sense of justice, for example, its notion of personhood, its understanding of the obligations of persons to one another and of one generation to the next.[5]

"The Death of the Lion" seems to juxtapose conflicting conceptions of circulation and care—the public pursuit of reputation versus the private cultivation of art—but these opposites are uncanny doubles that share the same will to power. In the world of newspapers, dinner parties, and country weekends, rival projects of self-creation compete for control over the process of circulation. The hostess and kingmaker Mrs. Weeks Wimbush creates nothing herself, and this absence leaves her free to use the making and unmaking of others' reputations as the material for her own ascendancy. "Lions" may come and go, but the "proprietress of the universal menagerie," as the narrator unkindly calls her (123), gains power and stature as the figure who regulates their rise and fall. The mutability of others, their susceptibility to changes in status and condition, allows her to claim a transcendent position above the vagaries of contingencies she manipulates and controls. This claim even extends, as it logically must, to death. When Paraday dies, Mrs. Wimbush is "fundamentally disappointed in him. This was not the kind of performance for which she had invited him to Prestidge" (another almost too transparent name), but "none of the generous acts marking her patronage of intellectual and other merit have done so much for her reputation as her lending Neil Paraday the most beautiful of her numerous homes to die in" (152–53). Death itself does not transcend her powers but provides yet more contingent material to be worked into her project of self-assertion.

Although the narrator claims diametrically opposite motives—"Let whoever would represent the interest in his presence (I must have had a mystical prevision of Mrs. Weeks Wimbush) I should represent the interest in his work" (124)—he has essentially similar aims because he too seeks to control Paraday and to use him to assert his authority. He portrays his attempt to prevent the newspapers or Mrs. Wimbush from laying their hands on Paraday as a pure defense of art, but the language of battle, victimization, and ascendancy he employs suggests that he is playing the same game as his competitor—and that is why he fears and demonizes her with excessive images that suggest a deep identification he would rather not acknowledge. As his double, Mrs. Wimbush may know his secrets better than anyone else because, despite their

---

[5] Hence Derrida's argument, derived from Heidegger in *Being and Time,* that "justice" and ethics are learned "only from the other and by death": "No justice . . . seems possible or thinkable without the principle of some responsibility, beyond all living present, within that which disjoins the living present, before the ghosts of those who are not yet born or who are already dead" (*Specters* xviii, xix).

apparent differences, they think the same way and want the same things. He imagines her, for example, accusing him in the following terms: "To be intimate with [Paraday]'s a feather in my cap; it gives me an importance that I couldn't naturally pretend to, and I seek to deprive him of social refreshment because I fear that meeting more disinterested people may enlighten him as to my real motive" (140). This imagined charge worries him only because it is true. Or, similarly, as he contemplates with pleasure the prospect of editing Paraday's works after his death, the narrator frets: "I couldn't have the matter out with Mrs. Wimbush, for I didn't want to be taunted by her with desiring to aggrandise myself by a public connexion with Mr. Paraday's sweepings" (153). Once again his paranoid self-defensiveness suggests the depth of his identification with his antagonist. His anxiety about these accusations reveals that he and Mrs. Wimbush are rivals and doubles who share the project of using the contingent rise and fall of another's identity to advance their own.

The narrator can't simply promote Paraday's work heedless of what the newspapers and high society think because, in the game he is playing, one side can win only if another loses. The narrator's exclusionary insistence that his victory requires her defeat betrays the will to power in his claim to care selflessly for art. Having Mrs. Wimbush for an opponent oddly invigorates him not only because it helps define his mission and purpose but also because having an antagonist is necessary to his own sense of power and accomplishment. If she did not exist, his will to power would have to invent her—and to some extent it does as he turns a relatively innocuous social climber into a monster and a demon through his paranoid attributions to her of strength and stature that are the mirror of the ascendancy he himself seeks.

From the beginning, the narrator exhibits an obsessive insistence with controlling how Neil Paraday is presented and defined. Parallel to the deployment of power by naming and placing that elevates Paraday to temporary divinity, the narrator seeks ascendancy by regulating how the author is seen. This is true not only of his efforts to protect Paraday from the prying eyes of newspapermen but also of his impassioned plea for intrinsic criticism:

"The artist's life's his work, and this is the place to observe him. What he has to tell us he tells us with *this* perfection. My dear sir, the best interviewer's the best reader."

Mr. Morrow good-humouredly protested. "Do you mean to say that no other source of information should be open to us?"

"None other till this particular one—by far the most copious—has been quite exhausted. Have you exhausted it, my dear sir? Had you exhausted it when you came down here?" (119; original emphasis)

He seems to speak for the author and to ask that the artist be recognized on his or her own terms. But the presumptuousness of his assertion of privileged knowledge about how to approach Paraday's works exceeds the author's own claims. Paraday is willing to let interest in his life or in his opinions about politics and art provide access to his works. Although his hopes that cultivating other interests may lead the public to read him are ultimately overly optimistic, they show that an author needs readers and cannot control or predict how they will find their way to him.

The narrator's uncompromising plea for intrinsic criticism is a political pronouncement about the privileges of a particular mode of interpretation that would exclude other approaches. Such exclusionary negation may define his own sense of authority—he knows how to read as others do not—but it would doom Paraday to a smaller coterie of admirers than he wishes for his work. Because the narrator wants to own and control Paraday, he seeks to define and limit proper access to him, and so an elite group of privileged readers would satisfy his interests as it would not the author's. Speaking for Paraday without listening to him, he claims to know his interests better than the author does. In an uncanny replication of the communicative irrationality of the world of drawing rooms and newspapers, the defense of the absolute integrity of the literary work constitutes a recognition of the artist that lacks reciprocity. The narrator's exclusionary aesthetic is a radical insistence on the power to know that constructs his own privilege by claiming the right to construct the author. Like Mrs. Wimbush and *The Empire*, the narrator asserts his will to power by attempting to regulate how the author is valued and seen.

The narrator's will to power is painfully evident in the kind of tutelage he gives to his disciple, the young woman who arrives seeking Paraday in person ("I've come for his autograph," she says, and "to look straight into his face" [126, 129]), but whom he converts to his way of seeing.[6] This is negatively defined as *not* seeing the author, renouncing contact with his presence, and disciplining oneself in an ascesis of reading. Fanny Hurter ("ominous name," as the narrator himself observes [133]) proves herself adept at restriction and self-punishment in service of a higher calling:

> We read him together when I could find time, and the generous creature's sacrifice was fed by our communion. There were twenty selfish women about whom I told her and who stirred her to a beautiful rage. . . . They received

---

[6] See Cooper's argument that the narrator uses his disciple to emulate and displace his own master: "In effect, by seducing a woman originally attracted to Paraday, he sexually usurps Paraday's subject position" (79).

invitations and dined out, and some of these occasions enabled Fanny Hurter to perform, for consistency's sake, touching feats of submission. Nothing indeed would now have induced her to look at the object of her admiration. Once, hearing his name announced at a party, she instantly left the room by another door and then straightway quitted the house. (134)

On another occasion, when they find themselves at an opera Paraday is attending, she refuses to look at him through binoculars: "To torment her tenderly I pressed the glass upon her, telling her how wonderfully near it brought our friend's handsome head. By way of answer she simply looked at me in charged silence, letting me see that tears had gathered in her eyes. These tears, I may remark, produced an effect on me of which the end is not yet" (134). This display of sado–masochistic tutelage is not gratuitous. Rather, it demonstrates that the private sphere is not a pure domain of disinterested, free appreciation but a disciplinary construction produced by acts of exclusion and regulation.

One of this couple's keenest pleasures is their sense of exclusionary differentiation. They enjoy the privileges of their communion by not seeing as others do, and the bond this negation creates is the constructive achievement of her acts of renunciation. Again disciplinary power that may seem merely repressive is creative and productive. Analogous to the public construction of authorship that creates a community of spectators by triangulating a common object, the narrator and his model pupil build their communion by joining in a shared way of seeing, together regulating proper behavior toward it. Their ascendancy is based not on the incorporation of values intrinsic to the works they read but on their opposition to other ways of knowing the author. Their private aesthetic realm is a political province constructed in opposition to different modes of seeing that it negates in order to define its own privilege. The private is not essentially different from the public, then, but is itself political through and through, because it is a form of community that conflicts with other forms of community and that regulates acceptable modes of behavior.[7]

Is there no way of caring for art that does not subordinate it to a contest between rival wills? Can art mediate between members of a community only by instituting structures of dominance? "The Death of the Lion" criticizes the uses of art in the service of power, as exemplified by Mrs. Wimbush in the public sphere and the narrator in the realm of aesthetic privacy, but it leaves open the question of whether alternative ways of using art to construct

---

[7] James would not subscribe, then, to Rorty's attempt to segregate the private pursuit of self-creation from the public responsibilities of citizenship (see chap. 1 above).

community might get beyond the battle for ascendancy. The role of the reader is crucial here. Like so many of James's ambiguous first-person narrations, "The Death of the Lion" does not identify the reader's position with the narratee projected by the narrator, a sympathetic listener who would accept without question his account of Paraday's history. Resisting the narrator's version, the reader may expose his narration as an attempt to dominate retrospectively, through interpretation, events he could not control when they occurred. This distance would give the reader room to maneuver and to imagine alternatives to the unsatisfactory opposition dramatized in the story.[8] The danger of this resistance, however, is that it may replicate the narrator's quest for ascendancy and control by making us his competitor, thereby perpetuating the rivalry between conflicting wills instead of overcoming it. The challenge to the reader is to negate the image of power as dominance in the uses of art dramatized in "The Death of the Lion" without in turn using the power and privileges of reading to assert dominance.

A way to avoid this contradictory trap would be to build a form of community with the author and with other readers based on mutual recognition and reciprocity rather than competition for ascendancy. "The Death of the Lion" offers the reader the opportunity to develop such community, but it cannot unilaterally establish it precisely because reciprocity requires a to-and-fro between partners who are both necessary to the exchange. Reading against the narrator constitutes an attempt to forge a bond at a deeper level with the author who created him, to discover his intentions beneath the designs of the narrator. But the authorial meaning we may seek in this way is absent, nowhere manifestly present in the text. We can never know for certain that we have reached it because it is only offered ironically and indirectly. Construing it consequently requires a leap of faith on our part—an exercise of trust in what we cannot know, an extension of belief that can never be fully justified. As a projection of meaning based on reasoned guesswork, such a reading is not outside the workings of power. It is exclusionary (negating other possible hypotheses) and regulative (seeing the text as a particular configuration of implications). But as a guess about another's absent meaning that can never be certain of itself, this use of power is not a quest for ascendancy but an attempt

---

[8] See Chambers's argument (esp. 16–18) that the distinction between the "narrative function" (the narrator's attempt to win over the narratee) and the "textual function" (the meaning the author may seem to be communicating to the reader different from the narrator-narratee relationship) allows for "oppositional reading" that may posit interpretations or imagine possibilities against the apparent will to power of the persona telling the story. On the ambiguity of James's stories of writers, see Rimmon's careful narratological analyses of "The Figure in the Carpet" and "The Lesson of the Master."

to subordinate one's own ends to the recognition of another's aims. Because of the very indeterminacy of another's intention as something we can never know but can only guess and reconstruct, there is an element of humility in such an act of recognition, a paradoxical acknowledgment of the need to efface oneself even as one actively engages the text by projecting a meaning nowhere straightforwardly evident. Making oneself vulnerable even while energetically wagering guesses, the reader deploys power to create mutuality rather than to perpetuate rivalry between mutually exclusive claims to dominance.

The uncertainty about the author's absent, only inferable intention in this story cannot be overcome by finding a single right reading that would put an end to interpretation. Instead, the uncertainty calls on us to extend our conversation about the text to include other readers, whose confirming or disconfirming opinion would throw new light on a matter we can never know unequivocally. There are once again forms of community with other readers that would replicate the errors the tale urges us to avoid—not only elite, exclusionary couplings like the narrator's with his disciple, but also forms of consensus that seek dominance through the sort of collective power of opinion that reputation-building requires. To try to win assent for one's reading is to use power through persuasion, but in service of an answer to a question that reveals the insufficiency of the questioner. If the other has a confirmation or disconfirmation I lack, he or she is necessary to me, and the possibility of a community based on reciprocity exists. Because the meaning of the tale is nowhere present, but only inferable against the narrator's version, it is open to an endlessly extending exchange of views. No single reader, or pair or group of readers, is sufficient unto itself. Any grouping is at most a community of belief that can in turn only find confirmation elsewhere in an interminable process of circulation and deferral. Recognizing that the uncertainty of knowing requires other readers and prevents final agreement can thereby give rise to a reciprocal exchange of interpretations that would constitute a different form of community than the conflict between rival wills dramatized in "The Death of the Lion."

The result of this kind of circulation may be that the author's works are preserved through continuing conversations about them, but in forms he or she cannot predict or control. If the author dies, as authors must, he or she can live on only by ceding power to the community of future readers.[9] Creating the possibility of community is the claim to preservation of "The Death of the Lion." But it cannot guarantee its fate because building community can be the

---

[9] For a further exploration of this point, see my essay "Reading James's Prefaces and Reading James."

work of no single agent. It is an act of power that goes beyond anyone's will to power. Community does not exist in "The Death of the Lion" except as a battle for ascendancy. But by inviting readers to use their powers to imagine and create other forms of community, James's tale refuses to impose a meaning in a gesture of humility that could make possible a community of readers other than what it represents. In doing so he transforms the historicity of reading from a threat to the author's ascendancy into an opportunity for collaboration and reciprocity.

5. HISTORICIZING CONRAD

Temporal Form and the Politics of Reading

Conrad wrote often and provocatively about political themes: imperialism in Africa and Asia, anarchism in England, revolution and reform in Latin America, subversion and surveillance in imperial Russia, and so on. The assumption that political fiction is primarily mimetic has led critics to connect the representational content of these works to events in Conrad's own varied history or to issues important at his time. Tying his political fictions to the past in this way, however, has often made Conrad's political thinking seem incoherent or contradictory. He has been praised as a courageous critic of imperial exploitation in the Congo, for example, even as he has been lambasted as a racist example of European cultural hegemony. He has been seen as a radical opponent of Western capitalism and as a conservative defender of traditional institutions. His irony, always sharp and often dark and scathing, has seemed oddly unstable, and as a result Conrad has been regarded as a curious political writer who is passionate about politics without it being at all clear what his politics are.

The problem, I propose, lies not with Conrad but with his critics—and, in particular, with their understanding of what it means to interpret fiction historically. When Conrad's political fictions are interpreted mimetically, the historical emphasis on "meaning-then" limits evaluation of his position to an appraisal of conditions existing at the time. Conrad's fiction is less simply mimetic and less one-dimensionally evaluative than such past-oriented historicism understands. He typically offers contradictory perspectives to the reader that refuse to cohere into a straightforward image of the past, and he does so because he wishes to expose the limitations and inadequacies of his time without alleviating the reader's responsibility to struggle with their complications. The contradictions in his political fiction are an incitement to future audiences to engage problems that Conrad refused to contain in the past. The notorious ambiguities of Conrad's political novels are not instances of confusion but strategies for speaking across historical distance.

To support this claim I will analyze the defining contradictions of three of Conrad's political novels and the challenges they pose to the reader. I have chosen texts that represent the range of his political writings and engage a variety of issues: the politics of imperialism in *Heart of Darkness,* the politics of identity and community formation in *Under Western Eyes,* and the politics of irony and commitment in *The Secret Agent.* In each case, Conrad refuses to simplify the issues at stake by taking a univocal stance. Instead he dramatizes contradictions that he cannot see his way clear to resolving, but he gets beyond the stalemate he would otherwise find himself in by transforming these contradictions into challenges for future generations of readers. This is not simply an act of evasion on Conrad's part, because his challenge to future readers is based in each instance on a rigorous confrontation with the limits to what he, in his own situation, can resolve. If we are no better able to see our way past these dilemmas than Conrad was, our shared plight not only attests to Conrad's perspicacity in revealing intractable problems but also points out the common ground that still exists between his period and ours.

Heart of Darkness and the Contradictions of Imperialism

The history of the reception of *Heart of Darkness* has been divided over whether to regard Conrad's text as a daring attack on imperialism or a reactionary purveyor of colonial stereotypes. One of the most important recent examples of this contradiction is Edward Said's split depiction of Conrad as an insightful critic of the cruelty and exploitation of imperialism who nevertheless replicates the very blindness and inhumanity he exposes. Although Conrad was able "as an outsider . . . to comprehend how the machine works," Said argues, he "does not give us the sense that he could imagine a fully realized alternative to imperialism": "Conrad's tragic limitation is that even though he could see clearly that on one level imperialism was essentially pure dominance and land-grabbing, he could not then conclude that imperialism had to end so that 'natives' could lead lives free from European domination. As a creature of his time, Conrad could not grant the natives their freedom, despite his severe critique of the imperialism that enslaved them" (*Culture* 25,

30). This judgment is surely unreasonable in expecting that Conrad might have risen above the limitations of his own period and attained some realm of transcendental understanding that Said's own insistence on the historical worldliness of writing would question. (If Conrad is indeed "a creature of his time," why should we expect him to be able to imagine "grant[ing] the natives their freedom," and why is it a "tragic limitation" rather than a sign of his historical position that he can't?)

To fault Said for evaluating Conrad against an ahistorical, utopian standard, however, is not to suggest that we read him solely with reference to his contemporaries' ability to understand themselves. The contradictions in Conrad's depiction of imperialism are evidence of an attempt to point beyond a situation it would be unreasonable to expect him to fully transcend. By using Marlow to dramatize contradictions that neither the author nor his narrator can resolve, Conrad poses future readers with the challenge of creating conditions of reciprocity whose absence he bemoans but that he does not know how to produce. Understanding Conrad's contradictory representation of imperialism as an attempt to reach beyond his situation by engaging it is a way of reading *Heart of Darkness* historically by seeing the time of writing and the time of reading in a mutually determining relationship across its history of reception.

These two temporal horizons, of writing and of reading, are starkly opposed—and insufficiently related—in the conflict between Chinua Achebe's well-known, controversial claim that the depiction of the Africans in *Heart of Darkness* is racist and xenophobic and James Clifford's praise of Conrad as an exemplary anthropologist. Where Achebe finds prejudice and dismissive reification in the representations of the Other in *Heart of Darkness*, Clifford sees in the text a heteroglossic rendering of cultural differences without any attempt to synthesize them. "Joseph Conrad was a bloody racist," Achebe claims, and *Heart of Darkness* is "a story in which the very humanity of black people is called in question"—"a book which parades in the most vulgar fashion prejudices and insults from which a section of mankind has suffered untold agonies and atrocities" (788, 790). By contrast, Clifford holds up the novella as an epistemological model for ethnographers because it "truthfully juxtaposes different truths" and "does not permit a feeling of centeredness, coherent dialogue, or authentic communion" that would give the misleading impression that understanding another culture can be accomplished once and for all (99, 102). According to Clifford, "Anthropology is still waiting for its Conrad" (96).[1]

---

[1] For particularly useful analyses of Achebe's charges, see Hawkins, "Racism"; and Watts, "Racist." Astonishingly, Clifford makes no mention of Achebe. Among those who see Conrad as a foe of imperialism, see especially McClure; Hawthorn; and Hawkins, "Conrad's Critique." For indictments of his bigotry and implicit endorsement of colonial attitudes, see Brantlinger; Torgovnick; and Parry, *Conrad*.

If *Heart of Darkness* can be viewed as an exemplar of epistemological evil and virtue—as a model of the worst abuses and the most promising practices in representing other peoples and cultures—that is because its enactment of the dilemmas entailed in understanding cultural otherness is strategically contradictory. Achebe wrongly assumes that *Heart of Darkness* offers a finished representation of the colonial Other to the metropolitan reader. Instead, the text dramatizes the need for an ongoing reciprocity between knower and known through which each comments on, corrects, and replies to the other's representations in a never-ending alternation of positions, but it does so by showing this reciprocity to be everywhere absent in the novel's world. Achebe is right to fault the text, then, because it dramatizes a pervasive state of cultural solipsism that it does not itself overcome, and it consequently abounds in representations of the Other that are one-sided and prejudicial. In yet another turn, though, Achebe's very act of writing back to Conrad is already anticipated by the text to the extent that its narrative structure calls for future criticism of and response to the absence of reciprocity it displays. Clifford is right that Conrad offers key guidance to anthropological knowing—not, however, because his novel is an ideal ethnography, but because its textual strategies aim to educate the reader about processes that might make possible a dialogue with the Other that is absent from Marlow's monologue. If Achebe fails to recognize how Conrad attempts to reach beyond the horizons of his imperialist situation, Clifford errs in crediting the text with fulfilling epistemological ideals that it leaves as an open and uncertain question for the future.

Marlow both criticizes and replicates the blindness and will to power of nonreciprocal approaches to alterity: for example, the scientist who oddly measures only the outside of the skulls of those traveling to Africa, and only on their way out, or the French man-of-war that shells invisible "enemies" in the forest. The absurd one-sidedness of these engagements with the unknown suggests that Marlow would endorse Achebe's complaint that "travellers with closed minds can tell us little except about themselves" (791). Marlow indicts the closed-mindedness of nondialogical encounters with otherness but then nevertheless duplicates it, reproducing the solipsism he exposes and laments. He remains for the most part an observer who does not communicate with the objects of his observation. His contacts with Africans are sufficient to reveal his self-enclosure and to educate him about the dangers of nonreciprocal impositions of power and knowledge. But they are insufficient to remove the alienness of alterity through dialogue, so that he remains a tourist who sees the passing landscape through a window that separates him from it, and he consequently commits the crimes of touristic misappropriation of otherness even as he is aware of and points out the limitations of that position.

This doubleness is evident in Marlow's complaints about the injustice of naming the Other without allowing revision or response. After seeing a chain gang of imprisoned Africans, Marlow remarks: "these men could by no stretch of imagination be called enemies. They were called criminals and the outraged law like the bursting shells [of the man-of-war] had come to them, an insoluble mystery from the sea. All their meager breasts panted together, the violently dilated nostrils quivered, the eyes stared stonily uphill. They passed me within six inches, without a glance, with that complete, deathlike indifference of unhappy savages" (19). The absurdity of the tag "criminals" shows the will to power in the right to name, which is especially visible when seemingly anomalous or arbitrary labels remain in force by the sheer power of the authority behind them. Once again replicating what he criticizes, however, Marlow challenges this authority by invoking a figure—the death-in-life of the "unhappy savage"—that is just as much a stereotype as the labels he unmasks.

Marlow tries the tactic of ironic counterlabeling, calling the crimes of imperialism "these high and just proceedings," or referring to the guard as "one of the reclaimed, the product of the new forces at work" (19). But the irony is offered to Marlow's audience—and, across them, to the reader—and is not part of a process of negotiation in which the right to name is tested and shared among those directly concerned. Marlow's awareness of the power of language to impose perceptions on the Other is not matched by a faith in language as an instrument of reciprocal exchange to mediate conflicting perceptions or by a belief that the circumstances of imperialism would allow such a to-and-fro. Marlow can only counter the right to name with strategies of reverse labeling that fight what they oppose by repeating its lack of dialogue. The reader is left to wonder whether this contradiction represents a moral inconsistency we could avoid, an epistemological problem (the need for types and categories) no one can escape, or a commentary on the power of social conditions to overwhelm an individual's best intentions.

Marlow takes the first steps toward a dialogical understanding of Africans by recognizing that their mystery and opacity are a sign of their humanity. Africans are a hermeneutic problem for him because he acknowledges that they have a world that he can construct only by reading signs—filling in gaps in the evidence, imagining hidden sides, and engaging in the other kinds of interpretive activity we invoke when we encounter phenomena that we assume are intelligible because they are evidence of other human life. When he tells the story of his predecessor Fresleven's death, for example, Marlow creates from scant evidence a narrative of mutual misunderstanding that tries to reconstruct how the baffling, terrifying European must have appeared to African perceptions (see 12–13). The very mystery of African thought processes that makes their world an interpretive challenge presents them as fellow human beings whose lives can be made intelligible by fitting them to narrative patterns that might also apply to one's own life. Marlow's interpretive efforts also demonstrate, however, that the hermeneutic circle can become vicious and self-enclosing unless it is opened up by making the object of interpretation an interlocutor. Marlow's attempts at recognition end in rejection because he does not move from intuited similarities to reciprocity:

> Well, you know that was the worst of it—this suspicion of their not being inhuman. It would come slowly to one. They howled and leaped and spun and made horrid faces, but what thrilled you was just the thought of their humanity—like yours—the thought of your remote kinship with this wild and passionate uproar. Ugly. Yes, it was ugly enough, but if you were man enough you would admit to yourself that there was in you just the faintest trace of a response to the terrible frankness of that noise, a dim suspicion of there being a meaning in it which you—you so remote from the night of first ages—could comprehend. (37–38)

The hermeneutic pursuit of self-understanding by understanding others is initiated only to be abandoned here as Marlow acknowledges a relationship with the Other only to refuse its claim to equal dignity and worth by consigning it to the remote past or to subterranean moral regions.[2]

Marlow's ambivalence dramatizes the sometimes ambiguous double nature of hermeneutic encounters with other cultures. The experience of alterity can be both frightening and invigorating—a threat to the self and an opportunity for self-recognition and self-expansion. Discovering unexpected similarities with radically different ways of being entails a disorienting and perhaps distressing loss of self-understanding—one turns out not to be exactly who one thought one was—even as it opens up new possibilities of self-knowledge, self-creation, and relationship. Marlow's sense of threat and loss paralyzes him, however, and does not allow him to conceive of the destruction of his previous certainties as a prelude to new constructions of himself and his world.

Once again the contradiction between the communicative possibilities Marlow's experience suggests and his failure to realize them is a way for Conrad to point out the limits of the situation he saw around him and to point beyond them without undertaking the utopian act of imagining the world as totally otherwise than he skeptically saw it to be. Marlow's contradictions are a challenge to the reader to imagine that the world might be otherwise and to reflect on the changes in the material conditions and epistemological practices

---

[2] Benita Parry oversimplifies when she claims that "both Kurtz and Marlow look upon blacks as another genus" (*Conrad* 34). Marlow senses a resemblance with the Other here, and that is why he reacts defensively. If the Other were not somehow the same as he is, the apparent differences of the Other from what he would like to think about himself would not be so threatening.

dramatized in *Heart of Darkness* that would bring about such a revolution. Conrad's refusal (or inability) to offer a materialized imagining of such an other world is a sign of his historical situation (he was writing near the zenith of imperialism's hegemony), even as the contradictions in Marlow's encounters with Africans represent a provocation to the future of readers—a future dimly but powerfully imaginable across the horizon of Conrad's act of writing—to engage those dilemmas with whatever mixture of skepticism and hope their differing circumstances, aspirations, and frustrations might allow.

The Politics of Identity and Community Formation in *Under Western Eyes*

As a writer who made his career far away from his native land, Conrad was especially self-conscious about the paradoxes and contradictions of cultural identity. His anomalous situation—neither English nor Polish but somehow still both—foregrounded in his self-consciousness the doubleness of being and not being the identities to which one is assigned. As an exile (he was forced to flee Poland at an early age because of his father's activities as a revolutionary), he was acutely aware that membership in a community is paradoxically both a necessity and a contingency—defined ineradicably by birth and family but also susceptible to change by education, migration, and allegiance (to recall Said's terms, a matter of both "filiation" with one's natal community and "affiliation" with groups to which one is aligned by virtue of social, political, or professional practices [see *World* 24]).[3]

The paradoxes of belonging to a community are a prominent theme of *Under Western Eyes*, Conrad's novel about national identity. As an orphan, his filiative place uncertain, Razumov is especially open and vulnerable to be claimed by the various affiliations competing to define Russian identity. That the relation between filiative bonds and affiliative allegiances is an issue of some urgency for him is evident in his insistent claim: " 'Russia *can't* disown me. She cannot!' Razumov struck his breast with his fist. 'I am *it!* ' " (215; original emphasis). The tautology here is meaningful only because the equivalence is not as transparent as he insists. "Russia" both is and is not who Razumov is, and that contradiction makes his identity problematic for himself and for others, a matter of uncertainty, anguish, and contestation. Like

---

[3] Hence the title of Frederick Karl's biography of Conrad, which attributes to him not one but "three lives" because his original filiation with his Polish homeland was replaced and displaced (but of course never completely erased) by his affiliations with the men of the sea in his profession as a mariner and then with the tradition of English letters in his career as a writer.

Conrad, Razumov feels himself a "homo duplex" because he is not at one with his available affiliations even as they are who he is and wishes to be.

The role of negation in cultural belonging is evident in Louis Althusser's useful notion that the cultural subject is formed by "interpellation or hailing," as in "the most commonplace everyday police (or other) hailing: 'Hey, you there!' " (174). In turning around and recognizing the call, we both are the person named and not it ("Does he mean me?") because it could be anyone, different from us. If, as Althusser argues, "Before its birth, the child is there- fore always-already a subject, appointed as a subject in and by the specific fa- miliar ideological configuration in which it is 'expected' once it has been conceived" (176), those filiative roles are susceptible in greater or lesser de- grees to affiliative confirmation or contestation because they may be experi- enced by the subject in question as convergent or divergent with who he or she is or desires to be. Razumov is "hailed" by a variety of parties who recog- nize him as "Russian" and therefore "one of us," and he invariably experi- ences such recognition as a misrecognition because he both is and is not the identities they assign to him.

Under Western Eyes explores the alternative outcomes that may ensue from the negativity and doubleness of cultural identity. National identity can feel alien because we are not the various roles in which we may find ourselves as members of a community to which we have not asked to belong. Nevertheless, the very contingency of these roles—the fact that they are not necessarily who we are—can leave room for creativity, criticism, or even rebellion. The gap be- tween one's interpellated role and one's sense of self may mean that one's self- presentation can be a lie. This may mean that one's status as a member of a culture can feel like a misrepresentation, or it can open up the possibility of manipulating or playing with one's identity. The differences and doubling constituting identity may be unsettling, but they may also allow negotiations, revelations, and exchanges that could not occur if both parties were locked in homogeneous, self-identical monads. Razumov's story does not resolve these oppositions. Instead, the disjunctions and ambiguities in the structure of the narrative displace them onto the experience of the reader and stage for the reader the contradictions of cultural identity.

These textual complications begin with the narrator. Most readers of *Under Western Eyes* wonder what to make of this obtuse figure, the "teacher of languages" (55), through whose self-avowedly "occidental" perspective we see the story ("this is not," he often reminds us, "a story of the West of Europe" [72]).[4] His repeated generalizations about Russia call attention to his own

---

[4] Among the most interesting analyses of the narrator's obtuseness are Lothe 263–93; Berthoud; and Erdinast-Vulcan 120–24.

incapacity to understand the story he tells: "I confess that I have no comprehension of the Russian character. The illogicality of their attitude, the arbitrariness of their conclusions, the frequency of the exceptional, should present no difficulty to a student of many grammars; but there must be something else in the way, some special human trait—one of those subtle differences that are beyond the ken of mere professors" (56).

Despite his plea of ignorance, the narrator offers a veritable catalogue of Russian traits which seems sometimes odd, sometimes profound, and often not justified by the facts of the story.[5] In this passage, for example, his own lack of comprehension quickly gives way to a sweeping assertion about the irrationality and fundamental strangeness of the Russian people. His narration is a compendium of authoritatively stated prejudices that simultaneously prove and deny his professions of ignorance.

Curiously, the Russian characters in the novel also repeatedly make pronouncements about Russian cultural identity that seem just as homogenizing, exoticizing, and misleading as the narrator's stereotypes. Different in function although similar in form to Orientalist typing by an external party, generalizations like these by Russians about Russian character and culture are instruments of pedagogical self-performance—declarative acts that establish cultural identity through the very process of enunciating it. Instruments of cultural subject formation, these generalizations are ways in which Russians call on one another and themselves to conform to or to acquire cultural traits. Sometimes the element of coercion in pedagogical hailing is painfully obvious, as when Peter Ivanovitch attempts to bully Nathalie by an appeal to national needs: "You must come out of your reserve. We Russians have no right to be reserved with each other. In our circumstances it is almost a crime against humanity" (152). The disciplinary force of interpellation is harder to see when cultural typing enunciates an ideal, articulating the nation's values by interpreting its destiny, as when Nathalie explains: "We Russians shall find some better form of national freedom than an artificial conflict of parties. . . . It is left for us Russians to discover a better way" (136). Here too, however, the enunciation of a mission "hails" Russians to an identity that may be described as their fate, and therefore inevitable, but that they must be educated to recognize, accept, and perform.

---

[5] For example: "I suppose one must be a Russian to understand Russian simplicity, a terrible corroding simplicity in which mystic phrases clothe a naïve and hopeless cynicism" (134); "they detest life, the irremediable life of the earth as it is, whereas we westerners cherish it with perhaps an equal exaggeration of its sentimental value" (134); "Russian natures have a singular power of resistance against the unfair strains of life" (191), and so on with an ultimately tedious and even annoying repetitiveness.

Such statements display the differential structure of cultural identity because their articulation of "Russianness" depends for its power and significance on the gap between the image they project and the subjects interpellated to it. These self-descriptions uncannily resemble the Western narrator's misrepresentations of Russian character because of the role of the negative in cultural identity. Only because Russian traits do not absolutely and uniformly define who Russians are is it possible and necessary for Russians to create their community and themselves by talking about themselves. Only because they both are and are not who they say they are do the definitions they exchange have meaning and force. That difference, the doubleness of cultural belonging, is what enables a people to perform themselves and to teach themselves their identity.

It also makes their community more heterogeneous than the frequent generalizations about the Russian people suggest. Razumov thinks of himself at one point as a servant of "the mightiest homogeneous mass of mankind with a capability for logical, guided development in a brotherly solidarity of force and aim such as the world had never dreamt of . . . the Russian nation!" (287–88; original ellipsis). The revolutionary Peter Ivanovitch declares: "Everything in a people that is not genuine, not its own by origin or development, is—well—dirt!" (217). If a nation is homogeneous, then everything not at one with its essence is an impurity to be eradicated. Both conservatives and revolutionaries use this logic of purification because both envision culture as a unified totality, with a single defining origin and goal, rather than a heterogeneous ensemble of projects with differing beginnings and ends.

Their conflict leaves Razumov caught in the middle of "a furious strife between equally ferocious antagonisms" (301). The uncompromising will to power on both sides suggests that homogeneity is not a given or a natural state but an artificial structure that can be forged only through strenuous acts of exclusion and discipline. Such acts employ negation in a self-contradictory attempt to erase differences. This is Razumov's impossible double bind—that he can establish an identity in either of the communities he is caught between only by eradicating the very differences that define him. Fearing the eradication of difference as much as he desires solidarity, Conrad depicts the intent of both sides to homogenize and purify the nation as a dangerous threat to the very conditions that make identity possible, even as he shows how unsettling and destabilizing the differences within a community can be.

What Razumov needs is reciprocity based on mutual recognition that would disarm the will to power in conflicts over cultural identity and enable an uncoerced exchange of differences. In a moment of profundity, the narrator declares: "A man's real life is that accorded to him in the thoughts of other men by reason of respect or natural love" (63). This formulation suggests once again the double structure of identity, inasmuch as we are our being-for-others, not our being-for-ourselves (our "real life" is what others think of us, not what we ourselves think or feel). Unless made the basis of a to-and-fro exchange through "respect or love," that doubleness can be disabling because it locates the power of self-definition elsewhere, outside the self. Without reciprocity with others, our life will not be our own.

The act of reading *Under Western Eyes* uncannily duplicates the absence of mutual recognition that maddens Razumov even as it offers the only site where the novel suggests reciprocity might be enacted. In a wonderfully contradictory narratological moment, Razumov angrily declares: "I am not a young man in a novel" (197). Even to us as readers, then, his identity is double because he is not who he is (he is *not* a fictional character, he tells us) even as he is who he is not (despite his denials, he is of course "a young man in a novel" all the same). We recognize him in a role, that of a character in a novel, which he explicitly repudiates—even if he does so as a character in a novel. This paradox displays once again the doubleness of identity and calls on the reader to recognize Razumov as he is for himself (*not* "a young man in a novel"), even as it simultaneously insists on the barriers to perfect recognition because his being-for-others (as a character to the reader) can never coincide with his being-for-himself.

The temporal displacement between the first and second parts of the narrative (beginning in Russia where Razumov betrays Haldin, then skipping ahead to Geneva where he reappears as a trusted and admired member of the exile community) creates for the reader a double vision of who Razumov is and who he is not that reenacts his sense of duality in the experience of reading. The text stages this doubleness by giving the reader parallel discordant perspectives of Razumov as he appears to Nathalie and other Russians in Geneva—the mysterious, polite young man whom her brother's letters have praised as "unstained, lofty, and solitary, . . . an intimate friend" (158)—and as we know him from "Part First" as Haldin's betrayer and murderer. We are both inside, sharing his secret, and outside, observing how he is misconstrued. This doubleness may not allow true reciprocity with a character we cannot converse with, but it may nevertheless make possible for us as readers the sort of to-and-fro movement between different perspectives, neither one sufficient in and of itself, through which the justice of competing representations can be negotiated. Such an oscillation of perspectives, never stabilizing into a rigid frame, can keep exchange going and thereby prevent the doubleness of identity from reifying into the one-dimensional trap Razumov experiences when others fix him by their definitions. Razumov's tragedy is that this nonreifying play of identities can only occur in his relation to the reader, as a character in a novel, and not in relation to the others in his world (ironically, if only he were "a young man in a novel," and only that, then he would be redeemed).

This dilemma shows that Conrad cannot imagine social conditions that would establish reciprocity once and for all. He suggests, rather, that such negotiation is a contradictory practice that cannot simply be produced by political structures. Instead, and for this very reason, Conrad shapes the social space of reading to create paradoxical challenges that give the reader practice in negotiating the differences that define identity and culture. Recognizing the difficulties of doing justice to a character in a novel who denies he is a character in a novel constitutes a provocation and an appeal to us as readers to reflect on the dilemmas of doing justice to other people and cultures. We can hope to do better than Razumov does in transforming the dilemmas of doubleness from an alienating bind into a space for reciprocal exchange. Conrad cannot do this for us, but by recreating these dilemmas in our relation to his text he instructs us about their challenges and contradictions.

The Secret Agent and the Politics of Irony

The key words of the title of Rorty's book on liberalism—"contingency," "irony," and "solidarity"—are also central issues for Conrad. Liberals should read and ponder Conrad, I think, because he has a tonic, illuminating anguish about the contradiction Rorty would have us embrace—the contradiction, namely, between an ironic awareness of the contingency of all norms, beliefs, and values and the necessity nonetheless to affirm a commitment to community, compassion, and self-invention.[6] Conrad refuses to accept this contradiction, whereas Rorty thinks we must simply learn to live with it. The way Conrad wrestles with it exposes vulnerabilities in Rorty's politics that liberalism can forget only at the risk of falling into political complacency and epistemological naiveté. Although I think of myself as a "liberal ironist" in Rorty's sense, I find Conrad's rigorous bitterness and unrelenting anguish about the contradiction between contingency and commitment more revealing and defensible than Rorty's commonsensical advice that we should stop worrying about a problem we cannot solve.[7]

Let me briefly recall Rorty's argument before exploring how Conrad translates his anguish into challenges and provocations for his readers. According to Rorty, "the citizens of [his] liberal utopia would be . . . people who combined commitment with a sense of the contingency of their own

[6] See the discussion of "liberal irony" in chapter 1.

[7] For critical analyses of Rorty's position, see Malachowski; and Rajchman and West.

commitment"—people who recognize the ultimate groundlessness and relativity "of their language of moral deliberation, and thus of their consciences, and thus of their community," but who nevertheless maintain their faith in ideals they realize they cannot justify (*Contingency* 61). He credits such people with an ironic sense because an ironist is, in his view, "the sort of person who faces up to the contingency of his or her own most central beliefs and desires" (xv). Conrad is an ironist in this sense because he recognizes that he can provide no foundation for his beliefs in such values as mastery, honor, and fidelity.[8] But he is not what Rorty calls a "liberal ironist" because he doubts what such a person believes, even though he shares a desire to believe it: "Liberal ironists . . . include among these ungroundable desires their own hope that suffering will be diminished, that the humiliation of human beings by other human beings may cease." For Rorty, liberals "think that cruelty is the worst thing we do" (xv). A figure like Stevie in *The Secret Agent* is perhaps the archliberal, then, but the paralyzed "convulsive sympathy" with which he utters the powerless if profoundly moving words "Bad world for poor people" expresses Conrad's skepticism about the prospects for reducing human misery (*Secret Agent* 167, 171). A large part of Stevie's problem may be that he lacks an ironic sense ("Being no sceptic, but a moral creature, he was in a manner at the mercy of his righteous passions" [172]). Conrad is not by any means deficient in irony, but the extremity of his skeptical vision in *The Secret Agent* suggests that an irreducible antagonism divides compassion and irony, faith and suspicion, commitment and contingency.

   The Secret Agent deserves close scrutiny not only because it is one of Conrad's most important political novels but also because the experience of reading this bizarre, intriguing work challenges us to confront the impossibility of reconciling such oppositions. From Verloc's distressing meeting with Vladimir near the beginning to Ossipon's overwhelming inability to fathom Winnie's madness and despair at the end, the characters in this novel repeatedly experience astonishment at finding they can no longer count on what they believed, assumed, and trusted. The typical consequence of such bewilderment is the disorientation Ossipon feels after finding Verloc murdered: "he was incapable by now of judging what could be true, possible, or even probable in this astounding universe" (288). *The Secret Agent*'s narrative strategies—especially the frequently hyperbolic irony of the narrator—attempt to stage experiences for the reader that are similarly disorienting.

   The effect of these strategies is perhaps not to astonish and overwhelm us so much as to leave us wondering whether any beliefs, values, or norms can be trusted, whether sympathy and compassion are noble ideals or dangerous

[8] See my *Challenge* 140–48.

deceptions, and whether faith and suspicion can be reconciled. The narrator suggests at one point that "true wisdom . . . is not certain of anything in this world of contradictions" (84). The force of this negative conclusion is not simply to urge upon the reader an all-encompassing skepticism but to confront us with a classic dilemma of liberalism—that is, how to act in a world of conflicting ideologies where no beliefs can claim unequivocal authority. Because Conrad cannot resolve this contradiction, he stages it for the reader. Whether there is any way beyond it for us is a question the novel does not answer, and that is one reason why reading *The Secret Agent* is such a bewildering and provocative experience.

Conrad's use of ironic strategies to change the reader's consciousness suggests that Rorty's conception of the philosophic uses of literature should be expanded and liberated from its dependence on a mimetic model. According to Rorty, ironists read literature and literary criticism to increase their "range of acquaintance" and to compare their own vocabulary with other possible languages: "Ironists are afraid that they will get stuck in the vocabulary in which they were brought up if they only know the people in their own neighborhood, so they try to get acquainted with strange people (Alcibiades, Julien Sorel), strange families (the Karamazovs, the Casaubons), and strange communities (the Teutonic Knights, the Nuer, the mandarins of the Sung)" (*Contingency* 80). This description of the value of literature suggests that we learn from books because of *what* they represent—the alien worlds they bring to our ken. But *how* a book represents is equally instructive. Its narrative strategies can enact its vocabulary so as to induct the reader into a different way of seeing through the very experience of inhabiting its procedures for making sense. To read a novel or a poem or a work of philosophy is not only to observe a different vocabulary and to watch the pictures it produces but also to learn how to speak its language and to have one's own assumptions and conventions challenged in the process. Reading *The Secret Agent* offers an education about the dangers and the necessities of irony not only because of what Conrad portrays in its world but also because of the strategies of narration he employs, calling on us to read ironically in order to enmesh us in the contradictions of irony.

The narrator could be describing his own ironic method when he declares at one point: "in truth there is a sort of lucidity proper to extravagant language" (220). He later notes that "to exaggerate with judgment one must begin by measuring with nicety" (249–50). At times, however, it is difficult if not impossible for the reader to be sure of the precise evaluation intended by the narrator's ironic characterizations because of their extremity. One of his earliest extended descriptions of Verloc, for example, is almost gratuitously unflattering: "He generally arrived in London (like the influenza) from the Continent, only he arrived unheralded by the Press; and his visitations set in with great severity. He breakfasted in bed, and remained wallowing there with an air of quiet enjoyment till noon every day—and sometimes even to a later hour. But when he went out he seemed to experience a great difficulty in finding his way back to his temporary home in the Belgravian square" (6–7).

The reader may respond to this characterization with sardonic amusement at the lazy, inept Verloc who has already been described as excessively fond of domestic comforts and as looking like he had "wallowed, fully dressed, all day on an unmade bed" (4). But a reader might also be somewhat surprised and disconcerted by the narrator's mockery because it could seem unjust. Surely Verloc has done nothing yet to deserve being compared to the flu—and to say that the only difference between him and this disease is that the newspaper takes no notice of him might also seem to pile on insults unnecessarily. Later we find (as a reader might already suspect) that Verloc stays out late not because he cannot find his way back to his hotel but because he has business to attend to, but a reader may already feel at this point that the imputation of navigational incompetence to Verloc is unfair, not because we know it is unfounded, but because it is consistent with a general attitude of sarcastic disdain that may increasingly seem excessive.

The narrator's lack of fellow feeling for Verloc may prompt the reader to try to sympathize with him, but the problem with extending compassion and understanding to this character is that he is too ludicrous a figure to deserve them. Our dilemma is that we can be humane only at the cost of being stupid, but we can be smart only by being inhumane. The problem is *not* that Verloc deserves a sympathy that the narrator withholds from him but, more disturbingly and contradictorily, that the extremity of the irony through which the narrator exposes his flaws may make readers uneasy even as they cannot resist its conclusions. This is one of the reasons why some readers (Avrom Fleishman and Irving Howe) have criticized the narrator's irony as "hysterical" or "peevish" and therefore not fully acceptable even when it is authoritative. The problem is that the irony is indeed both authoritative and unacceptable—and this contradiction is a provocation to the reader to reflect about the opposition between suspicion and sympathy behind it.

The first chapter of the novel repeats and reinforces this impasse with the story about Stevie on which it ends—the anecdote about how (in a grim foreshadowing of the way he meets his death) he lit firecrackers in a stairwell after some "office-boys in the building had worked upon his feelings by tales of injustice and oppression till they had wrought his compassion to the pitch of that frenzy" (9–10). The cynical mockery of the office boys is uneasily similar to the attitude of detached, derisive amusement that the narrator encourages us to take toward Verloc. Accepting the narrator's irreverent criticisms turns out to be a trap, then, because compassion and sympathy are what this world lacks and needs. This anecdote punishes readers who had earlier laughed with the narrator by exposing the potential cruelty of a cynical lack of fellow feeling. In a further ironic turn, however, Stevie's story does not offer us an alternative we can rest with because his pity and compassion are themselves portrayed as ludicrous. The anecdote discredits fellow feeling as much as it calls for it. Once again, but now from the standpoint of sympathy rather than cynicism, the reader is blocked in the attempt to find a workable alignment of suspicion and care, a synthesis uniting criticism and compassion.

The pattern of reading that I have tried to suggest in these two early examples is typical of the novel as a whole. The reader is tossed back and forth between negating and affirming movements without being directed toward a reconciliation of them. The narrator's mockery encourages a hermeneutics of unmasking that may seem cruel and heartless. But attempting to understand by extending faith and sympathy to others is an interpretive strategy that the novel invites us to assume only to expose its naiveté and ineffectuality.

The novel's refusal to let the reader's perspective stabilize brings to mind an image that Chief Inspector Heat invokes when the assistant commissioner surprisingly and unaccountably refuses to accept his interpretation of the bombing incident:

> He felt at the moment like a tight-rope artist might feel if suddenly, in the middle of the performance, the manager of the Music Hall were to rush out of the proper managerial seclusion and begin to shake the rope. Indignation, the sense of moral insecurity engendered by such a treacherous proceeding joined to the immediate apprehension of a broken neck, would, in the colloquial phrase, put him in a state. And there would be also some scandalized concern for his art, too. (116)

This example might seem to support Rorty's commonsensical advice that we simply act on our beliefs and not let our ironic sense of their contingency paralyze us. The liberal ironist will be better able to walk the tightrope of contingency and commitment, after all, by moving confidently ahead instead of worrying about the dangers of the performance or about the lack of a net below.

Conrad is well aware that self-consciousness can be crippling rather than enabling (recall, for example, how Lord Jim's dreams of grandeur prevent him from acting when the moment for heroism arrives, or how Marlow feels paralyzed and uncertain about what to do with Kurtz's revelation of the horror). But Conrad nevertheless believes that shaking the tightrope is necessary to combat complacency—"our agreeable somnolence," as the Marlow of *Lord*

Jim calls it, the "dullness that makes life to the incalculable majority so supportable and so welcome" (143). Although a certain willed ignorance of the risks he is running may help the tightrope walker execute his performance successfully, to stop worrying altogether is to risk falling into a state of complacency that is equally dangerous because it increases one's vulnerability to disorienting, sometimes disastrous shocks and surprises.

Once again caught in contradictions, Conrad's reader is asked to recognize that there is no remedy for contingency and that self-consciousness about its dangers can be debilitating—but at the same time we are presented with images of complacency in Verloc, Winnie, and others that urge us to remember the fragility of any set of arrangements or to risk the despair and even madness they suffer. *The Secret Agent* validates Winnie's "philosophy" of "not taking notice of the inside of facts"—"her tragic suspicion that 'life doesn't stand much looking into' "—even as it scathingly criticizes her ignorance and asks the reader to transcend it (154, xiii). The novel's contradictory treatment of irony and commitment refuses, however, to lay out for the reader a philosophy more adequate than hers. Like many of Conrad's greatest works, *The Secret Agent* suggests that an ironic awareness of the ubiquity of contingency is knowledge one cannot necessarily do anything with, even if it is also knowledge one cannot do without. Rorty's advice to stop worrying and simply act on one's commitments is more useful knowledge, but its very practicality risks the smug somnolence that Conrad so rigorously unmasks.

Cultivating a sense of irony in the reader, with full awareness of the danger and possible uselessness of the knowledge he is conveying, is Conrad's purpose when, like the manager of the music hall, he shakes the reader's rope anytime a reliable, univocal perspective seems to suggest itself. Like the chief inspector, however, the reader might feel that the authority in charge is not fulfilling his proper function and has broken faith with the performer. Conrad's unusual defensiveness in his "Author's Note" suggests not a little anxiety about being accused of violating the reader's trust: "I have always had a propensity to justify my action. Not to defend. To justify. Not to insist I was right but simply to explain that there was no perverse intention, no secret scorn for the natural sensibilities of mankind at the bottom of my impulses" (viii). He explicitly singles out his "ironic method" for defense—or justification (despite his denials, each implies the other here): "Even the purely artistic purpose, that of applying an ironic method to a subject of that kind, was formulated with deliberation and in the earnest belief that ironic treatment alone would enable me to say all I felt I would have to say in scorn as well as in pity" (xiii). His concluding statement is curiously (and defensively) phrased: "I will submit that . . . I have not intended to commit a gratuitous outrage on the feelings of mankind" (xv). The implication of the redundancy, of course, is that he has indeed committed an outrage, but not a purposeless and unnecessary one.

The "Author's Note" suggests some of the risks accompanying Conrad's ironic strategies not only in *The Secret Agent* but also in the other texts I have analyzed. By tossing the reader back and forth between contradictory alternatives that refuse to synthesize, Conrad might seem to be playing games with us. Manipulating us into impossible dilemmas and then refusing help might seem to show a lack of fellow feeling on his part. Repeatedly shaking the rope we are walking on might suggest the same condescension and scorn toward the reader that the narrator sometimes displays toward his characters. If these are risks Conrad's irony runs, they might result in anger and resentment of the sort his note defensively worries about.

Conrad's best defense would be to argue that his ironic strategies show a basic respect for the reader that the narrator frequently does not display toward Verloc and the anarchists. Although Conrad's irony may play games with us, it also invites us to play along with him, and it will not have its full effects unless we cooperate. The paradox of irony is that it is manipulative but that it also requires mutuality. Without the reader actively filling in what it does not specify, irony cannot work. Jean-Paul Sartre calls reading "an exercise in generosity" because the writer must recognize the reader's consciousness and freedom as necessary to constitute the work. In the spirit of reciprocal partnership, "the writer should not seek to overwhelm; . . . if he wishes to make demands he must propose only the task to be fulfilled" (*Literature* 45, 43). The challenge of Conrad's ironic method is to manipulate and direct the reader's consciousness without dominating us.[9]

Although Conrad's narrative strategies push us toward a knowledge of unresolvable contradictions we might be inclined to resist, he recognizes our freedom and equal status as knowers by relying so heavily on us to work things out for ourselves. The indirectness of his ironic method does not identify the reader's perspective with the narrator's, and that gap leaves us free to formulate the text's implications on our own. The liabilities of irony and the dangers of sympathy are not specified by the text but are blanks through which Conrad signals his respect for the reader—his generous acknowledgment of our capacity to develop an understanding of the inescapable contradictions of skepticism and commitment that no one in his novel (not even his narrator) enjoys. In an expression of solidarity with his audience, Conrad's use of irony shows faith in the reader's ability to be a partner in the epistemological and moral explorations set in motion by *The Secret Agent,* even if his anxiety in the

---

[9] See chapter 1 on Sartre's theory of reading. For an analysis of the democratic ideal of uncoerced dialogue in light of the uses and dangers of power, see my *Conflicting Readings* 134–50.

"Author's Note" betrays residual doubts that this trust may be misplaced because his gesture of confidence may not be understood and reciprocated. By
writing ironically, Conrad demonstrates a generous belief in the reader's capacity to develop not only an ironic sense but also an ironic awareness of the
problems of irony. The result of this generosity is a gift of knowledge that
might leave us uncomfortable and that we might not much like, but this is not
Conrad's fault.[10]

---

[10] That is not to say, however, that an analysis of the effects of reading always redeems the author. For a counterexample, see my analysis of the failure of *Chance* in the next chapter. It is difficult to distinguish between risks that succeed and those that fail, but a risk is a risk for the very
reason that it can go wrong, and *Chance* is a case in point.

6. MISOGYNY AND
THE ETHICS OF READING

The Problem of Conrad's Chance

Marlow's misogyny is a serious problem for most contemporary readers of *Chance*. Even readers who find much in the novel to admire typically temper their praise by faulting Marlow's all too insistent and obtrusive prejudices against women.[1] A brief list of some of his more egregious statements may suggest the extent of the problem:

[1] For example, Daniel R. Schwarz, who takes issue with Thomas Moser's influential argument that the late Conrad undergoes a marked decline, nevertheless concedes that "in *Chance*, Marlow becomes an unintentional caricature of his former self"—"an opinionated, cranky, indifferent and rather dense speaker" (42). Marlow's flaws are a major reason for Moser's judgment that *Chance* is "the first clearly second-rate work that pretended to be of major importance" (8). Like Moser (see 160), Cedric Watts provides a short list of Marlow's misogynist statements and notes that such remarks "may repeatedly tempt the reader to scribble angry rejoinders in the margin" (*Conrad* 119). Although F. R. Leavis finds *Chance* "a remarkable novel," he too complains of "irritation with Marlow" (225, 224), as does John Palmer: "The reflective, self-qualifying moralist of *Lord Jim* has become a more dogmatic philosopher and a crueler ironist; and . . . these changes are distinctly for the worse" (199). Rare exceptions to this pattern are William W. Bonney, who takes Marlow's comments on women as serious philosophizing about gender ("like the phenomenal world, the potent essence of woman partakes of a disorienting unity of opposites" [97]), and Gary Geddes, who tries to make Marlow's misogyny dramatically appropriate: "What would be more fitting, and ironic, than the fact that out of this irritating, philosophizing sceptic, who hides behind a cloak of misogyny and scorn for the world of commerce, religion, government, and even justice, should come the most genuinely sympathetic voice in the novel?" (34). Bonney's strategy of recuperation ignores the dismissive anger behind much of Marlow's misogyny. Whether Marlow should be read ironically, as Geddes proposes, is an issue I will explore in some detail.

As to honour—you know—it's a very fine medieval inheritance which women never got hold of. It wasn't theirs. Since it may be laid as a general principle that women always get what they want, we must suppose they didn't want it. In addition they are devoid of decency. I mean masculine decency. (63)

Hers [referring to the governess] was feminine irrelevancy. A male genius, a male ruffian, or even a male lunatic, would not have behaved exactly as she did behave. There is a softness in masculine nature, even the most brutal, which acts as a check. (100–101)

You [addressing the narrator] expect a cogency of conduct not usual in women. (103)

The secret scorn of women for the capacity to consider judiciously and to express profoundly a meditated conclusion is unbounded. (145)

Women don't understand the force of a contemplative temperament. It simply shocks them. They feel instinctively that it is the one which escapes best the domination of feminine influences. (155)

If women were not a force of nature, blind in its strength and capricious in its power, they would not be mistrusted. As it is one can't help it. (327)

Confronted with demeaning, dogmatic claims like these, a reader may very well ask: Are we meant to take these views seriously? Are they merely the dramatized opinions of a character, or does the author share them? Can they be discounted and neutralized by reading them historically as attitudes commonly held in the past but with no claim on the present? If we find such prejudices offensive, how should this judgment affect our evaluation of the novel?

These are important questions for the ethics of reading.[2] My intention is not to exonerate Marlow or to redeem *Chance*, which is, as I will try to suggest, a deeply flawed work. Its very shortcomings are interesting, however, as an occasion for reflecting about the role of ethical values and judgments in reading. What should the relation be between my moral values and those informing the work? When I read, should I suspend my beliefs about human beings and the right and wrong of conduct; if not, how should I deploy them? What should I do when (as commonly, even typically, happens) the values I encounter in a work contradict and contest my own? If the opportunity to enter radically different worlds is an important gain of reading, can challenges of this kind go too far or go wrong and justify the reader in rebuffing them? How should readers resolve conflicts between their obligation to open themselves up to ways of thinking and feeling other than their own—their responsibility to listen to the text and learn from it—and their commitment to beliefs

---

[2] For important recent statements on this topic, see especially Booth; Miller; and Siebers. Booth provides a helpful, comprehensive bibliography (505–34).

and standards that a work may offend (especially if it is innovative and provocative)? Are there norms transcending individual readers and works that could be invoked in problematic cases—standards that would entitle us to say to readers: "No, you're violating your responsibility to the work"; or to the work: "No, you're violating what you owe to the reader"?

Such questions cannot be made moot by appealing to historical differences. To begin with, although *Chance* was Conrad's first resounding commercial success, the novel's sales were more a sign of the promotional skill of the New York *Herald* and Doubleday's young editor Alfred Knopf than an indication that Marlow's views accurately reflected normative contemporary attitudes (see Watts, *Conrad* 114–16). By 1912, the year of the novel's serialization in the *Herald*, the suffragette movement was in full swing, and Marlow's claims about gender would have been as controversial to a significant number of readers then as now (see Gilbert and Gubar). In an otherwise laudatory review in 1914, when British and American editions of the book first appeared, Conrad's friend Sir Sidney Colvin dismissed Marlow's misogyny as "cheap and second-rate," and Edward Garnett similarly objected that "in Marlow's dislike of feminism the author's shadow is projected too obtrusively on the curtain" (quoted in Watts 117; Garnett 278). Curiously, though, Conrad claimed that he intended to write a book that respected the dignity of women as readers: "I don't believe that women have to be written for especially as if they were infants. Women, as far as I have been able to judge, have a grasp of and are interested in the facts of life. . . . [A]ny woman with a heart and mind knows very well that she is an active partner in the great adventure of humanity on the earth and feels an interest in all its episodes accordingly" (New York *Herald*, 14 January 1912, quoted in Watts 115–16). Wayne Booth asserts that "every literary work implies either that women can enter its imaginative world as equals or that they cannot" (387). Conrad claims that *Chance* passes this test, although the unmodulated stridency of Marlow's misogyny has caused many readers (like Garnett) to identify his views with the author's. In any case, looking back to the time of the novel's first appearance recreates rather than resolves the ethical question of how, and on what grounds, the reader should respond to the narrator's prejudices about women.

Even if the historical record unequivocally suggested that Marlow's views coincided with the norms of his period, problems of response would remain. One measure of the value of literature is its power to speak across historical distance. To neutralize Marlow's misogyny by rendering it historically specific would be to reduce *Chance* to the status of an artifact relevant only, or primarily, to its originating context. Literary works are "other"—uniquely bounded by their own historical and cultural horizons—even as they reach across those horizons to future audiences who appropriate them to interests and purposes their creators could not anticipate. A literary work is paradoxical because it opens up another world to us even as it speaks to contemporary concerns in ever-changing ways.

This paradoxical doubleness of a work's historical existence is reflected in what J. Hillis Miller calls "the double definition" of reading as "an ethical act": "It is a response to an irresistible demand, an 'I must,' and it is an act which is productive, a doing which causes other things to be done in their turn" (120). Reading entails a double ethical dimension because (first) it is a response to otherness whose distinctive difference we must attempt to recognize and do justice to, even as (second) the value and meaning of this listening will vary according to the interests and purposes we bring to our reading and the uses to which our understanding will be put. Booth describes the ethics of reading as similarly double: "I serve myself best, as reader, when I both honor an author's offering for what it is, in its full 'otherness' from me, and take an active critical stance against what seem to me its errors or excesses" in a paradoxical manner "that entails both surrender and refusal" (136).

This doubleness suggests that ethical reading is a to-and-fro activity, a back-and-forth movement between the work's demands on us and our demands on the work. Such an exchange requires reciprocity, mutual confidence, and respect even (or especially) when radical differences divide both parties. Echoing Gadamer and Iser, I have described such open-ended give-and-take as a particular kind of "play." An implication of this claim is that an act on either side that disrupts the reciprocity of play—stopping the give-and-take with a dominating intervention, for example, or refusing to recognize the other as an equal partner—would be an ethical violation of the very conditions required for understanding. If reading entails a to-and-fro play between my values and those encountered in the work, then the conduct of a "*Spielverderber*" (or "spoilsport," to recall Gadamer's term that I discuss in chapter 1) is a transgression of the ethics of reading.

The problem with Marlow's misogyny in *Chance* is that it is an unreciprocated act that labels women without allowing for a response. He claims to know women better than they know themselves, but the very willfulness of this assertion rules out a give-and-take that might test and modify his prejudices. The disappointment of *Chance* is that it does not transform this violation of reciprocity into an effective theme, although there is ample material in the plot and in the relations among the characters for doing so. The Conrad of *Lord Jim* and *Heart of Darkness* uses Marlow with great subtlety and ingenuity to challenge the reader to reflect about epistemological paradoxes that plunge him and us into productive bewilderment (see my *Challenge* 109–48). In similar fashion, Marlow's prejudices about women in *Chance* raise questions about the potentially blinding will to power of our hermeneutic categories whose fragility and deceptiveness we are for the most part oblivious to. Unlike Conrad's great novels of epistemological reflection, however, *Chance* is not an effective reciprocating partner in urging the reader to explore the ambiguities suggested by Marlow's prejudices. The reader is consequently left to speculate about the novel Conrad almost wrote but did not.

This is difficult to prove because, if the reader does do the work a novel doesn't, it is hard to demonstrate that the novel wasn't responsible. When I read *Heart of Darkness* or *Lord Jim,* I feel that the more Conrad demands of me, the more I can demand of him, and there will be a return. Reading *Chance* lacks this reciprocity. One reason why readers disagree about the value of this novel, however, is that some of them are willing to credit the text for work they are doing themselves. Others aren't, however, and their annoyance often suggests an angry disappointment with a partner who didn't live up to his part of the bargain. Again, it is hard to know where to draw this line because of the very nature of reading as a collaborative enterprise. Nevertheless, sometimes one can tell that one's partner is not doing his or her share, and *Chance* seems to me an instance of that. *Chance* is marred, then, by a double violation of the ethics of reading—Marlow's refusal of reciprocity with the Other in his reading of women, which is compounded in turn by the novel's failure to promote playful, reflective exchange about this matter with the reader.

The central but insufficiently developed theme suggested by Marlow's misogyny is the dangerous but necessary role of power in knowledge. In the statements that I listed at the outset, women are repeatedly referred to as "they"—a pronoun that marks "them" as Other even as it homogenizes them as a class. Marlow's dilemma (although he is too confident about his knowledge to recognize it as such) is that he can know the Other only by projecting beliefs that are constructions. These beliefs are generalizing schemata that try to make sense of an unfamiliar particular by assimilating it to a known type. As Marlow says of Flora at one point, "she was not so much unreadable as blank" (207). His misogynist statements are an attempt to read "woman" by filling in blanks and arranging anomalous, confusing elements into significant patterns.

Power is necessarily involved in compositional, gap-filling activity of this kind. Sometimes such power is productive, as when Marlow imagines the bafflement and suffering Flora must have experienced because of the collapse of her father's financial empire and the betrayal by her governess: "You may imagine then the force of the shock in the intuitive perception not merely of danger, for she did not know what was alarming her, but in the sense of the security being gone. . . . Even a small child lives, plays and suffers in terms of its conception of its own existence. Imagine, if you can, a fact coming in suddenly with a force capable of shattering that very conception itself" (117). This generalization seems much more revealing than Marlow's assertions about the psychology of women, but it is identical in epistemological structure. It fits the unfamiliar (the destruction of one's world) to a familiar category (a child's sense of security) and fills out inaccessible blanks (how Flora must have felt when her father went to prison and her governess angrily abandoned her). The danger—here avoided, I think—is that the will to power in such interpretive acts of composition and projection may run roughshod over the Other and become rigidly, circularly self-confirming.

An undeveloped theme of *Chance* is how, if at all, one can know that this is happening. If an illegitimate prejudice and a productive hermeneutic hypothesis have the same inherent structure, how can one tell them apart? Marlow is oblivious to this problem, and the novel provides little guidance to the reader about how to think about it. Illuminating hypotheses about otherness sit side by side with prejudices that seem to be unjustified assertions of power—but without a recognition anywhere in the text that their uncanny resemblance is an epistemological dilemma. If the reader wished to separate them—to list in different columns "Marlow's sexist prejudices" and "Marlow's valid psychological insights"—the novel gives no assistance in justifying such a distinction. The disturbing similarity between the kinds of statements in the two columns is something that *Chance* does not challenge the reader to reflect about, although it is deeply worth contemplating. Much of Marlow's experience in *Lord Jim* is devoted to reflecting about epistemological ambiguities of this sort, but similar dilemmas go unacknowledged in *Chance*. The ethical response of the reader to Marlow's sexist comments may be to wish for grounds to condemn them, but their similarity in structure to seemingly authoritative constructs suggests that objective grounds for such distinctions may not exist. The disappointment of *Chance* is that it does not play with this ambiguity to give rise to thought—either on the reader's part or on Marlow's—about the difficulty of distinguishing between blinding prejudice and revealing judgment.[3]

One way to have developed this theme would have been to have involved Marlow in give-and-take exchanges with the others he interprets as well as with other interpreters. These sorts of conversation are oddly absent in

---

[3] Robert Siegle's celebration of Marlow's epistemological reflexivity in *Chance* ignores this problem and, as a result, reproduces it—first rejecting Marlow's prejudices only to praise them as valid insights. Siegle condemns as "sexist" Marlow's "typing of male and female consciousness" but then in the very next breath affirms Marlow's analysis of the irrationality of women as a critique of phallocentrism: "Women, presumably because they have escaped the philosophical conditioning of workplace and university, perceive what idealism [defined as faith in 'the interpretive power of abstractions'] excludes" (92).

Chance, although they make up much of the interest in *Lord Jim,* where Marlow repeatedly finds his moral categories and interpretive hypotheses baffled during his exchanges with the enigmatic Jim and with the others he consults about him. Marlow's interlocutors in *Chance* are for the most part silent or ineffective. Even when Marlow talks with them, there is an absence of dialogue—of back-and-forth exchange that might challenge or test his assumptions and hypotheses and encourage the reader to ponder the conflicts between their views. The governess, whose betrayal of Flora occupies much of Marlow's interpretive energy and is the cause of many of his generalizations about feminine psychology, is absent and cannot defend herself or offer an opposing interpretation of her actions. Marlow's anger at Mrs. Fyne similarly prevents listening and exchange (a significant lost opportunity to which I will return).

Even his relation with Flora is largely built on silences: "In fact we had nothing to say to each other; but we two, strangers as we really were to each other, had dealt with the most intimate and final of subjects, the subject of death. It had created a sort of bond between us" (209). Marlow's shout that prevented her suicidal jump and established a "bond" between them is emblematic of the lack of reciprocity in their relationship. Yelling at someone on a cliff is presumptuous and may indeed cause them to fall. It is the sort of unsolicited act of generosity that, as Captain Anthony's proposal demonstrates, may have unintended, unwelcome consequences. When Flora tells Marlow about her misfortunes, he keeps his thoughts largely to himself. Even when his generalizations about her seem revealing, they are not offered for her reaction and response: "The world had treated her so dishonourably that she had no notion even of what mere decency of feeling is like. It was not her fault. Indeed, I don't know why she should have put her trust in anybody's promises" (236). This sounds plausible, but it is just as much an untested projection as his claim that she was grateful for small indications of affection from Captain Anthony: "It is lucky that small things please women. And it is not silly of them to be thus pleased. It is in small things that the deepest loyalty, that which they need most, the loyalty of the passing moment, is best expressed" (234). This assertion about feminine psychology may be less offensive than some of Marlow's other claims because it is essentially affirming, but it still treats Flora as an unreciprocating Other who is not given a chance to comment on and criticize descriptions of herself.

Without such reciprocity, even sympathetic readings can be usurpations, acts of power whose condescending authority is just as presumptuous as prejudices thrown out from an impersonal distance—and perhaps more irritating and intrusive because of the insinuation of intimacy. As unreciprocated acts of labeling, even his generous, sympathetic constructions of Flora's plight are consequently similar to the aggressive misogyny that Marlow directs at the women he dislikes (the governess and Mrs. Fyne). Once again, however, by not calling attention to this similarity, *Chance* misses an opportunity to provoke reflection about the ethics of understanding.

The first-person narrator might have been expected to supply the dialogue missing in the novel, but he too is silenced whenever he tries to speak up.[4] A to-and-fro exchange between equal interlocutors never develops between him and Marlow. The narrator claims at one point: "we were always tilting at each other." But the results are invariably one-sided, summarized in the words: "Marlow silenced me" (102, 117). Marlow's condescension is at times astonishing. After Marlow's claim that women lack "honor" and "masculine decency" but crave "power—the kind of thrill they love most"—the narrator interrupts: "Do you expect me to agree with all this?" To which Marlow replies: "No, it isn't necessary. . . . You need not even understand it" (63). When and if the narrator disagrees, it must be because he isn't smart enough to see what Marlow means. Reciprocity is impossible because the narrator is not granted the authority of an equal player, an epistemological partner like (say) Stein or the French lieutenant commenting on Jim.

One wonders why the narrator puts up with Marlow's put-downs. A possible reaction of the reader might be to step in for the ineffectual narrator and criticize Marlow all the more severely because he behaves so badly to the intermediary through whom we receive the story. But because Marlow's authority is nowhere effectively called into question in the novel, it is not clear that this is a step we are entitled to take. Moreover, if we do vent our anger at him in place of the too quiescent narrator, we risk duplicating the will to power we object to. This could be a provocative dilemma in which to place the reader: In our anger at Marlow's denial of reciprocity to an Other, we reject his authority, and thus we do to him what we object to him doing to the narrator. Playing this sort of game with the reader for our ethical and epistemological edification is, however, yet another opportunity that *Chance* misses.

To develop it, the novel would have had to explore more thoroughly and subtly the ambiguities of the narrative contract. The ineffectuality of the narrator, unwilling to take Marlow on, suggests a desire to preserve the narrative contract at almost any cost. There seems to be no price the narrator will not pay to get Marlow's story. But what are stories worth? By granting their

[4] Aaron Fogel unfortunately gives only passing mention to *Chance* because he claims Conrad's interest in the role of force and coercion in dialogue wanes after *Under Western Eyes* (see 25). Marlow's use of talk and silence to dominate or do battle with others suggests, however, that this theme remains central—although whether it is handled effectively is another matter. See Fogel's analysis of Conrad's skepticism about the ideal of dialogue between equal, reciprocating partners (esp. 1–38).

attention, listeners pay a price even when storytellers narrate free of charge
(see Barthes 88–89; Chambers 16–17; Pratt 100–116). The very telling of a
story is thus a presumption (the implicit claim that what I have to say will be
worth your time) and an act of power (by taking center stage, invoking the sole
right to speak, rendering others silent). The question may therefore arise: Is a
story a gift or an imposition—or both? The reader of *Chance* may feel that he
or (especially) she gets a story we might rather not have had (at least in this
version) at a cost we are not happy to have paid. That disappointment signals
that a violation of the bond between teller and listener has occurred—that obligations on both sides have not been equally honored. Thematizing that problem—what obligations are involved in the narrative contract, and when their
violation might warrant breaking it off—is an opportunity that could have
been grasped if the conflict between Marlow and the narrator had been developed further. As it is, the one-sided "tilting" between them is more likely
to result in frustration and confusion for the reader than in provocatively or-
chestrated reflection about the ambiguous mix of generosity and presumption
implicit in the act of narration.

The question of what teller and listener owe one another when a tale seems
objectionable is analogous to the problem of the civility to which opposing interpreters are entitled. After one of Marlow's more egregiously misogynist
statements, the first-person narrator intervenes: " 'Do you really believe what
you have said?' I asked, meaning no offence, because with Marlow one never
could be sure" (94). The narrator's hesitant deference and reluctance to quarrel suggest a willingness to tolerate difference that is commendable in a world
of conflicting interpretations. Conrad suggests in a letter to Garnett that "two
universes may exist in the same place and in the same time—and not only two
universes but an infinity of different universes—if by universe we mean a set
of states of consciousness" (*Letters* 2:95). In such a pluralistic world, the danger of violent collisions or disruptive jostling for position seems ever-present.
But if Marlow's prejudices about women are manifestations of a will to power
that seeks mastery through unreciprocated categorization, the reader can resist this will only by engaging in a battle that calls into question the liberal
ideal of tolerance of opposing views. The first-person narrator's desire to give
"no offence" invokes this ideal, but his desire for peaceful civility is questionable if combating prejudices requires attacking them by a counterstrategy of
categorization that labels them intolerable. The problem that the novel suggests but once again does not adequately dramatize is whether the civility
desired by the narrator is a naive and dangerous denial of the unavoidable
interdependence of knowledge and power, or whether decorum is all the more
necessary to prevent violence and disruption once this interdependence is
recognized.

The narrator's observation that "one never could be sure" if Marlow is serious suggests that perhaps we should take his opinions with a grain of salt.
Marlow's reply to the narrator's query about whether he means what he says
is odd and intemperate, however, but not exactly ironic: " 'Only on certain
days of the year,' said Marlow with a malicious smile. 'Today I have been simply trying to be spacious and I perceive I've managed to hurt your suscepti-
bilities which are consecrated to women. When you sit alone and silent you are
defending in your mind the poor women from attacks which cannot possibly
touch them. I wonder what can touch them?' " (94). Instead of lending credence to the notion that his attacks on women might be intentional rhetorical
excess whose very hyperbole should lead us to discount them, Marlow renews
his disparagement of the opposite sex with an angry vindictiveness that is difficult to evaluate. The narrator repeatedly asserts that "Marlow had the habit
of pursuing general ideas in a peculiar manner, between jest and earnest" (23).
But if this is teasing, it misfires. He does not seem to be joking; or if he is, his
humor does not undermine or debunk his misogyny, the force of which remains unchecked or even redoubles.

Because the signals offered by the text are confusing (crediting Marlow
with "jesting" when it isn't clear that he is), it is difficult to have confidence
that we as readers should view him ironically. The dilemma readers face is that
it is always possible to take someone ironically, but here the warrant from the
text for doing so is unclear even though it claims to give us explicit instruc-
tions. If readers choose to view Marlow as an unreliable narrator and discount
the authority of his claims about women, they are free to take this tack—but
they are acting on their own, unreciprocated by the text, inasmuch as the text
botches the signals it gives about how to classify Marlow's tone. Here as before, it would have been interesting if the text had made this problem into an
explicit theme: What are the marks of irony? If ironic reading is often a risk
because there may not be clear-cut signs calling for it, when is this wager justified? These are vexing and perhaps ultimately not answerable questions, but
the problem with *Chance* is that it seems oblivious to them.

A further obstacle to treating Marlow as unreliable is that his hermeneutic
constructions are nowhere called into question by his experiences as an interpreter. Unlike the Marlow of *Lord Jim* or *Heart of Darkness,* the Marlow of
Chance does not find his epistemological categories or moral values unsettled
by the story he tells (see my *Challenge* 9–11, 112–19). Unlike Jim or Kurtz,
Flora does not cause Marlow to doubt deeply held convictions. Flora is frequently bewildered by events in her story, but Marlow never is.[5] Because his

---

[5] Schwarz similarly observes that "Marlow is fundamentally unaffected by his tale, as if it
were peripheral to his values" (42).

certainty is never shaken, *Chance* misses the opportunity of staging the question of whether convictions can be held ironically, under erasure, simultaneously affirmed and questioned. The tone the narrator attributes to Marlow—a "tone between grim jest and grim earnest" (150)—would seem marked by such doubleness, but Marlow's unchallenged security about his views belies this claim.

The double act of suspending belief in convictions that one nevertheless holds is not effectively dramatized in *Chance*, and this failure may indicate that such bracketing is an impossible feat.[6] The novel suggests, however, that the alternatives are undesirable. Marlow calls "soothing certitude" deceptive in its very complacency about itself (273). The self-certainty of a prejudice marks its will to power by ruling out in advance the possibility of reciprocity. But if irony about the contingency and contestability of one's convictions is a valuable counter to dogmatic aggressiveness, Marlow also warns against "the madness of universal suspicion" and "the mortal weariness of bewildered thinking" (175, 183). Doubt is a germ whose spread is hard to check, and suspending belief in one's beliefs may issue in inaction. Avoiding the twin dangers of the violence of unchallenged certainty and the enervating paralysis of aimless bafflement, can one simultaneously discount one's assumptions and values even as one deploys them with conviction? Marlow's failure to synthesize "jest" and "earnest" leaves this question unanswered, although the novel asserts that this is a doubleness he has achieved.

If Marlow were more capable of self-critical irony, he might have recognized and been amused by the surprising similarities between his own views about Flora and "Mrs. Fyne's feminist doctrine" (58). The epithets that he applies to Mrs. Fyne—"a ruthless theorist," "an offended theorist" (126, 190)—are stones thrown from a glass house. If there is a will to power in her generalizations about sexual difference, as these labels imply, the same is true of Marlow's misogyny. Mrs. Fyne is Marlow's unrecognized double. *Chance* fails to take advantage of this doubleness, either by dramatizing it as an unconscious identification that, unacknowledged, could bring Marlow grief, or by staging it as a duplication of consciousness that could give rise to self-consciousness. Both kinds of doubleness are, by contrast, integral to the drama of Marlow's relation to Jim and Kurtz.

---

[6] Whether one can simultaneously hold and suspend one's beliefs has recently been a crucial point of contention. As I have noted, Rorty advocates this sort of doubleness in his posture of "liberal irony" (see *Contingency* xv, 61). Although frequently identified like Rorty with "pragmatism," Stanley Fish claims that such duality is inherently impossible because one cannot not believe one's beliefs (see 436–67). Part of my disappointment with *Chance* is that it raises this problem without exploring its complexities. See my discussions of Forster and Joyce in the following chapters.

Marlow's treatment of Mrs. Fyne is a model of how not to conduct hermeneutic disagreements. By labeling and dismissing her, Marlow refuses her
reciprocity and cuts off any chance of productive conflict between them—a
give-and-take through which a mutually enlightening articulation of their
similarities and differences might emerge. Even in the caricatured form in
which Marlow renders what he calls her "naively unscrupulous," "atrocious"
"knock-me-down doctrine" (62, 59), her theory seems worth taking seriously
as a commentary on Flora's tragic story:

> it was something like this: that no consideration, no delicacy, no tenderness, no
> scruples should stand in the way of a woman (who by the mere fact of her sex
> was the predestined victim of conditions created by men's selfish passions,
> their vices and their abominable tyranny) from taking the shortest cut towards
> securing for herself the easiest possible existence. She had even the right to go
> out of existence without considering any one's feelings or convenience, since
> some women's existences were made impossible by the shortsighted baseness of
> men. (59)

This is not at all implausible as a reading of Flora's plight. Her father, after
leaving her to fend for herself when he is sent to prison as a bankrupt fraud,
selfishly and tyrannically insists on her total devotion when he is released, despite years of neglect. Further, if even the generosity of Captain Anthony is
tainted by an element of aggressive imposition, a dominating solicitude that
Flora is powerless to resist, then the frank practical cynicism of Mrs. Fyne's
argument that helpless women should look out first and foremost for themselves is not inappropriate (ironically enough, since for reasons never fully
made clear, she objects to her brother's proposal, although her own doctrine
suggests that Flora is fully within her rights to accept it).

Marlow's blind fury at Mrs. Fyne's feminism prevents him from recognizing the common ground between them, with one significant exception. Mrs.
Fyne laments: "I've never had such a crushing impression of the miserable
dependence of girls—of women. This was an extreme case. But a young
man—any man—could have gone to break stones on the roads or something
of that kind—or enlisted—or—" (172). Marlow interrupts what he calls
"Mrs. Fyne's tirade" here and changes the subject, but he thinks to himself:
"It was very true. Women can't go forth on the high roads and by-ways to pick
up a living even when dignity, independence or existence itself are at stake"
(172). Once again Marlow remains silent with an interlocutor and suppresses
his views when announcing them could have led to a give-and-take that might
have had surprising and unpredictable results. If the "dignity" and "independence" of women are values he appreciates, shouldn't he worry that he violates them when he labels women without giving them a chance to reply?

Although Marlow elsewhere grudgingly acknowledges the "undeniable humanity" of Mrs. Fyne's "pure compassion" toward Flora (135, 140), he cannot credit a similar solicitude toward helpless suffering as a justification for her feminist pedagogy. But if he thinks that her theory of feminism conflicts with her practice of compassion, is there not a revealingly parallel contradiction between his misogynist generalizations and his sympathy for Flora?

These are missed opportunities for self-consciousness that the uncanny duplication of Marlow and Mrs. Fyne might have prompted if Marlow had credited her otherness as worth taking seriously and responding to openly, even playfully, with the sort of jesting self-irony the narrator attributes to him. Marlow the misogynist might then have discovered a secret sympathy with feminism that might have called into question the hostility and disrespect toward women of some of his more insulting prejudices. Marlow says at one point: "nothing is more disturbing than the upsetting of a preconceived idea" (289). Recognizing unexpected similarities with an Other is one way of unsettling prejudices about them, but Marlow here as elsewhere insulates himself from potentially tonic challenges.

Marlow's hostility to Mrs. Fyne is so blinding and unrelenting that it must have unconscious sources. Noting that Marlow confesses "there is enough of the woman in my nature to free my judgment of women from glamorous reticency" (53), Daniel R. Schwarz speculates that "perhaps Conrad is uncomfortable with this androgynous identity that he perceives within himself" (52). The flaw in this otherwise plausible hypothesis is that Marlow is fully conscious of his androgyny, and it therefore seems hardly capable of unleashing the distorting, uncontrolled ferocity he exhibits toward Mrs. Fyne. Thomas Moser attributes the misogyny in the later Conrad to his "hostility to feminine self-assertion": "Woman in action, woman as the competitor of man, is insufferable" (162, 160). Again this reading is plausible, but it does not quite fit the Marlow of *Chance*. What irritates Marlow about Mrs. Fyne is not her actions but her associations, in particular her friendships with other women:

> The girl-friend problem exercised me greatly. How and where the Fynes got all these pretty creatures to come and stay with them I can't imagine. I had at first the wild suspicion that they were obtained to amuse Fyne. But I soon discovered that he could hardly tell one from the other, though obviously their presence met with his solemn approval. These girls in fact came for Mrs. Fyne. They treated her with admiring deference. She answered to some need of theirs. They sat at her feet. They were like disciples. It was very curious. Of Fyne they took but scanty notice. As to myself, I was made to feel that I did not exist. (42)

What most offends and disturbs Marlow about Mrs. Fyne's feminism is the way it bonds her with others of her sex. As the breathless sense of scandal in

Marlow's commentary implies, bonds of this kind have a homoerotic component that some feminist theorists explicitly stress.[7] As Judith Fetterley argues, "lesbianism is a key issue in feminism because . . . in the lesbian the formidable power of woman's sexuality is set not against but for herself"; the assumption is that "women will never be free to realize and become themselves until they are free of their need for man, until they know that their basic bonds are with each other, and until they learn to make a primary commitment to each other" (152–53). Mrs. Fyne's relations with her "girl-friends" establish an exclusive community of women in accord with the lesbian ethos of some kinds of radical feminism.[8]

Although the Fynes produced three children ("all girls" [39]), the husband and wife seem to lead separate lives, with Fyne's libido displaced onto restless, frenetic walking that Marlow oddly resents. His anger at Fyne's energetic pedestrianism makes sense, however, if it is of a piece with his outrage and resentment at the homoerotic charge in Mrs. Fyne's relations with other women. Instead of dissipating his libido by walking, Fyne should be expending it at home. Part of Marlow's anger at Mrs. Fyne's feminine friendships is the resentment of an excluded party. If her community of women is formed by making men Other, his misogyny fights back by returning the favor. But given the homoerotic quality of these bonds, and if Mrs. Fyne is in many ways Marlow's unconscious double, it is perhaps not unreasonable to speculate that his anger also expresses and defends against his own desires. The force of his hostility would be fueled by his need to negate and deny wishes and feelings of his own that he distressingly sees his double acting out.

If this speculation is plausible, it raises some interesting questions about the ideal of community, which Conrad frequently celebrates in his works with just as much energy as he derides Mrs. Fyne's lesbian bonds in *Chance.* Is solidarity for Conrad a masculine value? And does it have a libidinal, homoerotic component?[9] Those are questions that Marlow's hostility toward Mrs. Fyne

---

[7] On the relation between feminism and lesbianism, see especially Jay and Glasgow; Rich; and Stimpson 97–110, 140–54.

[8] Critics have disagreed about whether Mrs. Fyne is lesbian. Jocelyn Baines asserts that "she is given all the lesbian's most distinctive characteristics" without specifying what these are (386n), but Frederick Karl dismisses this as unwarranted speculation, although he too gives no reasons (685n). B. C. Meyer's classic psychoanalytic study is oddly silent on this issue.

[9] Marlow's irrational anger and resentment of Mrs. Fyne would therefore be a variety of what Eve Kosofsky Sedgwick calls the "male homosexual panic" that can result from the resemblance of "homosocial" and "homosexual" ties—bonds between men for cultural, political, and economic purposes and relations motivated by desire. As Sedgwick explains, "Because the paths of male entitlement, especially in the nineteenth century, required certain intense male bonds that were not readily distinguishable from the most reprobated bonds, an endemic and ineradicable state of what I am calling male homosexual panic became the normal condition of male hetero-

masks and suppresses. The camaraderie on board ship is explicitly gendered masculine—the bond of "the men of the sea" in their "service of a temple . . . detached from the vanities and errors" of the world (33, 32). What is excluded in forming this community is women, except for the object that unites them, the "she" of the ship—the heterosexual object of their shared affection and desire as a collective masculine subject (the mate says of the *Ferndale* "she was more than a home to a man" [287]). Hence the mate's distress at the disruption of this bond when the captain brings a woman on board: "His impression had been that women did not exist for Captain Anthony. Exhibiting himself with a girl! A girl! What did he want with a girl?" (267). If solidarity is a pact between men, it would not be available to women, and Marlow explicitly says as much: "There is not between women that fund of at least conditional loyalty which men may depend on in their dealings with each other" (209). The lack of the possibility of solidarity among women signals that it is a male possession.

A number of memorable women in other works from Conrad's canon show that loyalty is not exclusively a masculine value, but their fidelity is inevitably not to other women but to men: Mrs. Gould's unstinting and increasingly unreturned devotion to her husband in *Nostromo*, Jewel's unwavering and disappointed allegiance to Jim in *Lord Jim*, Lena's ultimately futile sacrifice of herself for Heyst in *Victory*, Nathalie Haldin's faithfulness to her dead brother in *Under Western Eyes*, or Winnie Verloc's care and concern for her brother Stevie in *The Secret Agent*. Conrad's greatest exploration of community at sea, *The Nigger of the "Narcissus,"* is an exclusively male story, but the crew's self-indulgent and self-destructive identification with James Wait powerfully suggests the unconscious and sometimes dangerous energies that can fuel solidarity. This story explores with rigorous honesty how narcissistic desires can inhabit and subvert the ideal of community, and such a commitment to subjecting values Conrad cherishes to unflinching skeptical scrutiny is a hallmark of his greatest works. *Chance* does not belong in this company, however, because it suggests the subterranean presence of homoerotic desire in some kinds of community but then draws back from exploring it.

It is a very Conradian theme that identifications and bonds are often motivated by unconscious desires, wishes, and needs. The disappointment of *Chance* is that—unlike, say, Brierly's unconscious identification with Jim, or Jim's unrecognized sense of a secret bond with Gentleman Brown—this

sexual entitlement" (*Epistemology* 185; see also *Between* 1–5, 88–90). I am not arguing that homosexuality produces misogyny. Rather, my point is that fear of the homosexual undertones of homosocial bonding can, by the reversals and projections I am about to trace, result in hatred of women.

doubling of Marlow with Mrs. Fyne has no tragic outcome that might call attention to its repressed workings and focus them for thought. As a result they remain hidden unless the reader works against the text, or at least independent of its prompting, to ferret them out. Instead of staging unconscious identifications that give rise to thought on the reader's part about their disguised motivations, as *Lord Jim* so skillfully does, *Chance* allows them to stay hidden, surfacing only as distortions to the text in the flaws and missed opportunities caused by Marlow's misogyny. One can only assume that the anger of Marlow at Mrs. Fyne's lesbianism is a topic Conrad cannot bring himself to examine because to do so would reveal the homoerotic energy behind one of his cherished ideals.[10]

To a considerable extent, then, Marlow's misogyny may be a product of his fear of his own repressed desires and wishes. As in all symptom formation, a contradictory process of disguise and disclosure is at work here. The paradoxical logic of this kind of misogyny declares a bond with other men, a homosocial relation that can be homoerotically charged, but it does so by making women Other, thereby giving as the reason for the male bond not desire for the same sex, but heterosexual difference from the Other. The assertion of a male-male bond, the creation of the manifestly homosocial and latently homoerotic subject of misogyny, is strategically contradictory inasmuch as attention is directed elsewhere, toward the Other under attack, in a manner that deflects recognition from the same-sex bond it affirms. The negation of the Other through aggressive disparagement reflects and reinforces the repression of the same-sex desire that misogyny simultaneously expresses and disguises. The problem with *Chance* is that Marlow cannot play with his prejudices about women and ironically put them at risk, and the reason is that he has so much invested in them unconsciously.

[10] In life, Conrad's attitudes toward homosexuality seem to have been a mix of condemnation and tolerance. Although the extremely proper, fastidious Conrad was disgusted by Oscar Wilde and abandoned his former friend Roger Casement when his sexual inversion was revealed, he also had a number of openly homosexual friends, including the reckless Norman Douglas, whose son Robin frequently stayed with the Conrad family. See Meyers 225–26, 315, 318.

7. LIBERALISM AND
THE POLITICS OF FORM

The Ambiguous Narrative Voice in Howards End

Although queer theory's attention to E. M. Forster has primarily been directed at the explicitly homosexual text *Maurice,* the epistemology of the closet would suggest that the most interesting and important evidence of this author's sexual identity might be found in less obvious places.[1] For the very reason that *Howards End* has for so long seemed unusually normal, it is therefore a likely site for discovering effects of Forster's duality as a writer who is self-conscious about passing. Eschewing the pyrotechnics of other early modern novels, *Howards End* has seemed to many a holdover of Victorian conventions of realistic, omniscient narration. Some readers have sensed, however, that this appearance is deceptive. As Elizabeth Langland notes, "Forster is a difficult writer to approach because he appears simple" (252). Pointing to "the unease that lurks below the groomed surfaces of this book," Kenneth Graham finds that "along with the strong sense of masterful control in plot and in general analytic intelligence, there is unsteadiness of an enlivening kind that challenges the reader's attention at every moment" (161, 159). This indirectness and strategic instability manifest Forster's doubleness "as a queer artist [to quote Robert Martin and George Piggford], as one who seeks to disrupt the economy of the normal" even as he tries to avoid being exposed, "a Queer Forster who remains elusive, sharp-witted, and multifarious" and "is far too

---

[1] For example, the index to the anthology *Queer Forster* lists seventy-two pages on *Maurice* and only twenty-two pages on *Howards End.*

slippery to be contained within any simple category" (4, 6). The ambiguous narrator of *Howards End* is elusive in just this way. He invokes the powers of narrative authority even as he undercuts them, he offers definitive wisdom even as he exposes its partiality, and he pretends to mediate oppositions even as he demonstrates the ineluctability of difference. These contradictions convert the double structure of the closet into a way of playing with the reader's assumptions about the normative—normative beliefs and normative relations—but in a game so subtle and slippery that it can pass without notice or can seem to be a failure in the use of conventional techniques.

My analysis of these contradictions is in the first instance an attempt to make sense of formal features of Forster's novel that have been insufficiently appreciated, or have seemed flawed or incongruous, because their function as expressions of his closeted identity has not been understood. In the end, however, the purpose of this formal analysis is to suggest a reconsideration of Forster's politics. I want to work through form to politics because in *Howards End* the most interesting and important commentary on social relations, power, and ideology is located in the contradictory, elusive relation between the narrator and the reader. If the ambiguities of the novel's narrator act out Forster's ambivalences about accepting or refusing his community's conventions, then this is more than a personal drama. The games the narrator plays with the reader stage the defining oppositions of Forster's liberalism.

This politics is more subtle and complex than is typically credited because it envisions a mode of community based not on unity or solidarity but on nonconsensual relationships of mutuality that do not erase difference and heterogeneity. Such a vision is inherently contradictory and, I think, deeply informed by Forster's closeted sense of belonging to a community with which he was not at one. Forster's contradictory liberalism imagines a mode of nonconsensual reciprocity that is represented nowhere in the text itself but that defines the narrator's relationship to the reader. And this is why elucidating the politics of *Howards End* requires first of all an analysis of form. The contradictions of Forster's narrator make sense of the contradictions of his liberalism (and the reverse is also true).

As is well known, Forster did not fully recognize his homosexual orientation until after publishing *Howards End* in 1910, and he did not have his first sexual experience with another man until 1916. There is nevertheless ample earlier evidence of his self-consciousness about a defining difference from others that must be kept hidden. Consider, for example, the following entry in his *Notebook Journal* for 31 December 1907:

> Shall scarcely write another "Longest Journey," for it vexed people and I can with sincerity please them. Am anxious not to widen a gulf that must always remain wide; there is no doubt that I do not resemble other people, and even they

notice it. Have been strongly attracted . . . to acquiesce in social conventions, economic trend[s], efficiency, etc., and see that others may do right to acquiesce and that I may do wrong to laugh at them, and that great art was never a conscious rebel. A rebel, surely. (269)

It is difficult to know from this passage exactly what displeasing aspects of *The Longest Journey* should be avoided in the future, although one might guess that a secret of some sort betrays itself in the odd series of accidental deaths that either thwart heterosexual love (Agnes's husband-to-be Gerald dying while playing soccer; Rickie's mother's lover drowning during their brief elopement) or that cut short a too-intensely-charged homosocial relationship (Rickie run over by a train while saving his drunken half-brother Stephen). What this passage does make clear, however, is the double structure of conforming while rebelling that informs Forster's narrative art. He will acquiesce—try not to seem too different—but he will not suppress his otherness entirely or deny its subversive power (although "great art was never a conscious rebel," it was "a rebel, surely"). The double structure of Forster's closeted sense of self inspires a double game of disguising difference and allowing its potential disruptiveness room to play.

The role of the narrator is an especially important site for this game because of the narrator's functions as the voice of truth and as a mediator (not only between different perspectives in the text but also between the text and the reader). In both of these functions, the narrator of *Howards End* affirms the normative even as he tacitly questions and undermines it. He claims the privilege of speaking with definitive wisdom while ironically criticizing the will to power and partiality of all assertions of epistemological authority, including his own, and his efforts to establish community and connection demonstrate the inevitability of exclusion and the dangers of the homogenizing force of consensus. A critic as perceptive as Barbara Rosecrance sees these contradictions but doesn't know what to make of them:

> Despite the narrator's brilliance, his persuasion must ultimately be regarded as unsuccessful. He does not achieve a harmonious integration of ideology and dramatic representation, of content and form. His reflections are often disconnected from the action, so that the novel appears to present an uneven alternation between essay and scene, comment and action. To a degree found in no other Forster novel, the narrator's diction is abstract, metaphorical, hyperbolical; the anxiety and inflation of his tone suggest the desperation of his attempt to harmonize and persuade. (134)

If something seems odd about the narrator's efforts to "harmonize and persuade," this has to do with the two functions of narration Forster plays with in *Howards End*—the narrator's mediating role in forming social wholes and his epistemological claim to offer authoritative beliefs. Rosecrance sees that Forster's narrator invokes these traditional functions, and she also senses that he does not follow through on them to deliver the persuasive interpretation of the novel's world or the harmonious integration of its elements he seems to intend. But she regards the narrator's duplicity as a sign of his failings rather than as a subversive criticism of their claims because she does not understand the contradictions of his closeted position, attempting to pass for normal even while secretly rebelling against the normative.

It takes an unusually insightful critic like Rosecrance to note that the narrator fails in the normative roles of voice of truth and figure of unity—to see through the pose he is striking and to reveal its falsity. Attuned to the closet's double game of conforming while rebelling, however, a reader can understand the contradictions in the narrator's performance as a provocation to reflect about the functions they disrupt rather than a failure to execute them. The attribution of aesthetic failure keeps Forster's secret safe (the narrator is pathological, not the author), but it would prevent us (as it does Rosecrance) from recognizing the opportunity offered by his double games to challenge normative assumptions about truth and community. Readers for whom the conventional is the unquestionable standard will see Forster as one of themselves either in meeting the norm or in trying to but failing. Readers alive to the secret meaning of the wink and the nod Forster offers, however, may appreciate the challenge to the normative his narrator's duplicities pose, even as those duplicities keep the author safe from being found out by the conventional position whose assumptions he questions.[2] The contradictions of this strategy make his rebellion a muted one whose power is thwarted by its self-protective denial of any intent to deviate from the acceptable. That, though, is precisely the disadvantage as well as the advantage of a protest that seeks to protect its secret at the same time that it subverts, mocks, and criticizes the norms it pretends to obey.

---

[2] Like all interpretation, this is an inherently circular, contextual process. One needs an anticipatory sense of the pattern to see how the parts combine, even as their fitting together gives evidence of the design that makes sense of them. See my *Conflicting Readings*, esp. 2–12. Without the biographical context of Forster's closeted homosexuality and the guidance of the theory of the closet, the pattern I am describing would be invisible—as it has been to many readers, including myself. In a much earlier essay on *Howards End* ("Existential Crisis"), I, like Barbara Rosecrance, faulted the narrator, the author, and the novel for offering syntheses that were unconvincing. More than twenty-five years later, guided by ways of thinking and knowledge about Forster (especially the conflicted attitude revealed in the crucial *Notebook Journal* passage) which were not available to me then, I now see a design and a functional strategy where before I saw incongruity and artistic failure. That a secret becomes visible only if one knows what to look for is, of course, precisely how the epistemology of the closet works.

If the narrator of *Howards End* seems conventional, it is because he seems to speak omnisciently and authoritatively, with the impersonal voice of wisdom. But he is also coy, quirky, biased, questionably reliable in his judgments, and distinctly a character with a perspective all his own. This contradiction invokes convention even as it undercuts it, claiming epistemological authority in order to expose and explore its constructedness, its vulnerability, its lack of necessity. The narrator's strategy of openly affirming while tacitly questioning his authority commences with his very first statement: "One may as well begin with Helen's letters to her sister" (5). The seeming nonchalance of this assertion is implicitly contradictory. Although its casualness suggests the absence of any subversive intent, its very carefree manner foregrounds the contingency of narrative authority—he could just as well start somewhere else. This arbitrariness in turn cuts two ways. It demonstrates the narrator's power (he is the one who gets to decide), but it also dramatizes the lack of necessity of his constructions (another way of telling the story might be just as plausible and effective). The narrator has an almost Jamesian self-consciousness about his role as a fabricator (for example: "If you think this ridiculous, remember that it is not Margaret who is telling you about it"; or "Young Wilcox was pouring in petrol, starting his engine, and performing other actions with which this story has no concern"; or "the discussion moved towards its close. To follow it is unnecessary. It is rather a moment when the commentator should step forward" [11–12, 14–15, 73]). The narrator is repeatedly coy about his powers in a way that calls attention to their artificiality—how they rest on conventions about what is appropriate to storytelling—without constraining his willingness to use them. There is of course a long tradition of narrators joking about the artificiality of their powers, and a reader might think that nothing else is going on. But this coyness becomes a defining, pervasive attitude rather than an occasional gesture, and as such it signals the narrator's closeted identity. Analogous to the doubleness of Forster's own sense of passing, his narrator knows that the conventions he pretends to conform to are artificial constructions, and he winks at the reader to acknowledge this is so, even as he self-consciously and ironically continues to play the game they make possible.

The epistemological status of the narrator's pronouncements is similarly double, invoking the convention of authoritative narrative wisdom only to expose it as artifice by demonstrating that its truth, like all truths, is a partial perspective. The narrator's perspective seems to have special standing as a transcendent, all-encompassing viewpoint nowhere else available in the novel (and thus different from any particular character's), but it is also repeatedly marked as a distinctive, even eccentric point of view and thus partial and incomplete.[3] Passing but rebelling, the narrator seems both the voice of the normative and a peculiar, idiosyncratic poseur. What, for example, is one to make of this opinion he offers:

> To speak against London is no longer fashionable. The Earth as an artistic cult has had its day, and the literature of the near future will probably ignore the country and seek inspiration from the town. One can understand the reaction. Of Pan and the elemental forces, the public has heard a little too much—they seem Victorian, while London is Georgian—and those who care for the earth with sincerity may wait long ere the pendulum swings back to her again. Certainly London fascinates. One visualizes it as a tract of quivering gray, intelligent without purpose, and excitable without love; as a spirit that has altered before it can be chronicled; as a heart that certainly beats, but with no pulsation of humanity. It lies beyond everything: Nature, with all her cruelty, comes nearer to us than do these crowds of men. (79–80)

The use of "one" and "us" seems to invoke the impersonality of truth and the consensus to which authoritative views are entitled. The narrator is attempting to express what everyone thinks, not challenge the normative standpoint. But this is also the rhetorical posturing of a clever conversationalist who, with Wildean irony, increases the effect of observations he knows to be unique by pretending they are conventional. The wittiness of the narrator's extended comparisons through which London is characterized by repeated, escalating paradoxes ("intelligent without purpose, excitable without love," and so on, and so on) is a dazzling display of verbal power that masks what he is up to, slyly refuting the conventional wisdom while seeming to endorse it, giving reason for preferring the country and Nature through his very explanation of the fascination of the town. Although he seems to be explaining why urban values have won the day, by the end he has reversed himself without acknowledging he has done so as he exposes the inhumanity of the London crowd. With a doubleness that recalls Forster's own contradictory desire to fit in but also to rebel, the narrator acts as if he is conforming to conventional opinion only to subvert it, seeming to accept what everyone thinks even as he allows his distinctive difference to express its quiet opposition.

---

[3] Michael Levenson sees a similar contradiction: "Forster gives us a narrator who constructs the fictional universe with all the resources of a narrating divinity, only to halt suddenly, and to gape at what he has made with the incomprehension of any other mortal" (85). For Levenson, however, this is not only an aesthetic failing in the novel but, worse, evidence of the inability of "a waning liberalism" to forge connections (93). I will argue later that Forster's contradictory play with narrative authority is related to a liberal politics that is more complicated and resourceful than Levenson suggests.

Although the use of an all-knowing narrator would seem to invoke the conventions of realism, the playful, self-undermining duplicities of Forster's narrator give *Howards End* unexpected affinities with the more self-dramatizing experiments of modernist narration. The great modernists typically invoke one or the other of the conventions of realism in order to play with it ironically and, in doing so, provoke self-consciousness about its implicit but disguised epistemological or ideological assumptions (see my *Challenge*, esp. 261–70). To foreground the contingency of narrative authority and question its epistemological limits even while employing its privileges, as Forster does in *Howards End*, are classic modernist maneuvers. That this has not been widely recognized suggests the extent to which Forster has "passed" as a realist despite his use of many (mildly) subversive strategies which, if he had employed them more boldly, might have offended constituencies whose sensibilities he was reluctant to affront. If Forster desires to conform and resist simultaneously, then a double game of employing the ironies and narrative self-consciousness of modernism while posing as a conventional realist is a way of achieving this contradictory aim.

The posing, the playfulness, the self-conscious staging of conventions, the coy denial and display of difference—all of these contradictions may surprisingly suggest affinities between Forster's closeted narrator and "camp." Piggford notes that Forster "does not typically exhibit a camp sensibility in his fictional writings" (101), and his reserved, decorous manner is far from the extremity, flamboyance, and ostentation often associated with camp (see Bergman; Robertson; Sontag). Nevertheless, the inherent contradictoriness of camp—its fascination with artifice, its parodic relation to the norm, its love of double meaning—similarly depends on the vulnerability of convention to having its workings exposed and criticized simply by playing with it and taking it a step further (and further, and further . . .). In both cases the defining contradiction is that adoption of a convention becomes a way of transgressing it. Forster is more subtle, certainly, than Madonna or Mae West in how he plays with the norms of the conventional to undermine and challenge them, because he does not want to be found out and consequently lacks their eagerness to put themselves on display. But a similar appreciation for how artifice opens room for subversive play and a similar joy in creating double meanings by parodic invocation of the norm is evident in Forster's narrator and in camp. As Sedgwick observes, a frequent contradiction of the closet is "the conjunction of an extravagance of deniability and an extravagance of flamboyant display" (165), inasmuch as the "open secret" simultaneously seeks to protect itself and to announce its duplicity by tweaking the nose of the conventional. The greater ostentation of camp has stopped trying to pass, as Forster still

does, but the contradictions of camp are fundamentally similar to his duplic-
itous use of artifice to seem conventional even as he rebels.

Posing as normative in a manner that subverts the norm characterizes the
narrator's practice in other areas as well. One of the most important of these
is his use of myths and symbols. Here again he exposes and questions how
their rhetorical power is generated even as he invokes it. The narrator's contradictory use of symbols offers readers beliefs to share while subtly suggesting that they are nothing more than beliefs and therefore as much worthy of
skepticism as of acceptance and credulity. He will pass as one of us by circu-
lating beliefs we may hold in common even as he exposes the artificiality and
contestability of the bond established by a community's shared myths.

The symbols that the narrator invokes both assert and question the ability
of signs to act as mediators by showing that this power is neither intrinsic to
them nor based on any transcendental authority but instead depends entirely
on our willingness to accept and circulate them. This double strategy helps to
explain why many readers have felt that the claims made for Mrs. Wilcox's
mythic status are oddly unpersuasive.[4] The narrator asserts that "she seemed
to belong not to the young people and their motor, but to the house, and to the
tree that overshadowed it. One knew that she worshipped the past, and that
the instinctive wisdom the past can alone bestow had descended upon her"
(18). Undercutting this invocation of the powers of the past and the land as
embodied in this symbolic woman, Mrs. Wilcox's specific actions in the novel
often seem more like those of a whimsical eccentric than a force for transcendental synthesis, and her inability to inspire spiritual growth in her husband
and children also casts doubt on her powers. The narrator's invocation of similar synthesizing powers for the house, the wych elm, and its embedded pigs'
teeth also seems contradicted by their lack of efficacy as unifiers.

The questionable persuasiveness of these assertions of the connecting
powers of myths and symbols reveals mediation to be a strictly finite, rhetorical process and not a transcendental mystery. Like the miraculous healing
force of the pigs' teeth, Mrs. Wilcox has only the powers others—specifically
Margaret and the narrator—invest in her through their beliefs. For those who
do not believe—like the other Wilcoxes and many readers—her powers lapse.

---

[4] Even Lionel Trilling finds Mrs. Wilcox "a little trying" (90). Alan Wilde calls her not "completely believable" (*Art* 102), and Rosecrance argues that the real Mrs. Wilcox does not justify the
symbolic value attributed to her: "Assertion seeks unsuccessfully to bridge the gap between intention and presentation" (135). Wilde finds that the novel suffers throughout from a disparity
between what it claims "rhetorically, in terms of plot, symbolism, and motif" and what it demonstrates "psychologically, through the dramatization of the search for meaning" (100–101). Norman Page is almost alone in praising the novel's "integration of local realistic detail with
long-term symbolic purpose" (84).

That is why, as with the teeth, the border between vitalizing myth and ridiculous superstition is inherently permeable and changeable. By calling for a belief in symbols that the reader may question because the narrative only partially sustains it, Forster's narrator exposes the rhetorical basis of their epistemological authority while nevertheless making a rhetorical appeal. He asks us to share a belief in various unifying myths but at the same time he lays bare the epistemological structure on which social symbols depend for their power.

This doubleness replays in a different area his strategy of pretending to employ traditional narrative functions even while exposing their status as conventions through the very act of mimicking them. He winks at us as if to acknowledge that the beliefs he offers are only that—beliefs that can be played with and used to create a posture—although he still asks that we accept them as true, which they may or may not be if they are only constructions. If indeed myths of the land and the past were endowed with transcendental synthesizing powers, their homogenizing force as the true source of social unity would leave no space for difference to evade and manipulate the norms defining the community. Only because even the symbols and myths Forster values are nothing more than contingent creations is it possible to play the double game of passing and rebelling. The status of symbols as contingent rhetorical conventions may prevent Mrs. Wilcox, the house, and the wych-elm from miraculously saving her community, but it allows Forster and his narrator the room to maneuver they need in order to play games with what we believe signs mean.

The sense of place is similarly not intrinsic to it but a product of investments of belief. The narrator enacts and exposes this process when he asks what one would do "if one wanted to show a foreigner England" (120) and then engages in an extended geographical peroration which is difficult to interpret (unembarrassed patriotism or purple prose ironically parading and parodying its own extravagance?). The narrator invokes the power of place by creating it before the reader's eyes and, carried away by his own rhetoric, seems to lose the ironic self-control that elsewhere characterizes his persona:

> Seen from the west, the Wight is beautiful beyond all laws of beauty. It is as if a fragment of England floated forward to greet the foreigner—chalk of our chalk, turf of our turf, epitome of what will follow. And behind the fragment lie Southampton, hostess to the nations, and Portsmouth, a latent fire, and all around it, with double and treble collision of tides, swirls the sea. How many villages appear in this view! How many castles! How many churches, vanished or triumphant! How many ships, railways, and roads! What incredible variety of men working beneath the lucent sky to what final end! The reason fails, like a wave on the Swanage beach; the imagination swells, spreads, and deepens, until it becomes geographic and encircles England. (121)

Listing places one after the other, the narrator makes a series of attributions of value, investments of meaning affirmed with a mounting rhetorical intensity that culminates in an explicit recognition of the poetic processes at work ("reason fails . . . ; the imagination swells . . . and encircles England"). Place seems magical when these processes of meaning investment are invisible and its values seem to emanate from within, as they do when myths are simply believed and their poetic origins are no longer on display. The irony of the extravagant prose in this passage is that, in invoking the powers which can give patriotic value to place, it exposes them for critical scrutiny through the very extremity of the narrator's rhetoric.

The narrator's complaints about "the civilization of luggage" and Margaret's feeling that she lost "the sense of space" while driving in a motor-car (109, 145) are similarly contradictory in that they demonstrate that the meaning of space is a variable social, historical construct but nevertheless express longing for the presumably absolute value of place that has been lost. Margaret and the narrator both prefer the rural, traditional values of place that they feel are being dislodged by urban, cosmopolitan restlessness and technological change, but a battle of cultural meanings can occur over the issue of how space is constituted only because its meaning is not simply given but is produced by social investments of belief. Space is not only where opposing worlds meet but also where they act out their conflicts in their different constructions of it. The novel's demonstration that locating particular meanings in particular places is a contingent and culturally variable activity exists uneasily, unstably in tension with its nostalgia about the rural traditions of England and the house and the tree that embody them.

The values the narrator and Margaret attribute to place are affirmed even as the novel reveals the contingency of their commitments. The recognition, however, that such values are merely constructions questions their claim to absoluteness. If community is built out of traditions, the irony of Forster's narrator shows that this process of construction can be played with and that it is probably not what it claims to be, but the narrator nevertheless expresses a desire for the bonds that traditions can establish, and this longing is genuine and urgent. Once again double in his yearning to belong and in his reluctance to submerge his otherness, Forster creates a contradictory narrator who simultaneously desires unity and resists assimilation, protecting the possibility of difference.

Forster is in my view consequently more skeptical of the patriotism sometimes espoused by the narrator than Brian May recognizes when he claims that "Forsterian nationalism in *Howards End* is not an ironic performance but an imperial one" (15). It is instructive, I think, that the Merchant-Ivory film, which does convey a romanticized, nostalgic picture of England, leaves out of its adaptation of the novel the quirky, playful narrator. His self-undermining invocation of patriotic sentiments is much more complex and ironic than Merchant and Ivory's idealization of a land that never existed except on Masterpiece Theater.[5] Forster is a very English author who is skeptical of the values of "Englishness"—someone who feels the appeal of his country's traditions but is also wary of defining himself by allegiance to national identity, a writer who can express with unembarrassed sentimentality his love of particular English places (like his boyhood home Rooksnest, the model for Howards End) but also acknowledges the provinciality of local patriotic pride. As Forster will write later, "the English character is incomplete. No national character is complete. We have to look for some qualities in one part of the world and others in another" ("Notes" 14–15). Forster's self-undermining patriotism knows that John Bull can become a bully because he does not have an ironic sense of the incompleteness of his values, traditions, and loves. This suspicion that something is lacking in his nation's (or any nation's) defining beliefs and conventions gives evidence once again of Forster's doubleness as an author who both is and is not identical to the pose he assumes of conforming to the norms of his community. The knowledge that claims of wholeness leave something out—the other, the different, the nonconforming—conflicts in Forster with a desire for oneness. Fundamentally dual once again, he can wax lyrical in patriotic expressions of love for the land and the traditions of the past even as he skeptically exposes their artificiality and limitations.

The opposition of passing and rebelling makes Forster especially attuned to the contradictions of mediation. A pervasive doubleness informs the narrator's function as a mediator among the perspectives within the novel and between the narrative and the reader. The novel's famous motto "Only connect . . ." is deeply ironic (with emphasis on the "only") because the narrative invokes the ethos of connection while at the same time calling it into question. When Margaret lashes out at her husband at a climactic moment and declares, "You shall see the connection if it kills you, Henry!" (219)—and it nearly does—she inadvertently exposes the will to power in efforts to merge perspectives and forge unity out of differences. Resisting the homogenizing force

---

[5] For a sampling of the film's critical reception, see my Norton *Howards End* 459–68. Anne Billson's response, though extreme, is revealing: "If *Howards End* [the movie] is supposed to be an indictment of snobbery and greed, it fails, because it revels in the snobbish and greedy way of life: the idyllic country cottages, the grand mansions, the perfect lawns. The qualities of such illustrated English Lit are not cinematic, but are those of the Edwardian theme park. This film should be bought up by the National Trust, though it doesn't need to be preserved. It has already been pickled in the formaldehyde of nostalgia" (468). Although this hyperbole is perhaps not entirely fair, such a lack of irony in the representation of English upper- and middle-class customs and values certainly does not characterize the novel, and the absence of the narrator—or a cinematic equivalent—is at least in part responsible for this difference between it and the film.

of consensus that would wipe out differences even while seeking the possibility of relations that would respect and value alterity, Forster makes his narrator a paradoxical mediator who brings perspectives together—including his own and that of the reader—but also holds them apart and insists on their irreconcilable separateness. As I will argue later, a similar doubleness characterizes Forster's contradictory liberalism, which values relations even as it warns against the tyranny posed by ideologies of solidarity, conformity, and assimilation. Analyzing carefully the narrator's enactment of the contradictions of mediation is important for political as well as formal reasons.

These contradictions inform one of the narrator's most controversial statements: "We are not concerned with the very poor. They are unthinkable, and only to be approached by the statistician or the poet. This story deals with gentlefolk, or with those who are obliged to pretend that they are gentlefolk" (35). This is a shocking and surprising acceptance of class-based social exclusion that contradicts the ethos of connection that the novel would seem to endorse, and the reader may be reluctant to identify with the narrator's apparent cruel condescension. One response might be to credit the narrator with a tough-minded realism about how far social contact can be extended, as opposed to the idealistic self-deception that leads Helen to wreak havoc in the lives of those she would help. Perhaps it is better, a reader might think, to be clearheaded about the limited sphere in which one can productively pursue connection and focus one's attention there. But this attempt to restore connection with the narrator's perspective confronts the reader with another kind of trouble, because such constriction of relationships is not connection but exclusion, limiting us to a self-enclosed sphere instead of extending us beyond the horizons of our worlds. Abandoning the project of overcoming differences, we would be condemned to join only like with like. The reader's dilemma here is that we can adopt the narrator's perspective and overcome differences in relation to him only by accepting radical exclusion in another direction that sets us at odds with other perspectives and renounces in advance the ideal of community that the narrative seems to endorse.

This contradiction, however, enacts dilemmas central to Margaret's story. If, as she discovers to her sorrow, it is so hard to establish connections between different ways of being even within a single class (and one relatively free from the distractions of fiscal hardship), then what are the chances of extending community beyond it? That skeptical conclusion is disturbing for the very reason that it violates the ethos of connection, and the unease the reader experiences about accepting it—or about approving the narrator's acknowledgment of the necessity of exclusion—reinforces our sense of the value of connection without promising that it can be delivered. An appropriate response to the narrator's unabashed confession of the limits of his social imagination is both to reject it and to accept it, and this contradiction may make the reader uncomfortable—leaving us oscillating indeterminately between indignation at his exclusionary brutality and grudging respect for his tough-minded honesty.

Such discomfort is an invitation to think further about the paradoxes and problems of mediation. Forster plays with his narrator to suggest that these are not only economic and epistemological but also linguistic. The narrator scathingly exposes the inadequacies of the Victorian high style to describe Bast's impoverished existence. Orwellian simplicity and directness seem more appropriate than the ornateness of Ruskin: " 'My flat is dark as well as stuffy.' Those were the words for him" (38). The narrator's own language is subject to the same critique he makes of *The Stones of Venice,* however (and his unabashed confession of limited social range admits as much). After he shows that elevated aesthetic diction cannot effectively interpret Bast's world, the narrator is hoisted on his own petard when his language breaks down in trying to describe Jacky:

> A woman entered, of whom it is simplest to say that she was not respectable. Her appearance was awesome. She seemed all strings and bell-pulls—ribbons, chains, bead necklaces that clinked and caught—and a boa of azure feathers hung round her neck, with the ends uneven. . . . As for her hair, or rather hairs, they are too complicated to describe, but one system went down her back, lying in a thick pad there, while another, created for a lighter destiny, rippled around her forehead. The face—the face does not signify. It was the face of the photograph, but older, and the teeth were not so numerous as the photographer had suggested, and certainly not so white. Yes, Jacky was past her prime, whatever that prime may have been. She was descending quicker than most women into the colourless years, and the look in her eyes confessed it. (39)

Confronted with Jacky, the narrator is curiously both hyperbolic and speechless. Words pour out of him listing her accoutrements in abundant, extravagant detail, but he is also at a loss for words to describe her, his linguistic helplessness marked by a series of confessions of the limits to what his language can capture ("too complicated to describe," "it does not signify," "whatever that may have been").

The narrator's stuttering condescension exposes the interpretive limits to language by dramatizing them in his own discourse in a way that invites the reader to turn on him the same critique he has just used on Ruskin. If a powerful image emerges of Jacky and of her husband's disappointment and desperation, this is because we as readers can project it in the blank spaces of what the narrator cannot say directly with the language at his disposal. Like Ruskin's, the narrator's style cannot claim universal scope but will disclose some states of affairs congenial to its grammar and vocabulary while disguising others (the same holds for the plain style Orwell endorses). This point would have been less effectively made—and would even have been contradicted—if Forster had endowed the narrator with language fully adequate to render the Basts' existence with the simple directness and immediacy the narrator himself recommends but cannot employ.

Bast pursues connection by reading, and the failure of his acquisition of cultural literacy has similar implications for the limits of language as an instrument of social mediation. The inability of language learning alone to make him one with the groups he aspires to join dramatizes the irreducible multiplicity and differential powers of the discourses that make up a culture. When he speaks books, his attempt to make another language his own ironically marks the differences of his own native speech all the more distinctly. His awkwardness shows that he is speaking the language of another, which, as such, he cannot use with the facility of a native speaker, so that his very attempt to transcend his linguistic position reveals it. His insecurities about how to speak this foreign language and his inability to get what he wants by using it also demonstrate how discourses are linked to power. Learning the texts of the privileged class cannot by itself give Bast the authority the Schlegels enjoy. His efforts to enhance his social standing by extending his literacy are ultimately ineffective because learning a discourse does not necessarily convey the entitlements that those at home in it possess.

Just as Bast's acquisition of culture shows that there is no universal language that can synthesize all the speakers in a community, so the narrator cannot claim to possess a discourse that can bring everyone in the novel together (not to mention those he explicitly excludes). The narrator's position in the text is constructed to dramatize the problems of language as an instrument of social mediation. His coy self-consciousness about the arbitrariness of his powers reveals that they are the product of discourse (the result of the conventions establishing his authority), and he thereby participates in the differential entitlement to social power correlated to the discourse one employs that characterizes all of the other perspectives in the text, even if the conventions of narration give greatest authority to his position. A transcendental language of social mediation does not exist in the world of *Howards End*—not for Margaret, not for the narrator—but instead the novel suggests that language has a double structure that both holds people together and keeps them apart. It allows Forster to reach out and establish relations with others different from himself even while disguising his otherness, and this in turn makes it possible to play games with his readers that they may or may not catch.

This doubleness parallels the doubleness required by the text's encouragement of an identification with Margaret that it then contests by exhibiting all of the problems that thwart her project of connection. "There was something uncanny in her triumph," she thinks at the end; "She, who had never expected to conquer anyone, had charged straight through these Wilcoxes and broken up their lives" (241–42). The contradictoriness of the text here is an index of the epistemological ambiguities of mediation. On the one hand, from the loneliness of the closet, Forster desires to expand the possibilities of relationship, but on the other hand, guided by his sense of the ineluctability of difference and the need to preserve the safety of the hidden, he suggests that the will to harmonize and unify is not only unrealistic but also potentially dangerous. The irony of Margaret's failure to create an all-encompassing synthesis is that, in seeking to overcome partiality, she reproduces it. This irony suggests that her project of fostering relations between seemingly incommensurable forms of life is not able to transcend differences but is rather just one position among others, whose claims it contests. Her failure to find wholeness and her entanglement against her will in partisan combat demonstrate that opposing forms of life are not fragments that find their completion in each other but incommensurable ways of being that resist assimilation in a single, harmonious unity. The question *Howards End* leaves open is whether modes of connection can be found that might join differences without removing them. The ambiguity of Margaret's project of connection that wreaks destruction, like the ambiguity of the reader's intimate relation with a narrator who espouses exclusion, is a provocation to ponder this question without promising that it can be answered affirmatively.

It is not surprising that, if Forster is a closeted writer who wants to pass for the same even as he wishes to protect and affirm his difference, he would fear the blending or suppressing of differences represented by the ethos of connection, even as he would desire the personal closeness with others that inspires it. The Forster who does not wish to widen the gulf he feels between himself and others, and who seeks to avoid unnecessary conflict, desires relationship despite and across the differences that isolate him from others, and this goal of mediating incommensurable worlds similarly inspires Margaret's attempt to reach beyond her sphere to make connection with its opposite. But Forster's fear that suppressing his differences from others may sacrifice his identity makes him aware that a bully may lurk in the ethos of connection. The will to power implicit in the project of forging consensus and community is evident in the destruction wrought by Margaret's well-intentioned efforts at mediation, and this threat would be felt strongly by someone who, like the Forster writing in his 1907 *Notebook Journal,* is torn between submerging his difference from others and rebelliously insisting on it because it is what gives meaning and value to his life as other than the normative.

A similar doubleness informs many of Forster's political declarations: his affirmation of the priority of personal relations over the claims of the state or the nation, his muted praise of democracy because it "admits variety" and "permits criticism," his resistance to ideological orthodoxies of all kinds (as in his credo "I do not believe in Belief") ("What I Believe" 70, 67). Forster's liberalism is based on a wariness of how the will to power of any ideal or norm threatens those secretly different—or, if not in hiding, at least not in power. Forster would like to leave space for differences even as he desires to create the possibility of relationships that would not be hegemonic. His liberalism has been criticized as too "soft" or weak and insufficiently radical in its recognition of the need for social change.[6] His pluralism is suspicious of the promise of unifying forces of any kind, however, whether conservative or radical, because the homogenizing implications of attempts to forge community or consensus threaten differences that may be too fragile, vulnerable, or weak to defend themselves but that are nevertheless (or for that very reason) valuable to us all. Hence his strategy in *Howards End* of making ironic the figure of common social values and norms, the authoritative narrator, and of using contradictions in that figure to invoke and question the unifying power of beliefs about the nation, the land, and the past.

Forster's liberalism projects a differential, heterogeneous ideal of community as a pluralistic, democratic structure defined not by positive allegiance to any particular set of beliefs or norms but negatively, diacritically, by relations that permit "variety and criticism." The social bond in such a world is not solidarity or synthesis but the reciprocity of mutual respect for differences. Nonconsensual reciprocity of this kind would provide a way of indirectly creating community without sacrificing the negativity and the heterogeneity that allow difference, in contrast to a positive embrace of a particular set of norms or values.

This mode of relatedness that preserves and encourages difference exists nowhere in *Howards End*—except in the relation between the narrator and the reader. Margaret seeks but does not find it and instead swings between suppressing her uniqueness in order to bond with her husband and then violently insisting on her perspective when Wilcox refuses to respond with the recognition and respect she desires. Her project of connection lapses into an

---

[6] Wilfred Stone offers a carefully balanced criticism and appreciation of the "softness" of Forster's liberalism. For more radical critiques, see Eagleton, *Exiles;* and Jameson, "Modernism." May faults what he sees as the individualistic "liberal ironism" of *Howards End* and prefers the "prophetic pragmatism" of *Passage to India*, which, he claims, endorses a universalizing vision of synthesis in the "Hindu sublime" (16). I think this judgment misses Forster's wariness of the homogenizing force of consensus. I will argue below that an abiding skepticism of the erasure of differences also informs Forster's later novel.

exercise of power because of this absence of reciprocity. By playing games with the reader, the narrator risks falling into a similar trap of manipulating others through an exercise of power that would thwart relationship. His slipperiness and elusiveness avoid this trap and instead enact the contradictory social relation Forster desires. The narrator's double games preserve the possibility of difference (the slippery narrator is never simply identical with the reader's position) even as they use power to smirk, wink, and play with power, to provoke us to reflect but not to cajole or coerce us into agreeing.

It is often difficult to know whom the narrator is speaking to because his explicit address is contradicted, subverted, or questioned by the implicit meanings he suggests. This duplicity creates the possibility for the reader of occupying a different position from that of the narratee whom a narrator may seek to overpower through persuasion or with whom a narrator may seek harmony and agreement (see Chambers 19–55). Instead of being persuaded by Forster's narrator or unifying our perspective with his, we are invited to see through and across his winking gestures to play a complicated game based on the premise that neither of us is in the position we seem to occupy. We are together, in the sense that we are both participants in the game, but the reciprocity of playing together does not collapse our differences. Among other things it requires that we respect the doubleness of his posture of seeming to conform while secretly rebelling. If we do not recognize the invitation to play that his doubleness offers (by regarding it as aesthetic failure, for example), the game is over before it begins because no relation is established. But the possibility of collaboration with the narrator is based on the difference between his position (in his closet) and ours as his secret allies outside who are offered the chance to learn, grow, and enjoy ourselves by participating in the play with conventions he offers. As an exercise in reciprocity that preserves and values the differences between the partners, this collaboration suggests a mode of relation different from the hegemony of connection or the homogeneity of consensus.

If the doubleness and duplicity of Forster's narrative voice in *Howards End* betray some anxiety about his dual identity, his narrator's ironic playfulness converts that defensiveness into a way of being toward the reader that is productive and creative.[7] Forster's nervousness about his closeted position is unquestionably evident in the *Notebook Journal* passage I quoted earlier where he worries about offending others by his perceived difference from them. But

---

[7] Langland similarly finds the "narrative stance" of the novel to be "ambiguous, uneasy, and defensive," but she sees this as a symptom of Forster's "confusion and dissatisfaction" about his sexual identity and his "fear of the feminine in himself" (253). She is right about Forster's anxiety, but I think she underestimates the extent to which he converts it into a strategic resource for playing games with the reader.

this anxiety coexists, as I have argued, with a stubborn, proud, if muted defiance. The contradiction between a wish to conform and a desire to rebel could have been paralyzing (and no doubt was to some extent). In creating the elusive, idiosyncratic narrator of *Howards End,* however, Forster converts this contradiction from a private dilemma into a strategy for playing games with the reader, games that can offer enlightenment and pleasure provided one figures out how to respond to their provocation. The nervousness of some of the narrator's coy gestures may be evidence of the author's uneasiness about his closeted position, but to the extent that the anxiousness of the narrative voice functions as a signal about the duplicities and ironies he offers us, it is a strategic and artful disquiet, less a symptom of the author's personal problems than an invitation to enter into a particular kind of relationship with an unusual narrative persona whose idiosyncrasies are both baffling and intriguing.

Speaking from a closeted position, and with the contradictory desire to conform and rebel, is inherently an anxious, unstable project. It would be simplistic and anachronistic, however, to fault Forster for not coming out and speaking directly. Instead, I think, we should recognize how he converts the nervousness and evasiveness of his position into the energy and purposiveness of play. In *Howards End* the means for making that conversion possible is the narrator. That is because the narrator is not the author but a device that an anxious, proud writer can use to transform the contradictions he personally feels into socially useful games. It is then up to readers to play along with these games if they can and will.

8. READING INDIA

The Double Turns of Forster's Pragmatism

When E. M. Forster is invoked by politically minded critics, it is often to attack or dismiss him. His name has become a token for error or lamentable naiveté, whether he is presented as an illustration of the fallacies of liberal humanism, or as a last remnant of British imperialism, or as a practitioner of traditional narrative methods who lacks self-consciousness about the epistemological ambiguities of language.[1] This caricature of Forster has prevented critics from appreciating the response his work offers to political issues of considerable contemporary relevance. As I have tried to suggest in my reading of *Howards End*, Forster's conflicted but ultimately resolute defense of liberalism reflects his recognition of the impossibility of reconciling different ways of seeing, a recognition he attempts to bring readers to share by his subtle play with narrative authority and point of view. In *A Passage to India*, where the conflict of interpretations is enacted in a conflict between cultures, Forster experiments with narrative techniques in a more complex and innovative manner than is often understood. He does this to educate the reader about dilemmas of mediating cultural differences that were an urgent problem in his day as they are in our own.

Lionel Trilling's classic assessment of Forster as a representative of the liberal imagination suggests why he is typically misunderstood but also offers a

---

[1] For examples of these charges see Parry, "Politics"; Suleri; Schleifer 54–55; and O'Hara 81. See also Jameson's attack on Forster ("Modernism" 12–22).

way toward a more adequate appreciation. Trilling regards Forster as an exemplary figure for educating the liberal mind to a suspicion of ideals and absolutes and to an appreciation of complexity and anomaly. But the language of
Trilling's praise of Forster's "moral realism"—his awareness of "the contradictions, paradoxes, and dangers of living the moral life" given "the inextrica-
ble tangle of good and evil"—may sound too temperate, balanced, and
cautious to be interesting (*Forster* 12). A closer look at Trilling's praise of
Forster suggests, however, that a dismissal of the novelist's social vision as
naively moderate is too hasty. Trilling finds in Forster a rigorously contradictory sensibility: "Forster refuses to be conclusive. No sooner does he come to
a conclusion than he must unravel it again" (16). This sense that the last word
must always be displaced and deferred lest its promise of truth be believed
leads, in Trilling's view, to "Forster's insistence on the double turn, on the
something else that lies behind," which "is sometimes taken for 'tolerance,' "
but "often makes the severest judgments" and "does not spring so much from
gentleness of heart as from respect for two facts co-existing" (17). According
to Trilling, contradiction in Forster is not a harmonious balance of opposites
but a double movement of asserting the possibility of making normative
claims and then calling them into question by doubting their definitiveness
and univocity. The notion of contradiction in a "double turn" is not complexity refining a more accurate approximation of truth but rather the invocation
coupled with the contestation of an interpretive or evaluative framework.

Exercising such double turns is the challenge of reading *A Passage to India*.
A work of much greater epistemological complexity than its seemingly conventional narrative form suggests, this novel invokes the ideal of nonreified,
reciprocal knowledge of other people and cultures only to show that interpretation invariably requires distancing, objectifying prejudgments. The novel insists that truth and justice can be determined unequivocally—Aziz is innocent,
and India must be liberated from the yoke of British oppression—but its manipulation of point of view demonstrates the difficulty (perhaps impossibility)
of attaining a lasting consensus about any matter or of discovering a final, un-
contestable meaning to any state of affairs. The result of these double movements is not paralysis but an appeal to the reader to act with an awareness, as
Trilling puts it, that "much necessary action is anomalous" (14). Forster's
great novel of India stages for the reader what it might mean to practice politics under erasure—to pursue ideals of justice and humanity with full faith in
their claims to validity, even as one recognizes that any norms (including one's
own) are perspectival constructs that cannot finally legitimate themselves.

Such a politics has much in common with Rorty's notion of "liberal irony"
that I have discussed before. Forster is an important precursor of Rorty, and
his liberalism is consequently less old-fashioned and has more relevance to

contemporary debates about freedom, belief, and justice than is often assumed.[2] *A Passage to India* attempts to dramatize for the reader the contradictions of liberal irony. Both Forster and Rorty desire a politics that would enable us to act with a sophisticated, skeptical awareness that all norms are provisional and contestable and that any consensus is potentially deceptive and hegemonic, but also with a defensible faith in ideals of justice and community as necessary guides for social change. After analyzing the narrative and epistemological double turns of *A Passage to India*, I will suggest Forster's affinities to a deliberately paradoxical "liberal irony" by imagining the position he would take in the debate between Habermas and Lyotard over the politics of legitimation, a debate I have frequently broached in this book because their opposition defines the conservative and the radical positions to which a politics of nonconsensual reciprocity (and, I think, Forster's tough-minded but self-deprecating liberalism) offers an alternative. Like Rorty, Forster would want to combine Lyotard's skepticism about the untranscendable heterogeneity of different perspectives with Habermas's affirmation of mutual understanding and uncoerced exchange as desirable ideals. Like Trilling, both Rorty and Forster believe that political action must be pragmatically contradictory and ironic about the ideals it pursues not because balance is the most realistic attitude but because truth is always deferred.

A Passage to India presents a clear, unequivocal image of its ideal of knowledge, but it does so negatively, in a way that questions it even while affirming it. The ideal is a respectful understanding of others that acknowledges their right to speak for themselves and that does not subordinate them to one's own interests and purposes.[3] This is precisely the opposite of the treatment Aziz

---

[2] Daniel Born and Brian May similarly see in Forster a sensibility akin to contemporary liberalism. Neither focuses as I do, however, on Forster's narrative strategies as a key locus where his politics are enacted, and both consequently describe his liberalism as more stable and univocal than I think it is—Born finding Forster wrenched by "liberal guilt" about the inability of democracy to deliver justice, May identifying him with a prophetic belief in unity that transcends ordinary pragmatism. Although they offer opposing versions of Forster (one with a tragic vision, the other with a vision of redemption), I would argue that both are half right (and half wrong) because his liberalism is constituted by "double turns" that challenge the reader to appreciate the difficulty and the necessity of simultaneously holding conflicting perspectives. Only by attending to the process of reading set in motion by Forster's narrative strategies can we appreciate fully how his texts oscillate between contradictory positions without ever settling down—and that oscillation, manifested primarily in the formal qualities of his narratives, is the ultimate meaning of his politics.

[3] This is an ideal shared by many contemporary critics of colonialism and imperialism. For a useful survey of their views, see Parry, "Problems." R. S. Khare calls this ideal "genuinely reciprocal representations": "The issue now is not simply to represent the Other but to recognize it anew, with its own powers of recognition, representation, and persuasion intact" (1–2). Or, as John Tomlinson argues, the decisive question about cultural imperialism is "Who speaks?" (98). See chapters 2 and 3 above.

receives in his very first encounter with the British in the novel, when two ladies take his carriage and ignore his very existence: "The inevitable snub," Aziz thinks; they "turned instinctively away" upon seeing him and, when "he called courteously" to them, "did not reply, being full of their own affairs" (11–12). Appropriating his object while denying his status as a fellow human subject, they act as if he were invisible. When Indians are seen, they are often similarly ignored because a lack of recognition is implicit in Anglo-Indian claims of privileged knowledge of native behavior. "I know them as they really are," the police superintendent tells Fielding. "The psychology here is different" (160). He then promulgates psychological laws that justify his right to treat Indians as objects of his administrative power. As laws that claim to know others better than they know themselves, these readings deprive others of the right to comment on or to shape a description that has power over them. Aziz identifies the link between knowledge and power when he calls the "pose of 'seeing India' . . . only a form of ruling India; no sympathy lay behind it" (296–97). Whether in the form of regarding others as beneath notice or of categorizing them according to preset ideas, knowing is an act of taking power over others if it is not based on reciprocal recognition.

The novel invokes this ideal, however, only to violate it. As is well known, the novel unleashed storms of protest from members of the Anglo-Indian community who felt that its portrait of them was prejudiced and unfair (see Furbank 2:126–30). At least two responses are possible to such criticism, and Forster made one of them: "If I saw more of Anglo-India at work . . . I should of course realize its difficulties and loyalties better and write about it from within. Well and good, but you forget the price to be paid: I should begin to write about Indians from without" (quoted in Furbank 2:129–30). This response suggests that knowledge is inevitably exclusionary, one's perspective necessarily setting one at odds with other standpoints. If such conflicts are unavoidable, however, then the ideal of mutual recognition between knower and known would seem doomed. Even if two parties overcome their opposition, their convergence only sets up differences between themselves and some other party. Because knowledge is necessarily perspectival, one can recognize another only by refusing recognition to someone else. Attaining mutuality thus means displacing rather than transcending difference.

Another response to the charge of partiality is that, although prejudices are inescapable, they are not always wrong. Rustom Bharucha asks on Forster's behalf: "Does the fact that he 'loathes' the Anglo-Indians imply that he doesn't know them? I think not, but then I speak as an Indian. Turton [the chief administrator in *Passage*] is not a one-dimensional caricature for me: he represents a particular combination of pomposity and power that was known to exist in colonial India" (163). Acknowledging that he and Forster share a perspective others might contest, Bharucha defends not only the inevitability but also the potential productivity of distinctly partial, even partisan portraits. To call an interpretation one-sided is not necessarily to dismiss its validity, if total, unrestricted knowledge is impossible. The beauty of this argument is that it turns the interpretive power of prejudice against the practitioners of it, but the resulting embarrassment is that one thus consents to the necessity of injustice and exclusion as the conditions for knowledge even though the lack of a reciprocal understanding of others is the crime against which one protests.

The Indian reception of the novel has also been controversial in ways that suggest that alienating acts of categorization and objectification may necessarily inhabit even a sympathetic reconstruction of the Other's world. One Indian reader praises the novel because "for the first time I saw myself reflected in the mind of an English author, without losing all semblance of a human face" (quoted in introduction to *Passage* xxiii). This reader recognizes himself in the mirror Forster holds up to India because the novelist represents his face as a "human" one (although seen from the outside) and not as a mere object of curiosity or instrument for manipulation.[4] Sara Suleri, however, lacks any sense of this respect for the integrity of the Other. She charges Forster with practicing "representation as a mode of recolonization" and finds in his novel "the subterranean desire to replay, in twentieth-century narrative, the increasingly distant history of nineteenth-century domination" (169).[5]

The narrator's interpretive practice sometimes lends support to this charge because of his use of objectifying categories. Sounding much like the police superintendent promulgating psychological laws, the narrator claims at one point that "suspicion in the Oriental is a sort of malignant tumour, a mental malady, that makes him self-conscious and unfriendly suddenly; he trusts and mistrusts at the same time in a way a Westerner cannot comprehend" (267). Is such a judgment a legitimate attempt to make unfamiliar behavior comprehensible to a reader from another culture by employing recognizable metaphors ("suspicion" figured as a "tumour" or "malady"), or does it turn the Other into an exotic exhibit for what the narrator elsewhere dismisses as demeaning, manipulative speculations about "Oriental Pathology" (208)? It

---

[4] Ironically, although this reader writes to proclaim that his identity has been affirmed, he is left semi-anonymous by the journal that published his words (*Nation and Athenaeum* [4 August 1928], 590). He is identified only as "A.S.B." (see introduction to *Passage* xxiii). Other Indian readers who have found in the novel an image of themselves they recognize, appreciate, and accept are G. K. Das, Vasant Shahane, Frances Singh, and Ahmed Ali.

[5] In a similar vein, Nirad Chaudhuri complained much earlier that "Aziz and his friends belong to the servile section and are all toadies" (22).

can be read both ways, and its ambiguity suggests that interpretive types are both a source of abusive prejudice and a vehicle of empathetic understanding.

The conflicts marking the reception of *A Passage to India* suggest that the novel offers a strategically ambiguous response to the question of how one can interpret other cultures in a nonrepressive, nonmanipulative manner. A liberating, noninstrumental understanding of others coincides with the ideal of a nonreified knowledge based on mutual recognition, which the novel endorses and, for some readers, achieves. But the objections of other readers, both British and Indian, to the way the novel knows them reveal important hidden contradictions in this ideal. If knowledge is always from a perspective, it cannot be completely nonrepressive and nonmanipulative precisely because its very partiality is necessarily objectifying and exclusionary. The attempt to recognize others as they themselves are to themselves must occur through an interpretive framework that distances and reduces them because, as a perspective, it is not identical with what it seeks to know. These epistemological dilemmas not only mark the history of the reception of *A Passage to India* but also are central themes in the work itself. In its portrayal of how both the British and the Indian communities know, the novel casts doubt on the very ideal—that of a nonreifying understanding based on mutual recognition—it urgently advocates and seeks to realize.

Forster's "double turn" in affirming and contesting the possibility of nonreifying knowledge can be seen in the novel's contradictory treatment of Anglo-Indian claims to interpretive authority derived from "experience" (the Collector cites his "twenty-five years' experience of this country," for example, as entitling him to speak with "the whole weight of . . . authority" when he condemns Aziz [155]). Much is made of the irony that such "authority" often leads to disastrous misreadings. When Ronny Heaslop tells his mother about what his experience as an administrator has taught him, Mrs. Moore "felt, quite illogically, that this was not the last word on India" (44)—as, indeed, it is not. But when she and Adela Quested seek to discover "the real India" (19), they make repeated and equally disastrous mistakes in reading that demonstrate their lack of experience—specifically, their ignorance of conventions necessary for construing potentially misleading signs. Two of these misreadings are the direct cause of the ill-fated visit to the Marabar Caves—first when the newcomers accept a Hindu family's invitation that was probably not seriously meant and was not in any case carried out, and then when they mistake the meaning of Aziz's attempt to make up for this slight by a polite gesture and take seriously his invitation to visit his home: "He thought . . . of his bungalow with horror. Good heavens, the stupid girl had taken him at his word! What was he to do?" (67). And in a desperate inspiration he invites them to the Caves, where further misreadings will result in his imprisonment on an unfounded charge of rape. If the Collector's erroneous interpretation based on his experience wrongfully convinces him of Aziz's guilt, the irony is that the two newcomers' misinterpretations based on their inexperience pave the way for his mistake.

The point of this "double turn" is that nonreifying knowledge cannot be attained simply by discarding all preconceptions, because without a prior understanding of the matter at hand one is not likely to make sense of it. What Adela and Mrs. Moore do not understand is that Indians do not always mean what they say—a discrepancy not unique to the East but characteristic of the doubleness and hence the possible duplicity of signs. The narrator (presumably speaking from experience) claims of Indians: "What they said and what they felt were (except in the case of affection) seldom the same" (103). Because what is said and what is meant do not necessarily coincide (as the naive newcomers mistakenly assume), an initiation into the conventions being employed as well as experience deciphering similar messages are requisite for reliable interpretation. Although experience can be a source of misleading prejudices, an anticipatory understanding of the probable meanings of the signs to be deciphered is necessary because their significance is not immanent within them. *A Passage to India* calls attention to this dilemma by both denying and affirming the importance of preconceptions for interpretation.

Forster suggests the ubiquity of the obstacles to the ideal of knowledge he seeks by portraying the Indians as guilty of the same acts of misreading that he finds among the British, and for the same epistemological reasons. After the novel accuses the British of misconstruing Indian signs, it then shows the Indians committing the same mistakes not only toward the English but also among themselves. When the Collector issues invitations to the bridge party, for example, "his action caused much excitement and was discussed in several worlds" (30)—setting off a series of conflicting interpretations as to what lies behind it. Is he acting on orders from above, or is the invitation a genuine gesture of friendship? No one assumes that the meaning of the invitation is simply what it says, but no agreement is reached as to what the inscrutable Anglo-Indian is up to, and no one comes close to deciphering his actual motive.

If Anglo-Indian officialdom is blinded by its preconceptions about the Indians even as it cannot do without them, so its misunderstandings are duplicated by the prejudices of the Hindus and the Moslems about each other. The Moslem Aziz, the novel's primary victim of Anglo-Indian prejudice, is full of his own prejudgments about his Hindu countrymen. As he tells Miss Quested and Mrs. Moore in explaining why the Hindu family's invitation fell through: "Slack Hindus—they have no idea of society; I know them very well because of a doctor at the hospital. Such a slack unpunctual fellow! It is as well you did not go to their house, for it would give you a wrong idea of India. Nothing sanitary. I think for my own part they grew ashamed of their house and that is why they did not send" (62). The irony here, of course, is that Aziz's own embarrassment about his "detestable shanty" (63) subsequently leads him to withdraw his suggestion that they call on him at home, and this irony in turn calls into question his prejudices about Hindus and his insistence on their radical difference from himself. His misunderstandings and conflicts with his subordinate, the Hindu Dr. Panna Lal, duplicate Aziz's own relation of mutual cultural opacity with his Anglo-Indian boss (who similarly thinks Aziz "slack" and "unpunctual"). Aziz reads the Hindus through his preconceptions about them, just as the Hindus do the Moslems ("I wish they did not remind me of cow-dung," Aziz thinks of a Hindu interlocutor, who in turn thinks of him, "Some Moslems are very violent" [256]), and as the Anglo-Indians do to both, and as the Indians do to the British. Some preconceptions may be more reasonable and more illuminating than others, and the powers of some prejudices over their objects may be more oppressive than others, but *A Passage to India* displaces the ideal of nonreifying knowledge through mutual recognition along a seemingly endless series of prejudices that include everyone.

Is the reader of *A Passage to India* simply to abandon the ideal that Forster calls up but then so powerfully criticizes and contests? Turning once again, Forster suggests that we can get beyond prejudice, but only by going through it—that is, by employing interpretive frameworks ironically, through a constructive act of negation that deploys epistemological categories and simultaneously suspects them. He repeatedly calls on the reader to undertake such a double movement in discounting the various interpretive constructs proposed in the novel and filling out what they do not include. The double movements begin with the very first paragraph of the novel, which describes the setting by negating the categories it invokes: "Except for the Marabar Caves—and they are twenty miles off—the city of Chandrapore presents *nothing* extraordinary. . . . There are *no* bathing steps on the river front, as the Ganges happens *not* to be holy here; indeed there is *no* river front, and bazaars *shut out* the wide and shifting panorama of the stream" (2, emphasis added; see also Beer 46–47).

Projecting what is the case by discounting what is not is also the way the reader needs to respond to the various constructions of race, gender, and culture in the novel—such as, for example, the Anglo-Indian interpretation of Adela Quested as "the English girl who had had the terrible experience, and for whom too much could not be done" (202), "an English girl fresh from England" (156), "our sister" (171), "my own darling girl" (171). There are many reasons for suspecting these categories as having more to do with Anglo-Indian sexual and racial stereotypes and mechanisms of cultural self-definition than with Adela's confusion, anguish, and pain, but for many chapters (16–21) they and prejudices like them are all the reader is offered while Adela is kept as inaccessible from us as she is from Fielding, who feels that a few words with her would clear everything up. Such directness and immediacy are unavailable, however, and the reader is left to imagine what happened to Adela and what she is feeling by negating the images through which the British "Club" depicts her.

Different categories require different kinds of negation. Some prejudices the reader must demystify and discard, like the construct of British purity under threat from a sexually dangerous racial Other (the danger implied by constructing Adela as "the English girl"). This notion reveals less about Adela than about how Anglo-Indian cultural identity is created by exclusion and projection. But even here something might be retained after the prejudice is discounted, if only because how Adela understands what occurred is shaped for her by the way the Anglo-Indian community receives her story. Other prejudices are more ambiguous, however, and require more subtle acts of negation coupled with recuperative appreciation. A contradictory combination of rejection and acceptance is necessary, for example, whenever the narrator invokes cultural types in his role as tour guide to India: "Religion is a living force to the Hindus, and can at certain moments fling down everything that is petty and temporary in their natures" (294). Without at least partially accepting categorical statements like this, the non-Indian reader can know nothing of the complexities of Indian life—but the novel's depiction of the will to power implicit in the tourist's desire to know the "real India" should lead the reader to suspect even benevolent generalizations, and such a response is appropriate because of the inevitable absences and exclusions that accompany any perspective.

Consistent with its implication that an ideal state of knowledge can be approached but only indirectly, through negation, *A Passage to India* affirms both the discoverability of "truth" and the necessity of endless interpretation. This is the epistemological paradox suggested by Forster's treatment of what happened in the Marabar Caves. On the one hand, Adela Quested's accusation against Aziz is unambiguously wrong. The reader is with Aziz in another cave at the moment the assault is said to have occurred, and we then see him discovering on the ground Adela's field glasses with the broken strap that is later taken as evidence of their struggle. From the moment Aziz is arrested, the reader knows he is innocent—the "truth" of the matter is clear. On the other hand, we are never certain what really did happen to Adela in the cave or how the strap on her glasses broke—and Forster himself claimed not to know: "In the cave it is either a man, or the supernatural, or an illusion. And even if I know! My writing mind therefore is a blur here—i.e., I will it to remain a blur, and to be uncertain, as I am of many facts in daily life" (quoted in Furbank 2:125). The echo she hears can be deciphered in any number of ways, and has been by readers of the novel (although it leaves her when she tells the truth and exonerates Aziz). The field glasses were physically present at the scene and, like a bullet hole, are an index bearing a trace of the event. Something happened, they tell us, but they are only a sign that must be deciphered to fill in the absent occurrence they point to, and they are subject to different interpretations, none of which ever reveal what happened.[6]

A similar doubleness is evident in his handling of point of view, through which he both affirms and questions the possibility of knowing other minds and of discovering a lasting consensus across different communities. The narrator moves freely among the minds of different characters with apparent faith in their intersubjective accessibility, but the effect for the reader is to stress the mutual opacity of worlds that only we and the narrator seem able to connect. Just before Adela's anguishing experience in the cave, for example, the narrator first shares with us the very intimate thoughts leading up to her question "Have you one wife or more than one?" and then reveals to us Aziz's shocked response that he attempts to disguise: "To ask an educated Indian Moslem how many wives he has—appalling, hideous!" (144). Only the reader and the narrator ever know both sides of this cultural and personal misunderstanding, which precipitates the major crisis in the novel. Our ability to explain the misunderstanding and to move back and forth between these two characters' tragically disjoined perspectives affirms the possibility of overcoming the mutual opacity of different worlds. But this is a privilege that should make the reader uncomfortable, because our inability to share what we see with the characters duplicates the gap between worlds that has such awful consequences in the novel.[7]

---

[6] Two comments suggest Forster's appreciation of epistemological multiplicity: "I don't myself like the phrase 'the real India.' I suspect it. . . . 'Real' is at the service of all schools of thought" ("India" 321). And: "Religious people are vigorous because they identify a certain set of opinions with divine will, and stick to them alone. They are just as human as the non-religious, but more consistent. The non-religious man is distracted by the variety of human voices, one speaking truth at one moment, one at another. It seems impossible to him that anything so powerful and sympathetic as a human voice can be wrong" (quoted in Furbank 1:112).

[7] By playing with point of view like this in order to stage epistemological dilemmas for the reader, Forster does precisely what Ronald Schleifer accuses him of failing to do: "E. M. Forster articulates a sense of failure of civilization in his work . . . but unlike the modernist writers, he does not present this crisis within the very discourse he offers us; his understanding of what is gone from the world is not enacted in his language" (54). Forster's experiments with narrative perspective may be less spectacular than those of some other modernists, but the very subtlety through which he offers and withholds knowledge is an enactment of complex epistemological dilemmas.

This gap is dramatized again in a series of clues that we understand differently from the interpretations offered by a character—the picture of Aziz's beloved wife that is assumed by the police superintendent to demonstrate the accused rapist's lust, the displaced collar seen by Anglo-Indians as proof of native sloppiness after Aziz generously lends his collar pin to Fielding, or the reference of a British officer to an anonymous Indian polo player (whom we know to be Aziz) as an example of a native who is "all right" in contrast to Adela's assailant.[8] In all these instances the reader connects worlds that are opaque to each other by correcting misinterpretations that divide them. In line with Forster's faith in the discoverability of truth, the reader's ability to set these mistakes right suggests that we can cross the boundaries dividing different perspectives. But intersubjectivity is thus affirmed through depictions of its absence that call it into question and demonstrate the stubborn resistance of different perspectives to reconciliation.

The moral and political norm implied by intersubjectivity is an ideal of justice based on consensus. This ideal is resolutely endorsed by the novel's depiction of Fielding's exemplary courage, compassion, and commitment to truth in allying himself with Aziz and his Indian friends against the prejudices of British authority. But just at the moment of Aziz's vindication, Forster questions the possibility of justice and consensus by splitting Fielding off from the celebrating Indian party (putting him in a carriage with Adela)— thus beginning his increasing alienation from Aziz over the issue of the compensation Miss Quested should pay. Fielding's pleas for mercy ("Do treat her considerately," he begs; "she really mustn't get the worst of both worlds" [240]) do not further the cause of reconciliation but instead breed dissension and mutual recrimination. The narrator reports of Fielding that Aziz's "insensitiveness about Adela displeased him. It would, from every point of view, be right to treat her generously" (249). The irony, however, is that Fielding is equally open to the charge of insensitivity—of myopically universalizing his own perspective on justice and failing to credit other reasonable views. After affirming the possibility of finding agreement about truth and right at Aziz's trial, Forster throws open the question of justice and consensus again in the debate about compensation that ultimately drives Fielding and Aziz apart, even after Aziz yields and agrees to let Adela off.

---

[8] For an insightful explication of these examples, see Hawkins, "Forster's Critique" 54–55. The conclusion Hawkins draws from them is not quite accurate, however: "The Anglo-Indians, as Forster presents them, act on emotional preconceptions rather than rational and open-minded examination of facts" (54). Although Forster thinks some prejudices are blinding, his novel questions whether "rationality" and "open-mindedness" are simple, straightforward epistemological attitudes.

Aziz for his part is unjust to Fielding in assuming that he had pecuniary motives in arguing against compensation. Here again Forster affirms the discoverability of a legitimate interpretation by eventually disabusing Aziz and the reader of the assumption that Fielding wanted Adela to keep her money so that he could marry her for it. But before Forster allows the narrative to clear up this misconception, the reader is kept inside Aziz's mistaken perspective for an extended period (see 282–92). We may wonder how Fielding could be guilty of such infamy—but he is as opaque to us as he is to Aziz until the error is accidentally exposed when Aziz mistakenly calls Fielding's brother-in-law "Mr. Quested" and finds he is actually Ralph Moore. If we have such doubts, they alienate us from Aziz's perspective even as we inhabit it and thus disturbingly recreate in our relation to him the dissonance between his world and Fielding's. Although truth finally prevails, Forster manipulates point of view to give the reader a subtle but revealing experience of how the opacity of others can lead to conflicts about justice, and that memory lingers for the reader even as it does for Aziz and Fielding, who never regain their former intimacy after suspicion has divided them.

The difficulties of discovering and sustaining agreement between different perspectives are not solely a sign of the unbridgeable divide between British and Indian cultures but are also characteristic of India itself. The unsynthesizable diversity of India is a repeated refrain in the novel: "No one is India," "Nothing embraces the whole of India, nothing, nothing," "There is no such person in existence as the general Indian" (65, 136, 255). Forster's depiction of India as a multifarious country that defies totalization is not an attempt to render it exotic and mysterious. Rather, the heterogeneity of India is a particular instance of a tendency toward internal diversity that can be found in many (perhaps all) cultures. Such a generalizing intention is evident when the narrator lists those not invited to the Collector's bridge party: "And there were circles even beyond these—people who wore nothing but a loincloth, people who wore not even that, and spent their lives in knocking two sticks together before a scarlet doll—humanity grading and drifting beyond the educated vision, until no earthly invitation can embrace it. . . . We must exclude someone from our gathering, or we shall be left with nothing" (32).

The endless series of differences suggested here is in part attributable to class (the description of poverty), in part to culture (if the choice of loincloth or nakedness is dictated by custom rather than scarcity), in part to religion (the worshipers of the idol). The challenge to the "educated vision" is to "embrace" more than the Collector's party does. This appeal is not limited to India, because differences of class, custom, and religion are not unique to it. Nor is the question with which the passage ends: Must something be excluded from any act of unification lest identity be abolished when differences are overcome? In raising this question Forster suggests not only that an all-encompassing consensus may not be possible but also that community may not be desirable if it requires negation and rejection.

When synthesis does occur in *A Passage to India,* it is often dangerous because of the exclusionary mechanisms that sustain it. The solidarity that the British community feels when it rallies to Adela's side is a state of communal solipsism based on scapegoating Aziz and banding together against the threat of a racially and sexually constructed Other. By the same token, Fielding begins to become uncomfortable with his Indian allies when their solidarity in a just cause seems to become vindictive and blinding: "Victory, which would have made the English sanctimonious, made them aggressive. They wanted to develop an offensive, and tried to do so by discovering new grievances and wrongs, many of which had no existence" (248). One of Fielding's reasons for asking for mercy for Adela is to prevent her from becoming the scapegoat to the Indian community that Aziz had been to the British. In order to act in concert against British oppression, the Indians need to overcome their differences, and such solidarity is facilitated by a sense of shared injustices and by the mediation of myths and symbols whose unifying force is unrelated to their basis in reality (hence the power of the absurd chant "Esmiss Esmoor, Esmiss Esmoor" [214]). But Forster worries that the mechanisms of exclusion and projection that bring about such unity may themselves mirror the unjust practices they seek to eradicate. Once again employing the particular circumstances of India to suggest a more general political problem, Forster asks whether the uses of consensus in the pursuit of justice can be protected from the abuses of a communal solipsism that practices violence on others by inventing exclusionary fictions about them.

Invoking and questioning the ideal of community throughout, the novel concludes by sounding the notes of concord and discord simultaneously.[9] In the Hindu festival that dominates the last section of the novel, all conflicts are transcended: "The festival flowed on, wild and sincere, and all men loved each other, and avoided by instinct whatever could cause inconvenience or pain" (294). But this image of achieved reconciliation is contested by the Moslem Aziz's detached, often uncomprehending perspective: "Aziz could not understand this, any more than an average Christian could," and he "felt bored, slightly cynical" because "these sanctities . . . had no connection with his

---

[9] Readers of the novel have been divided over whether it endorses unity because they have heard one or the other of these notes. For example, contrast Wilfred Stone, for whom the novel shows "that, for all our differences, we are in fact one" (339), with Alan Wilde, who finds in the ending "an acceptance of life's and the self's profound disunities" (*Horizons* 70), or with Barbara Rosecrance, who claims that "the perception of divine unity is not translatable into social or personal fulfillment" (236).

own" (295, 296). Analogously, Aziz and Fielding overcome their differences only to rearticulate them in their final conversation—rediscovering trust and intimacy even as they quarrel about Indian politics, a conflict that thwarts the declaration of friendship both seek. Whenever Forster invokes an ideal of community or mutual recognition, he questions it by asserting cultural or personal differences of perspective. The consequence, even to the end, is to invoke the ideal negatively, by deferring it: "No, not yet," and "No, not there" (312). The reasons for deferring a vision of synthesis are not only practical, having to do with the particular political problems of India, but also epistemological, a consequence of the irreducibility of different perspectives and the obstacle they present to univocal notions of justice and consensus.

Forster's "double turns" in *A Passage to India* imply that the quest for legitimate norms of truth and justice is more complicated and contradictory than either Habermas or Lyotard suggests in their debate about the politics of interpretation. The epistemological and social ideal invoked by Forster's novel has much in common with Habermas's goal of "uncoerced consensus arrived at among free and equal persons"—"a constraint-free intersubjectivity of mutual understanding, . . . a sphere of agreement free of violence" (*Modernity* 40, 220). As much as Forster shares this ideal, however, he is suspicious of it. The depiction in *A Passage to India* of the insuperable heterogeneity of the social world gives support to Lyotard's objection that Habermas's notion of consensus reached through intersubjective deliberation is naive, perhaps dangerously so, about epistemological and linguistic multiplicity. The stress must be placed on dissension, Lyotard argues: "Consensus is a horizon that is never reached" (*Postmodern Condition* 61).

Contrary to Habermas's claim that noncoercive mutual understanding will lead to agreement as the inevitable telos of a constraint-free exchange of views, *Passage* demonstrates that the result even among sympathetic interlocutors may not be the discovery of common convictions but an acknowledgment of the irreducibility and opacity of other worlds—or so Aziz and Fielding find when their quest for union at the end reveals the deep, abiding differences between them. Even more, Forster would agree with Lyotard that consensus may not only be elusive but oppressive. With a radically probing irony that Conrad would appreciate, *A Passage to India* suggests that the lack of intersubjective agreement leads to injustice even as it shows how the achievement of consensus can be blinding and destructive as well. The British Club's misreading of Aziz's guilt demonstrates the need for mutual understanding (the "truth" would emerge if everyone would only share what they know), but it also demonstrates that freely given mutual agreement (the Anglo-Indian community's reinforcement of its prejudices) may result in a blinding communal solipsism rather than a collective revelation of truth. The Indian demand for retribution similarly is lamentable for its lack of understanding of Adela's plight, but it also shows that uncoerced consensus can be homologous to bullying mob violence. Forster's skepticism about the exclusionary mechanisms through which social solidification is achieved suggests that freely given agreement may be not only irrational (and not, pace Habermas, proof of intersubjective rationality) but also violent and oppressive. If all gatherings achieve their identity by virtue of those they exclude, the uncoerced unification of one community can slip all too easily, by the logic of negation, into the forceful and repressive rejection of others.

Rorty's "liberal irony" is similarly contradictory on this score. On the one hand, Rorty recommends that "when we look for regulative ideals, we stick to freedom and forget about truth and rationality. . . . Whatever else truth may be, it is something we are more likely to get as a result of free and open encounters than anything else" ("Truth" 634). In his analysis of the Habermas-Lyotard debate he consequently supports Habermas's advocacy of uncoerced communication: "Social purposes are served, just as Habermas says, by finding beautiful ways of harmonizing interests, rather than sublime ways of detaching oneself from others' interests" ("Habermas and Lyotard" 174). On the other hand, Rorty—like Forster—doubts that universal agreement can be discovered: "To be ethnocentric is to divide the human race into the people to whom one must justify one's beliefs and the others. . . . Everybody is ethnocentric when engaged in actual debate" ("Solidarity" 13). For that reason Rorty accepts Lyotard's claim that different narratives for explaining the world (Rorty calls them "vocabularies") cannot necessarily be synthesized and that this heterogeneity is not a bad thing. Turning yet again, however, Rorty criticizes Lyotard for assuming "that the intellectual has a mission to be avant-garde, to escape the rules and practices and institutions which have been transmitted to him in favor of something which will make possible 'authentic criticism' " ("Habermas and Lyotard" 174). Consensus may not deliver truth, but the various forms of social discourse still have uses and should not simply be discarded. By the same token Forster continues to employ narrative forms that assume community with his reader even as he uses them to give us a sense of the unbridgeable differences dividing us.

Forster is less complacent than Rorty about the contradictions of liberal irony, however, and he worries that recognizing the contingency of one's ethnocentric convictions is not sufficient to eliminate their exclusionary violence. To recognize ironically that one must necessarily exclude others (as the narration of *Passage* does almost from the outset) is still, after all, to exclude them (as happens repeatedly throughout the novel on both sides of the British-Indian divide and within each community with a relentless logic of internal division). Not content to rest with a contradiction, but turning yet again, Forster responds to the dangers of communal solipsism by advocating the ideal of reciprocal, nonmanipulative knowledge even after he has unmasked its naiveté. Lyotard's endorsement of "dissensus"—of innovative countermoves that break the rules and create new games—portrays knowledge as inherently conflictual, an agon between perspectives from which one can liberate oneself only by an act of subversion that then itself becomes a new participant in the combat (see 40, 59). Forster's novel suggests, however, that there is invariably a human cost when perspectives conflict, whether the disappointment and confusion of a failed attempt to reach understanding with another (again the example of Aziz and Fielding comes to mind), or the loss of liberty and integrity one may suffer if one's perspective is denied (the novel's indictment of the epistemological will to power of imperialism). Lyotard is aware of these dangers, and they lead him to appeal for an idea of justice not tied to consensus—a mutual respect, for example, that would condemn "terror," the destruction or threat of exclusion of a player from a linguistic or epistemological game one is playing. In a Forsterian double turn, with the skeptical force of a Conrad combined with a Rortyan pragmatic will to carry on, the ideal of community as a principle of justice is thus both rejected and affirmed—negated as an impossible and perhaps dangerous dream of unity, but recuperated and embraced as an enabling condition of reciprocal recognition without which language and other games based on an exchange of differences could not long function.

My construction of Forster's position in the Habermas-Lyotard debate suggests, then, at least a negative answer to the question of legitimation. Although it may not be possible to discover norms of truth and justice that can claim validity across different perspectives, Forster and Lyotard agree that some acts can be judged illegitimate. "Terror," as Lyotard defines it, is wrong, even if this negative judgment cannot be translated into converse form—that is, it does not dictate unequivocally what is right. This contradiction reproduces Forster's double movement in affirming and contesting a univocal standard of justice. *A Passage to India* suggests that the ideal of nonreifying knowledge based on reciprocal recognition can legitimately and unambiguously condemn some epistemological and political practices. The novel never wavers in its rejection of manipulative, repressive Anglo-Indian prejudice and the exclusionary violence it perpetrates. But the ability to render such a negative judgment does not always allow us to decide whose version of justice is correct. Hence Forster's reintroduction of a dispute about justice (should Adela pay compensation?) after vindicating the innocent Aziz, and hence his portrayal of the unsynthesizable heterogeneity of India that the momentary consensus about Aziz cannot overcome.

The possibility of making negative judgments is not enough, however. Here Forster agrees with Habermas that positive norms are necessary to provide goals for social change. One positive imperative in Forster's condemnation of the refusal to recognize the integrity of differing perspectives is a call to work for conditions that allow free, equal exchange—the sort of uncoerced conversation that Rorty advocates as a substitute for the impossible dream of "truth" and "reason." Like other pragmatists, Forster finds such conditions in democracy: "So two cheers for Democracy: one because it admits variety and two because it permits criticism. Two cheers are quite enough: there is no occasion to give three. Only Love the Beloved Republic deserves that" (*Democracy* 67). Since we cannot have a world of all-embracing harmony that would deserve three cheers, let us encourage multiplicity and disagreement. These might seem obstacles to community, but because a synthesis of perspectives is impossible, allowing their differences free expression is the best alternative. With Rorty, Forster advocates uncoerced exchange, not because such "communicative rationality," to borrow Habermas's term, will result in agreement, but precisely because it won't. Forster's endorsement of democracy is modest and negative, based on skepticism about consensus and unity, but it nonetheless projects a positive image of social relations that people with different perspectives can join together to pursue. More skeptical than Rorty, Forster is deeply and temperamentally suspicious of declarations of faith (remember his resounding assertion: "I do not believe in Belief"). But with an irony that is ultimately more affirming than Conrad's, he also suggests that it is possible, indeed necessary, to believe in ideals after one has criticized them.

The "double turns" that define the experience of reading *A Passage to India* endorse a paradoxical but pragmatic course of pursuing goals that are impossible to justify or attain. Mutual understanding may be an illusion because of the irreducible opacity of other perspectives, but it cannot be approached unless one nevertheless believes in it. A nonreifying knowledge of others may always elude us because of the necessary role of preconceptions and categories in understanding, but again we forfeit any chance of realizing this ideal even partially and imperfectly if we refuse to commit ourselves to it. A consensus about truth and justice may not be possible, but this in turn gives different perspectives the right to pursue their own particular visions because no view can claim in advance special inherent privileges. Forster is a pragmatic ironist who suggests that we need to believe in ideals that we know we cannot justify because, if we did not, they would lose all meaning and force and we would be left with nothing. Reading *A Passage to India* is an education in the double movements necessary to sustain the contradictory attitude of suspecting ideals one believes in and believing ideals one suspects.

9. JAMES JOYCE AND
THE POLITICS OF READING

Power, Belief, and Justice in Ulysses

Throughout this book I have been arguing against two fallacies that characterize much politically oriented criticism. First, the call "Always historicize" is widely taken to privilege the originating context. The politics of a text is seen as a matter of how it addresses or portrays the social conditions of its period. This focus on the original time of writing neglects the ability of texts to speak across historical distance. Even the first writing is futural—an anticipation of an audience that has not yet received the text. Many especially innovative, provocative works challenge the contemporary audience's habits of understanding so greatly that the originating context lacks the means to make sense of them. By trying to change that context, works cross boundaries and open themselves to a history of future receptions that will understand them differently. This dimension of history is lost when "historicizing" privileges the author's period as the defining locus of meaning. The transhistorical usefulness of texts as instruments for thinking about problems readers face in their own day is diminished if we confine a work's historical meaning to its beginnings.[1] In order to appreciate fully the historical existence of texts, we must pay attention to how they do cultural work across their histories of reception

---

[1] It is also important, however, to avoid the correlative error of "presentist" interpretation that projects contemporary meanings and values onto a text or judges it against current norms without regard for its temporal otherness. The mistake against which I am warning is the collapse of historical distance, an error committed either by reducing a text to its past significance or by ignoring its difference from contemporary concerns.

by being interpreted in various ways that make them relevant to changing problems and concerns.

The second fallacy is to neglect the literary dimensions of texts. Much politically engaged criticism reads like sociology. It is, of course, notoriously—and necessarily—difficult to define the "literary," but the political and social significance of a literary work goes beyond its mimetic content.[2] Innovations in structure and style can challenge the reader's conventions for understanding and behaving just as much as content. Indeed, the "what" of a work's mimetic content is available only through the "how" of its linguistic engagement with the reader's ways of making sense. Investigating the political implications of form is necessary to account adequately for the social existence of texts. As social beings, literary works do transformative work by communicating with readers. Studying the act of reading is not a formalist temptation to neglect historical reality. It is, rather, an area where literary critics can contribute to the understanding of social history with an expertise that sociologists, historians, or political scientists usually do not have.

The games James Joyce plays with the reader in *Ulysses* illustrate the dangers of these fallacies and indicate a different way of conceptualizing the politics of literature. This is a text that is often taken to reflect the conditions of Ireland in Joyce's day—the immediate social and political context of Leopold Bloom's and Stephen Dedalus's imagined lives in Dublin in June 1904.[3] But the text's elaborate experiments with style suggest that mimetic interpretation misses much of what is going on. The challenge of overcoming the seeming opposition between the historical and the formal dimensions of *Ulysses* can

---

[2] On the difficulties of defining "literature," see the chapter "The Variability and Limits of Value" in my *Conflicting Readings* 109–33.

[3] One of the best, most exhaustive analyses of this kind is Cheryl Herr. She explicitly associates her concern with Joyce's Irish backgrounds with the historical turn in contemporary criticism. On Joyce's politics, see also Cheng; Ellmann; Hawthorn; Manganiello; Watson; and McGee, *Joyce beyond Marx*. One of the most successful attempts to synthesize historical and formal criticism is Lawrence, " 'Beggaring.' " Another is Andrew Gibson's important recent interpretation of *Ulysses* as a protest against English nationalism: "Joyce works towards a liberation from the colonial power and its culture. . . . The styles in *Ulysses* are examples of this. They are wicked practices upon the colonizer's culture" (13, 15). Fredric Jameson's suggestive reading of *Ulysses* as paradoxically a metropolitan and a colonial text seems at first an attempt to avoid the fallacies I have identified—because he seeks to describe what its peculiar Irish "modernism" *was* in order better to understand what imperialism then and now *is*, and because he seeks "the traces of imperialism" not "in the obvious places, in content or in representation," but "as formal symptoms, within the structure of First World modernist texts themselves" (64). Nevertheless, the term "symptoms" suggests that for Jameson texts are captive of the past they bear witness to, and not that they can go beyond the limits of their period by proposing strategies for diagnosing or even remedying its deficiencies (which would make them not only sickness but, at least potentially, cure).

best be met, I think, by seeing Joyce's games with the reader as a strategy of engaging dilemmas in his own time that allows him to speak across his horizons to ours.[4]

Ulysses does this by staging the dilemmas opened up by the contingency and contestability of "truth" that the liberalism of Joyce's day was unable to accommodate and that are still a live issue for contemporary neoliberal thought. The provocations offered to readers of *Ulysses* foreground two inherently unresolvable problems that also preoccupy Conrad and Forster. First, is the ironic recognition that all beliefs are contingent a productive or destructive act, a way of making commitment possible or the first step toward nihilism? Second, if no form of life can claim absolute authority (even democracy is nothing more than a contingent cultural form), what standards can be invoked to resolve claims of injustice and adjudicate the competing demands of different forms of life? Less pessimistic than Conrad but less modest and coy than Forster, Joyce nevertheless responds to these dilemmas just as they do: he shifts them to the reader because he cannot resolve them. He does this by trying to overcome the challenges of contingency through an assertion of his own will to power even as he simultaneously demonstrates their insuperability by disclosing the limitations of any authority, including his own. This contradiction makes *Ulysses* both a coercive and an emancipatory text, as the divided reaction of readers over the history of its reception suggests. Joyce's masterpiece of linguistic subversion and innovation is both an instrument through which the author uses the reader for his own ends in his personal battle against contingency and an open-ended invitation to us to discover and play with the implications of an infinitely heterogeneous world.

Joyce is a master manipulator with an insatiable will to control, shape, and dominate through form, but he is also a rebellious, puckish anarchist who questions the claims of any discourse, even his own. Because no style or perspective can prove its necessity or its "truth," Joyce celebrates the infinite possibilities of giving form and creating meaning. But the absence of any ultimate origin or end tempts him to seek a kind of apotheosis by creating games that

[4] Technically, my invocation of "Joyce's day" may seem imprecise because it conflates the time of production ("Trieste-Zürich-Paris, 1914–21") and the time represented in the text (16 June 1904). This distinction is worth calling attention to, however, because it suggests once again, in a different way, the mutually constitutive interaction between present and past that makes interpretation a historical act. The meaning of the past will vary according to the present situation of interpretation, not only in the relation between the moments of writing and reading but also in the relation between the time represented by the text and the time of production. How a portrayal of the past testifies to the assumptions and interests of the author's period can be an especially important issue, obviously, with historical novels and plays. These two temporal moments are quite close in the case of *Ulysses,* however, and their differences do not affect my basic argument.

endow him with ultimate authority as a god whose powers extend limitlessly, as long as the games he initiated go on. Both attitudes can be seen in his much-quoted claim about *Ulysses:* "I've put in so many enigmas and puzzles that it will keep the professors busy for centuries arguing over what I meant, and that's the only way of insuring one's immortality" (Gifford and Seidman v). In a world where all meanings and values are contingent, the only way to achieve transcendence is to gain power over an endless series of others for whose enterprises one becomes both arche and telos. But then the limitless-ness of their exegetical work and the indeterminacy of their interpretive con-flicts demonstrate the inconclusiveness of any authority, even Joyce's. His power is both asserted and denied by the meaning-making activity it sets in motion (and the jocularity of his comment suggests he knows as much).

Some of Joyce's best critics acknowledge this contradiction in different ways. Karen Lawrence notes a similar doubleness when she argues that the disappearance of the author's "signature style" in *Ulysses* behind a "series of rhetorical masks leads us to doubt the authority of any particular style," even as Joyce nevertheless seems to have "a kind of fantasy of omnipotence, a de-sire to transcend all logical, formal, and emotional constraints" (*Style* 9, 119). The erasure of the author's "signature style" emancipates the reader's seman-tic powers, but it also, and at the same time, serves a strategy of dominance. John Paul Riquelme similarly argues: "For Joyce's all-powerful narrator, the choice of invisibility and the acts of withdrawing mark his presence. . . . the author's persona makes itself felt through its apparent invisibility" (132). Jacques Derrida also intuits this invisible will to power when he notes: "Yes, everything has already happened to us with *Ulysses* and has been signed in advance by Joyce" ("Gramophone" 48). The absence of a signature style al-lows Joyce to sign his name more ubiquitously than he could in any single mode of writing. Joyce the master stylist achieves apotheosis through his very disappearance.

Readers have responded to *Ulysses* with a combination of fascination and resentment, delight and anger, because Joyce seeks simultaneously to emanci-pate and overpower them. The complaints of even his most appreciative read-ers are legion. After noting that the reader probably cannot see a fraction of what Joyce put into *Ulysses*, Edmund Wilson grumbles that "Joyce has as lit-tle respect as Proust for the capacities of the reader's attention" (215–16). One of his most conscientious detectives, Robert Martin Adams, confesses that "the uneasy sense of missing something, of not quite getting the point, must be familiar to many people's experience of *Ulysses*—I am sure it is to mine"—and he suggests, finally, that "the book loses as much as it gains by being read closely" (9, 246). Weldon Thornton decided to devote much of his career to tracking down the book's allusions only after responding to his first reading of

Ulysses with an angry paper in which he "argued that by asking far more of the reader than he had any right to do, Joyce repeatedly and willfully violated the implicit contract that should exist between any writer and an audience" (124). (For this essay, Thornton remembers, he received a D-.) Wolfgang Iser claims that "perplexity should be regarded . . . as a stimulus and a provocation" in *Ulysses,* but he also notes that "the reader is not obliged to take the bait and will, indeed, ignore it if he feels himself to be overtaxed," as the text's demands seemingly make inevitable (*Implied Reader* 210). Even Derrida admits feeling ambivalence about Joyce's hermeneutic challenge: "Who can pride himself on having 'read' Joyce? With this admiring resentment, you stay on the edge of reading Joyce" ("Two Words" 148). "Admiring resentment" captures nicely the contradictory feelings of many readers about Joyce's display of authorial power.

In a way that has made readers feel exasperated and annoyed, *Ulysses* points out their limits, their inadequacy, their inability to meet its demands, and it thereby asserts its superiority. But it keeps drawing readers even as it frustrates and repels them.[5] Part of the attraction may derive from the sort of rivalry that resentment often spawns, an envious desire to become like Joyce by emulating his powers of semantic performance. But another part of the text's appeal is due to the emancipatory, self-expanding pleasures it offers by challenging our capacities—extending, enhancing, and liberating the reader's powers to mean.

Ulysses can make readers feel both powerless and powerful, and these are two sides of the same project. *Ulysses* exposes and demystifies the will to power of any particular style or perspective by orchestrating a potentially endless array of discursive strategies, none of which can claim priority. But Joyce's ability to generate and criticize all of these styles gives him a claim to foundational status in the very process of denying foundations. He goes beyond *Ulysses'* ensemble of styles in the act of pointing out their limits even as he demonstrates there is no place beyond the limits of style.

Explicating this contradiction will suggest, I think, how Joyce engages his own historical horizon by reaching across it. This is true of both the coercive

---

[5] The same could be said of *Finnegans Wake.* Contrast Margot Norris's praise for the *Wake* as a "decentered" and hence subversive emancipatory text with Colin MacCabe's complaint that the late Joyce's rarefied stylistic play lacks a sense of audience and cuts him off from potential communities that his experiments might change (156–57). I choose to focus on *Ulysses* because I think the contradiction between enabling and overpowering the reader is staged more productively in it than in the *Wake,* although that is, I admit, debatable. Both texts can be faulted for self-aggrandizing linguistic display, but the *Wake's* bolder experiments with language can also be seen as an extension of the same contradiction I find in *Ulysses* between a drive for personal apotheosis and a desire to emancipate the reader.

and the emancipatory sides of his project. His effort to escape contingency requires a future readership to manipulate, just as his invitation to reflect about
and play with the indeterminacies of meaning is also a way of engaging readers beyond his horizons. In both cases, the contradictions of power in *Ulysses*
cannot be understood if the politics of the text are equated with its originating context or its representational content. Understanding Joyce's games with
power means attending to the politics of reading.

Belief, Commitment, and the Epistemology of Irony

Ulysses simultaneously stages and seeks to transcend the problem of commitment in a world of contingent beliefs and values. Joyce distances himself
equally from Stephen Dedalus's paralyzed skepticism and from Bloom's benign faith in "love" and the progressive values of the "new Bloomusalem."
But it is consequently unclear where Joyce stands: Has he risen above the conflict between these alternatives by dramatizing it, or is he with us as an equal
player in the field of indeterminacy created by the inability to resolve this opposition? Is he our collaborator and ally in the game of playing ironically with
this opposition, or does he use us as instruments in a strategy to assert his ascendancy? In short, is he playing with us as partners or as pawns?

These contradictions are everywhere evident in the text's divided—maddening yet also liberating—dramatization of the dilemmas of belief and commitment. "Do you believe your own theory?" Stephen is asked about his views
on Shakespeare; "No, Stephen said promptly," but someone nevertheless immediately inquires: "Are you going to write it?" (9:1065–68).[6] Believing one's
theory is not a prerequisite for representing and disseminating it. Quite the
contrary, its lack of necessity invites inscription because a theory is simply a
construction, no more necessary than any alternative view that might be sub-
stituted for it. As a contingent construction, a theory participates in and testifies to the heterogeneity and variability of signification that the instabilities
of writing exemplify.

The pragmatic necessity of fixing an interpretation and taking a position is
a loss as much as a gain. It allows a particular view to elaborate itself with the
sort of complexity and subtlety Stephen's display in the Library demonstrates, but it does so only by excluding other equally tenable positions.
Stephen's facility in erecting artifices he does not believe in is not liberating
but disabling: "I believe, O Lord, help my unbelief," Stephen thinks. "That

---

[6] I follow the convention in Joyce scholarship of citing passages by chapter and line number
as designated in the Gabler edition.

is, help me to believe or help me to unbelieve? Who helps to believe? *Egomen.* Who to unbelieve? Other chap" (9:1078–80). The determinacy of either believing or unbelieving would be preferable to the limbo Stephen finds himself in. Others undermine his personal will and desire to believe, not only because their ideologies threaten to entrap him in constructs he has not made and cannot control, but also because their views demonstrate the lack of necessity of his own artifices. To stick fast to a belief, however—like the soldier in "Circe" who proclaims, "I'll wring the neck of any fucker says a word against my fucking king" (15:4597–98)—is more often than not either silly and simpleminded or violent and authoritarian because of its refusal to recognize the contingency of its assumptions and values. The weakness and shallowness of naiveté and the violence and rigidity of dogmatism are two sides of the same coin because both result from blindness to the contingency of what they believe.

As much as Joyce opposes absolutism that condemns as blasphemy any deviations from faith, he also mocks noncommittal pluralism that would evade the dilemmas and hard choices brought about by contingency. "All sides of life should be represented," says the quaker librarian to the disputants about *Hamlet,* and "He smiled on all sides equally" (9:505–6). Tolerance may be preferable to terrorism, but it can also be a mask for indifference. Recognizing that other "truths" may be as justifiable as one's own is a more insightful acceptance of the variability of beliefs and values than the blind intolerance of absolutism, but it can also be a way of dodging commitment—the need to choose between equally tenable but mutually exclusive "truths" on grounds that can never be entirely certain. One of Stephen's interlocutors, John Eglinton, says, "The truth is midway. . . . He is the ghost and the prince. He is all in all" (9:1018–19)—a counsel of moderation that earns him the mocking tag "John Eclecticon" (9:1070). Noncommittal eclecticism is a self-deceptive, unworkable attempt to escape the epistemological dilemmas of contingency. "Truth" is not some middle ground, nor is it attainable by syncretically combining "all sides." Rather, different "truths" that exclude one another compete for our undivided allegiance, and one must choose between them, which inevitably means sacrificing other possible views and setting oneself at odds with adherents of different beliefs.

Joyce is both attracted to and repelled by Stephen's radicalism: "with me all or not at all! *Non serviam!*" (15:4227–28). This refusal to compromise or to accept half measures is the opposite of the liberal imagination's tolerance of difference and appreciation of complexity. A disabling contradiction of Stephen's position, however, is that he is an absolutist in opposing absolutism. "You will not be master of others or their slave," he tells himself (3:295–96). Can his refusal of the alternatives of dominance or submission lead anywhere beyond the act of negation on which it is premised? Is there any possibility of affirmation that avoids dogmatism while nevertheless acknowledging that a commitment worth its name entails uncompromising demands? Stephen and Bloom share "an inherited tenacity of heterodox resistance," and they "professed their disbelief in many orthodox religious, national, social and ethical doctrines" (17:23–25). How does one translate this rejection of narrow dogmas in the name of "heterodoxy" into an affirmation that avoids the blindness and will to power of the orthodoxies whose hegemony they oppose? Resistance is as evasive of choice and commitment as tolerance and eclecticism can be. But is there any way of avoiding the dangers of an indifferent pluralism without falling into either fanaticism or paralyzed universal resistance?

Joyce responds to these questions by writing *Ulysses*, demonstrating their unanswerability by staging them as problems for the reader. On the one hand, this strategy is a rigorous, imaginative response to the epistemological and political dilemmas of a heterogeneous, fully contingent world. *Ulysses* enacts the constitutive contradictions of a neoliberal conception of democracy that has given up a consensus model of truth—a position that defines itself as accepting the coexistence of radically incommensurable standpoints, even as it is itself irreconcilably opposed to some positions (the varieties of dogmatism, absolutism, nihilism, indifferent tolerance, or syncretic eclecticism Joyce criticizes). This is a pluralism with a cutting edge that points out the need to make commitments one cannot perfectly justify while remaining always mindful of their lack of necessity. On the other hand, Joyce's strategy of dramatizing for others problems he cannot himself resolve may be perceived as evasive to the extent that he is trying to avoid being trapped in them by trapping the reader instead. If that is his game, then he risks the accusation that he is contradictorily refusing his own implication in dilemmas he dramatizes as inescapable.

This contradiction can be seen in the ambiguity of the novel's irony. The irony in *Ulysses* is often difficult to read, sometimes because of the inability of any position in a contingent world to justify itself absolutely, but sometimes because Joyce seems to seek through irony to evade responsibility for and involvement in the dilemmas he points out ironically. Frequently his irony seems like a way of getting beyond Stephen's paralysis by combining commitment with a recognition of the contingency of any set of beliefs. But just as often *Ulysses* seems to indulge the sort of paradoxical sleight-of-hand Stephen is expert in— playing games to ensnare others in impossible impasses as a desperate attempt to distance himself from them. The irony of *Ulysses* can be egalitarian and pragmatic, including us all as equals and attempting to give the reader useful tools for dealing with the dilemmas it dramatizes, but its irony can also seem superior and evasive, playing with the reader in order to escape impasses the text traps us in, and in the process claiming ascendancy through the ability to toy with us.

This duplicity is very difficult to pin down—indeed, evasiveness is its defining gesture. But what I am trying to suggest is like the distinct but sometimes hard to describe difference between a joke where the laugh is on everyone, teller included, and a joke where one knows from the manner of the telling that the teller is laughing at us and exempting himself. The comedy in *Ulysses* has elements of both. A good deal of the anger and resentment *Ulysses* has inspired over its history of reception results, I think, from its suggestion that it is different from you and me in its power to create meaning and its freedom from restrictions that limit us, even though it itself shows that it cannot be. Although Joyce criticizes Stephen's vanity and paralysis, he has seemed to some readers to share this young man's disdain for lesser mortals, his sense that his problems and his destiny must be special, not merely representative of the general human condition. But Joyce is not Stephen. He is also Bloom, and the democratic impulse in the text can be as attractive to readers as the aristocratic impulse can be alienating. Here too, however, Joyce is contradictory. He may share Bloom's sense of humanity, but he also seems superior to Bloom's foibles and mocks him more than would be strictly necessary in order to subject his values to an ironic criticism this character is not always capable of. Bloom is a democrat and a pragmatist who is not consistently aware of the contingency and contestability of the values he stands for, and part of the irony with which he is treated is an attempt to supply that awareness so as to protect and preserve his beliefs, but part of it seeks to rise above him—to achieve an apotheosis Bloom is mocked for aspiring to. And this contradiction, again, reflects Joyce's contradictory response to the challenges of contingency.

The irony with which the text treats some of Bloom's key pronouncements in "Cyclops," for example, is both a pragmatic instrument for dealing with contingency and a deceptive strategy for evading it. Here and elsewhere, Bloom is presented as a wise fool whose combination of silliness and profundity simultaneously mocks and affirms his philosophical comments and consequently makes it difficult to know what attitude to take toward them. The problem is not this undecidability as such but, rather, the ambiguity of whether it should be welcomed as a liberating provocation to the reader's reflection and creative play or suspected as a guise for the author's unremitting quest for ascendancy. In this chapter full of violent rancor, prejudice, and resentment, Bloom's criticism of the narrowness of nationalism seems a straightforward act of heroism: "Persecution, says he, all the history of the world is full of it. Perpetuating national hatred among nations" (12:1417–18). But then he trips over himself, in hilarious but very revealing fashion, when he tries to define a "nation":

—A nation? says Bloom. A nation is the same people living in the same place.

—By God, then, says Ned, laughing, if that's so I'm a nation for I'm living in the same place for the past five years.

So of course everyone had the laugh at Bloom and says he, trying to muck out of it:

—Or also living in different places.

—That covers my case, says Joe.

—What is your nation if I may ask? says the citizen.

—Ireland, says Bloom. I was born here. Ireland.

The citizen said nothing only cleared the spit out of his gullet and, gob, he spat a Red bank oyster out of him right in the corner. (12:1422–33)

Bloom's contradiction exposes the contingency of the category "nation" by revealing that it is not the fixed, determinate entity to which the citizen and the Nameless One have pinned their allegiances. A person's sense of national identity is both related to and independent of place because it is a narration that creates a self by telling a story of origins and affiliation. Nationality is therefore a variable cultural construct and not an essential, natural characteristic.[7]

Bloom's affirmation of his Irishness is misleading, however, not so much because it establishes identity by the link to place he has just questioned as because it suppresses the many other various aspects of his identity in asserting one side of himself. This simply reinforces the point, though, that national identity is a fiction. No story is ever the whole story, and Bloom both is and is not primarily Irish because his identity both is and is not tied to his geographical location. Bloom speaks truths about the contingencies of self-fashioning, then, truths that he himself might not recognize. By leaving readers to sort out for ourselves the wisdom in Bloom's bumbling self-contradictions, Joyce gives him more authority than "Mister Knowall" (12:838) would have if he were not mocked.

The evasion in this lesson in the pragmatics of national identity begins to become apparent, however, when one asks how one might use it. If national identity is not an essential attribute but a contingent construction, can that negative definition be translated into a positive affirmation of the self that does not fall back into the traps of reification and violence? Joyce both dramatizes and sidesteps this question. The citizen's violent refusal of Bloom's affirmation of identity—literally spitting it out in a dramatic gesture of rejection—

---

[7] See Anderson; Bhabha; and Said, *Culture* and *World*. G. J. Watson misses the wisdom in Bloom's fumbling by dismissing his definition of a nation as "humorously inadequate" (44).

suggests that, as a contingent fiction of affiliation, national identity depends as much on the Other's recognition as it does on one's stories about oneself. Until the narration is accepted, it is not finished. Because, as a narrative construct, identity is differential and figurative, it is based on acts of negation, and who is excluded from the community is as constitutive of it as who is included. The very contingency of communal identity makes it rest on violence and opposition. The persecution and scapegoating against which Bloom rightly protests enact this negation and attempt to naturalize it by depicting the Other as essentially and not just conventionally an outsider.

Joyce dramatizes this dilemma vividly, but his depiction begs a crucial question: Is this a problem irony can solve, or does it suggest the limits of irony as a response to contingency? Is Bloom's indirect, bumbling disclosure of the contingency of community and the constructedness of national identity usable knowledge? Or is the negation on which identity is based necessarily tied to the sort of exclusion that leads to the prejudice and violent hatred that fill the chapter? Joyce jokes about these matters at Bloom's and the citizen's expense but withdraws without answering them. That is his privilege—fictions don't have to resolve the problems they raise—but the difficulty is that the dilemma he is evading returns in his relation to his audience. Reading is characterized by dilemmas of affiliation and opposition similar to those dramatized in the text. Is some kind of reciprocity between reader and author possible without the scapegoating and exclusion "Cyclops" would have us reject? Or is the act of laughing with Joyce against the butt of his jokes premised on just this kind of negation of the Other? Is *Ulysses* aware that its comedy contains a violence not entirely dissimilar from the citizen's spitting? Appreciation may alternate with annoyance, to the extent that readers feel either that they can ally themselves with Joyce and other readers in a mutually enabling community that celebrates contingency (the community of Joyceans), or that they are excluded by a text and a circle of commentators who trade in secrets others are not privy to and who define themselves (whether intentionally or not) by their difference from ordinary readers.[8]

---

[8] Joyceans are a notoriously generous group who are very welcoming to newcomers ("as primal hordes go," reports Geert Lernout, "this must be one of the most open and democratic" [201]), but even this benign sense of identity, with its communal allegiances and shared practices (ritual observances of "Bloom Day" and the like), is exclusionary. Hence the resentments that are often expressed against the "Joyce industry." See Brannon for an interesting exploration of the "common reader's" relation to *Ulysses* and professional Joyceans. *Ulysses'* evasiveness and peculiarity suggest to readers that it is a hermetic text, and they are consequently ready to assume that experts in its mysteries belong to some sort of secret, exclusive society. That such resentments and suspicions persist against the overwhelming evidence of the inclusiveness of actual Joyceans

The contradiction between Joyce's pragmatic and evasive uses of irony is especially acute in Bloom's disquisition on love:

> —But it's no use, says he. Force, hatred, history, all that. That's not life for men and women, insult and hatred. And everybody knows that it's the very opposite of that that is really life.
>
> —What? says Alf.
>
> —Love, says Bloom. I mean the opposite of hatred. . . .
>
> —A new apostle to the gentiles, says the citizen. Universal love. (12:1481–89)

What is daring about this passage is how close Joyce comes, through Bloom, to a direct statement of value that borders on cliché. But Joyce skirts that danger in the sing-song parody that invokes the specter of banality in order to expel it:

> Love loves to love love. Nurse loves the new chemist. Constable 14A loves Mary Kelly. Gerty MacDowell loves the boy that has the bicycle. M.B. loves a fair gentleman. Li Chi Han lovey up kissy Cha Pu Chow. Jumbo, the elephant, loves Alice, the elephant. Old Mr Verschoyle with the ear trumpet loves old Mrs Verschoyle with the turnedin eye. The man in the brown macintosh loves a lady who is dead. His Majesty the King loves Her Majesty the Queen. Mrs Norman W. Tupper loves officer Taylor. You love a certain person. And this person loves that other person because everybody loves somebody but God loves everybody. (12:1493–1501)

The irony in this passage is harder to read than it might at first seem. Who is speaking here, and with what authority? It is not the chapter's nameless first-person narrator, whose sarcasm is more biting and less playful. The voice is more similar to the other digressive exercises in gigantism in the chapter, but the irony of most of those lists is relatively straightforward, mocking the citizen's delusions of patriotic grandeur by taking his exaggerations to extremes

---

suggests the depth and persistence of the role of exclusion and negation in identity formation. My point is that Joyce's text dramatizes this problem but does not escape it, although it tries to by adopting an ironic stance. As an example of this problem, note the contradiction between Bernard Benstock's claim that the concept "non-Joycean" has no "real function, since the purpose of the symposia has always been to bring others in from the 'outside,' thus diminishing the existence of the 'outside,' " and his description of how unique and valuable the 1984 Frankfurt symposium was because of the challenge "outsiders" posed to "insiders" (7–8). The contradiction whereby an "outsider" has his or her status marked precisely by the invitation designed to diminish the distance between "outside" and "inside" is also a theme of Derrida's "Ulysses Gramophone."

beyond even his pretensions. Here, however, the intention is harder to gauge because what the passage mocks is the sympathetic Bloom's pretensions to moral grandeur, not the citizen's bravado about Ireland. Does this list of love's loves mean to condemn love as a cliché or to rescue it through ironic indirection, affirming it by negating it?

That question reiterates a recurrent theme of the episode that love depends on negation for its meaning. The emptiness of the positive definition of what love loves suggests the perhaps surprising usefulness of Bloom's earlier description of love as "the opposite of hatred." As "not hatred," love is the negation of a negation. Does that implicate love in the opposition it opposes, however, or transform it, as a double negative, into something different, something positive? The contradictions entailed in love as an affirmative value constituted by negation recall Derrida's argument that "a certain narrativity is to be found at the simple core of the simplest *yes*. . . . *Yes* never comes alone, and we never say this word alone," if only because "*Yes* indicates that the Other is being addressed" ("Gramophone" 54, 63). Every simple affirmative is a diacritical structure that defines itself by what it is not and therefore implies the temporality of narrative articulation and deferral to unfold its sense. Love is similarly differential because it is always part of a structure of reciprocity, of appeal and reply to an Other. The repetitious sing–song dramatizes both kinds of differentiation through the game of substitution it plays with who loves whom. To tell what love is requires a chain of substitutions that enacts its story of relationship, and each part of the chain is itself a double structure with two partners in reciprocity.

Revealing ironically the differential contradictions of love is potentially useful knowledge. But the evasiveness of the passage becomes clearer when we press the pragmatic question further: Do the ironies here enable the reader to exercise love in full recognition of its arbitrariness and contingency as a structure of difference and repetition? Or does the repetition debunk any and all love by exposing how the structure of endless substitution inevitably trivializes a value that defines itself by the uniqueness of its object? If love is a differential structure of repetition, does that redefine love in a more usable way, or does it empty love of significance? Joyce plays with love in this passage, but it is unclear whether the results of the play are enabling to the reader or incapacitating, and the consequence of the ambiguity is that Joyce evades the issue and leaves us with it.

Joyce is the canniest of uncanny writers, however, and he suggests that, if his use of language is indeed deceptive and manipulative, the reason may be that all rhetoric is necessarily implicated in force, power, and duplicity, even (or most of all) when it explicitly opposes violence. In "Eumaeus" Bloom recalls his encounter with the citizen and, before going on to repeat his affirmation of love, makes a highly questionable point about rhetoric: "He called me a jew and in a heated fashion offensively. So I without deviating from plain facts in the least told him his God, I mean Christ, was a jew too and all his family like me though in reality I'm not. That was one for him. A soft answer turns away wrath. He hadn't a word to say for himself as everyone saw. Am I not right?" (16:1082–87). Well, no, he isn't. After all, the citizen threw a string of expletives after the fleeing Bloom and hurled a tinbox after him for good measure, doubly discrediting the cliché "a soft answer turns away wrath." It wasn't, and it didn't.

The aggressiveness of Bloom's rejoinder to the citizen is an admirable defense of his dignity, but it also ironically undercuts his opposition to force and violence by showing that even love's advocate must resort to them. This contradiction, however, recalls Bloom's earlier argument in "Cyclops" about the futility of trying to stop violence with violence: "isn't discipline the same everywhere. I mean wouldn't it be the same here if you put force against force?" (12:1360–61). The verbal and physical violence with which the chapter ends demonstrates the truth of this statement, even though Bloom has by then apparently forgotten it. Even a "soft answer" cannot defuse "wrath" because the rhetorical attempt to move others or to defeat antagonistic views replicates the structure that pits force against force. It is therefore implicated in the battle for power in the very act of opposing it. The rhetoric of gigantism in "Cyclops," for example, mocks the excesses of the citizen's patriotic language, but only through forceful language that takes the power of rhetoric to comic extremes. By using force against force to oppose the violence of exaggerated, prejudicial claims, Joyce's rhetoric anticipates Bloom's similar contradiction at the end. Joyce thereby acknowledges his own full implication in the problems he dramatizes. Although it is not at all clear that ironic self-criticism of the will to power of rhetoric is sufficient to defuse its use of force, the self-undercutting rhetoric of exaggeration in "Cyclops" shows that the self-contradictions of language allow no uncompromised position, no place to speak for love or any other value without engaging in a battle for power.

In depicting Bloom's apotheosis at the end of "Cyclops" and again more extensively in "Circe," Joyce not only invokes and mocks his own desire for godlike ascendancy but also reveals the will to power in even the most selfless, benign affirmations. "And they beheld Him even Him, ben Bloom Elijah, amid clouds of angels ascend to the glory of the brightness at an angle of fortyfive degrees over Donohoe's in Little Green street like a shot off a shovel" (12:1915–18). Bloom's ascension comically and aeronautically parallels the propulsive action of the citizen's violent throw as a way of dramatizing that the claim of "ben Bloom Elijah" to the status of a redeemer with a saving message of grace is directly related to a violent meeting of force with force. Similarly in "Circe" the mocking elevation of Bloom into an all-wise prophet, savior, and king suggests that the only apotheosis possible in a world of relative values is one that undercuts itself through the excessiveness of its claims:

> My beloved subjects, a new era is about to dawn. I, Bloom, tell you verily it is even now at hand. Yea, on the word of a Bloom, ye shall ere long enter into the golden city which is to be, the new Bloomusalem in the Nova Hibernia of the future. . . . I stand for the reform of municipal morals and the plain ten commandments. New worlds for old. Union of all, jew, moslem and gentile. . . . General amnesty, weekly carnival with masked licence, bonuses for all, esperanto the universal language with universal brotherhood. No more patriotism of barspongers and dropsical imposters. Free money, free rent, free love and a free lay church in a free lay state. (15:1542–45, 1685–93)

Bloom's apotheosis simultaneously asserts and mocks his vision of universal reconciliation and unrestricted freedom. It is part of a narrative structure of repeated elevations and deflations, rises and falls in Bloom's fortune, which occur throughout *Ulysses* but reach a feverish intensity in the rapid transformations of "Circe," where "from the sublime to the ridiculous is but a step" (15:2401–2). Elijah himself asks: "Are you a god or a doggone clod?" (15:2194), and indeed after Bloom is called "Emmanuel," a "Deadhand" writes on the wall: "Bloom is a cod" (15:1869–71). Both the ludicrousness of his ascendancy and his rapid alternations between "god" and "cod" undercut Bloom's seemingly harmless vision by depicting its triumph in absurd terms. If we are looking for a place to stand, Bloom's beliefs turn out to be just as vulnerable and precarious as Stephen's unbelief.

Nevertheless, although ridiculed, Bloom's utopia is not entirely discredited. Bloom's mock apotheoses are a way of invoking his values without being held responsible for them, debunking them without rejecting them altogether. If Bloom's ascendancy seems silly, it is not because his values are wrong or pernicious but because his vision seems naive and inflated. His pretensions as a reformer who would change the world are vain and betray a will to power contrary to the generosity of his vision, but that contradiction challenges his status as prophet without fatally damning the values of reconciliation and emancipation he preaches. Bloom's beliefs are mocked when his utopia is held up for ridicule, but they also survive the attack. In the light of these reversals, humanistic interpretations of Bloom as the novel's heroic figure of community and care appear overly simplistic, but so too do claims that the book has no beliefs or values, inasmuch as some endorsement of Bloom is implied in imagining his ascendancy even as it is taken away. In the mocking apotheoses, Joyce simultaneously affirms and refuses to commit himself to Bloom's beliefs and desires.[9]

One reason for this contradictory strategy is that Joyce is wary not only of the will to power of any particular set of beliefs but also of the tyranny and violence of consensus. Bloom's ascension is accompanied by popular acclaim for his views: *"Bloom explains to those near him his schemes for social regeneration. All agree with him"* (15:1702–3; original italics). This unity of opinion would seem to be the free granting of consent that immobilizes power by letting no force operate other than the force of the better argument. Bloom's wisdom prevails with no compulsion other than the intrinsic appeal of its own reasons and aspirations. But this consensus almost immediately disintegrates into dissent and discord—protests that suggest that even seemingly freely given agreement can constitute an oppressive regime. Only a few pages later the mob shouts: "Lynch him! Roast him! He's as bad as Parnell was" (15:1761–62). This reversal from harmonious consent to collective protest and opposition suggests that agreement is tainted by domination and coercion because it stifles difference. Bloom's vision of "union for all" clashes with his endorsement of absolute liberty—"weekly carnival with masked license," all varieties of freedom "in a free lay state"—because consensus suppresses the difference that emancipation asserts. Linguistic differences make possible strife and opposition (elsewhere Bloom reflects that there were "more languages to start with than were absolutely necessary" [16:352–53])—hence the political appeal to him of Esperanto as the linguistic correlative to his dream of social unity—but the multiplicity of languages is also a sign of freedom and possibility that consensus and community, even willingly assented to, may threaten. *Ulysses*, after all, could not be written in Esperanto.

---

[9] According to Lionel Trilling, for example, "the sweet disposition of Leopold Bloom's mind to imagine the possibility of rational and benevolent social behavior and the brotherhood of man . . . makes *Ulysses* unique among modern classics for its sympathy with progressive social ideas" (158). Similarly oblivious to the elusive complications of Joyce's irony here, Dominic Manganiello also finds in *Ulysses* an unqualified endorsement of Bloom's "vision of a classless, humanitarian, pacifist and cooperative society, devoid of all forms of hatred and sentimentality" (113). By contrast, Stuart Gilbert claims that Joyce "has no philosophical axe to grind" (39), and E. R. Curtius finds that "a metaphysical nihilism is the substance of Joyce's work" (quoted in Gilbert 226). Richard Ellmann claims that in this scene "Joyce is here exaggerating to the point of absurdity Bloom's kindness and good-hearted civic feeling" to distance himself from the naiveté of his hero's socialist program while accepting its core moral values (85–86). The difference of opinion among these and other readers over whether Joyce is a humanist or a nihilist suggests that his contradictions are more complex than this, however, and that his beliefs are more difficult to pin down—and strategically so, I would argue, inasmuch as he is trying to make and evade a commitment at the same time.

Truth is rhetorical in Joyce's view because knowing harbors a will to power over others who ratify one's beliefs by accepting them. This is why any set of commitments risks becoming tyrannical when it acquires adherents and achieves consensus. The problem, however, is that in a world of contingent values there is no better proof of the validity of a position than its ability to win assent. Joyce responds to this dilemma, once again, with a contradictory strategy. By deploying rhetorics that seek the assent of others, even as he depicts multiple contesting rhetorics, Joyce demonstrates that any commitment is a particular, partial perspective based on beliefs that are no stronger than the allegiance they inspire. But at the same time he denaturalizes and demystifies those allegiances by demonstrating their arbitrariness—others are equally defensible—thus criticizing their exclusive claims to authority and power.

Here as previously, Joyce dramatizes the contingency of any commitment even as he evades contingency by refusing to make a commitment. Stephen Heath describes Joyce's writing as "pastiche" rather than "parody"—"a copying that fixes no point of irony between model and imitation, that rests, in this respect, in a hesitation of meaning" (42). As "pastiche," Joyce's writing demonstrates the multiplicity of possible beliefs without stabilizing his own perspective the way "parody" does. But the "hesitation of meaning" that results is ambiguous, both a statement about contingency and an evasion of its consequences. He uses his privileges and powers as an author to point out epistemological dilemmas that should make any commitment wary of its tendency to rigidify, naturalize, and overreach itself. But "hesitating to mean" is a way of meaning that refuses the commitment to a perspective, which is a prerequisite for meaning. Constructing a "pastiche" is a signifying act that does not signify and a refusal to signify that signifies, and this contradiction is both a testimony to the intractable paradoxes of contingency and an attempt to transcend them. What Joyce believes is unreadable, both because he has an egalitarian respect for the viability of incommensurable perspectives and because he will not allow himself to be limited to any particular, contingent view, even though he shows such restriction to be our fate.

Joyce's hubris in seeking to exempt himself from paradoxes he shows to be inescapable differs from the respect for and sense of equality with the reader that characterize Conrad's irony even at its most savage or Forster's "double turns" even at their most subversive. Conrad's skepticism is ultimately generous because he assumes that the same limitations and contradictions affect both himself and his readers even as he tacitly wishes us well, in our different circumstances, in resolving problems that he cannot see past. Forster's resolute humility in defending democracy against the bullying stridency of absolutism is similarly based on a recognition of common cause with the reader, whose perspective, like Forster's own (even in his belief in the values of democracy), is necessarily partial, incomplete, and contestable. Conrad and Forster exercise power by playing games with the reader, but they do so in ways that acknowledge their own entanglement in the dilemmas they seek to implicate us in, and this recognition of a shared vulnerability about which they are trying to educate us establishes a fundamental reciprocity and equality as the basis of the narrative bond between writer and reader. This modest recognition of shared constraints and limitations is missing in Joyce's pride of authorship and his refusal to abandon the dream of apotheosis. For better or worse (and it can be both), he is bolder, more radical, and more defiant than they are in his confrontation with the contradictions of contingency.

To return to a point I made earlier, what I am trying to suggest is a distinction much like the subtle but undeniable difference between generous humor where the jokester is laughing with us and comedy that prompts resistance and protest because it masks a will to power that uses us for its own purposes. Joyce's humor is difficult to describe because it has elements of both. There is indeed a powerful emancipatory dimension to *Ulysses* because the games Joyce plays with the reader open up new possibilities of play for us as well. He is not just toying with us but, rather, makes it possible for us to acquire new powers of expression, interpretation, and criticism if we rise to the many challenges of his infinitely playful text. Nevertheless, his unwillingness to give up the quest for apotheosis contradicts this emancipatory dynamic by using the reader for Joyce's own ends (his transcendent triumph as the master gamesman) in the very kind of exclusionary one-upsmanship his text criticizes. Readers have had divergent responses to *Ulysses* depending on whether they have felt more strongly the emancipatory egalitarianism or the defiant drive for apotheosis that together define Joyce's contradictory project. The most that can be said in Joyce's defense—and it is not insignificant—is that the games he plays with us provide us with the critical tools to question and resist his prideful assertion of power.

Style, Authority, and the Problem of Justice

Jacques Derrida tells a wonderful story about overhearing an American tourist in a Tokyo bookstore proclaim: "So many books! What is the definitive one? Is there any?"—to which Derrida "almost replied, 'Yes, there are two of them, *Ulysses* and *Finnegans Wake*,' but I kept this *yes* to myself and smiled inanely like someone who does not understand the language" ("Gramophone" 35). This anecdote captures many of the contradictions of authority, justice, and the will to power of language in Joyce. If his books can claim definitive status, that is due in no small measure to all they reveal about the workings of knowledge and style, but in the process they refute the unequivocal authority of any single perspective that the tourist desiring reliable orientation seeks. By multiplying styles and juxtaposing their competing claims to truth, Joyce invokes and questions the assertion of privilege that language games have in common with Molly's suitors: "each one who enters imagines himself to be the first to enter whereas he is always the last term of a preceding series even if the first term of a succeeding one, each imagining himself to be the first, last, only and alone whereas he is neither first nor last nor only nor alone in a series originating in and repeated to infinity" (17:2127–31). *Ulysses* demonstrates that any assertion of uniqueness and priority masks serial participation in an endless chain of claims to originality, each of which contests the others by demonstrating their equivalence as substitutes. In this regard one of the nicest points about Derrida's story is that there are *two* "definitive books," so that the question he would answer is left open: Which of Joyce's two authoritative texts is indeed the authoritative one?

This anecdote epitomizes Joyce's contradictory strategy of acquiring authority by contesting it. Poststructuralist versions of Joyce that attribute to him an antiauthoritarian, antihierarchical attitude toward the knowledge claims of different languages capture only one side of this strategy. According to Patrick McGee, for example, the multiplication of styles in *Ulysses* produces a profoundly egalitarian text that "never values one style over another or says that one developed necessarily out of another"; and the privileges of the author are similarly questioned: "Joyce's writing suggests that an author cannot dominate language or its effects, through his will to power or the authority of a personal style. The author is constituted as author by words, which he can direct but never completely master" (*Paperspace* 71, 113). The contradiction that this perceptive observation misses is that, by deploying a carnival of styles to deny the priority of any language, Joyce asserts his own authority as a master of discourse. His example shows that making the antiauthoritarian move is one of the most powerful strategies for asserting authority. By creating and manipulating a panoply of styles that challenges the authority of any one language, Joyce demonstrates his incomparable powers as a stylist and epistemologist who not only knows how to use diverse rhetorics but who also knows their limits, and in so doing rises above them.

These contradictions in Joyce's relation to authority and language enact important contradictions about justice. In an insightful and provocative book, James McMichael denies that Joyce has any will to dominate others or assert superiority: "Joyce's case with me is that he wants justice for all," and "the last thing Joyce wanted was to be mistaken for an intelligence which . . . is above justice" (24, 22).[10] McMichael consequently identifies a figure he calls "Jamesy," who functions much like David Hayman's "Arranger" (see 88–104), as the indifferent, omniscient, sometimes imperious stylist whose injustice and will to power Joyce parodies. This attempt to separate out part of the text that seeks power and ascendancy in order to assert that *Ulysses* as a whole is unequivocally for justice suggests, however, that Joyce is not as straightforward and univocal as he seems in McMichael's depiction of him as an egalitarian defender of everyone's right to put forward claims.

Joyce and justice are both more contradictory than McMichael suggests. If no standards of right and wrong can claim absolute authority, then justice does not exist determinately or univocally but is always subject to contestation and renegotiation. According to McMichael, "*Ulysses* urges that every case be heard and responded to justly: beyond that, it advances no program for identifying injustice, nor could it be for justice if it did" (203n). What counts as "injustice" gets decided, as McMichael rightly argues, by parties making claims on one another. But those assertions typically have the force of uncompromising demands: "Do me justice—listen to my claim!" Precisely because no fixed, unequivocal norm for "justice" exists, then, it gets defined as a contingent value through the making and contesting of absolute, unequivocal assertions of entitlement.[11]

Ulysses dramatizes this process by setting against one another the uncompromising demands of different languages, each of which asks that we recognize the legitimacy of its perspective; but *Ulysses* itself cannot be above the process it describes, as it would be if "Jamesy" were not Joyce. To separate Joyce who wants justice for all from "Jamesy" who wants it for himself would not save Joyce as a defender of justice but, rather, put him outside the process through which the value of justice gets decided. The author of *Ulysses* makes unequivocal demands on us to do him justice and to recognize his authority for the very reason that, as his text demonstrates, all claims for justice—including his—are contingent and contestable, and the only way he can call for

[10] McMichael acknowledges the influence of Emmanuel Levinas, whose view of justice as a variable, contestable category having to do with one's responsibility to hear and respond to the claims of others is fundamentally similar to the thinking about "injustice" in the neoliberal tradition that has informed my argument (see McMichael 197–98). By contrast, the Lacanian arguments developed with great dexterity and complexity by Joseph Valente see "justice" not as a question of intersubjective negotiation but as a defining dimension of the psychological and linguistic order. As will become apparent, I think McMichael is insufficiently attuned to the ambiguities of such negotiations and consequently portrays "justice" as more univocal than Joyce (or Levinas, in my view) suggests.

[11] For further explorations of the necessary contradictions of "justice" as a contingent, contestable value, see the chapter "The Sense of Injustice" in Shklar, *Injustice.*

justice in such a world is by making demands that may seem imperious because they are total and exclusive.

Once again Joyce's appreciation of the contingency of language goes hand in hand with the absoluteness of his assertion of power. If he wants justice from us, as McMichael rightly says he does, that too must be an uncompromising demand. Otherwise Joyce won't receive the hearing he feels he is entitled to. If anyone is going to relativize that claim, it is not going to be Joyce; it has to be us, as readers, who set his demand for recognition and entitlement over against other claims we hear. But reading Joyce's text gives us good lessons about how to do that and shows why it is necessary not to take any claim to authority (even his) at face value.

These contradictions can be seen in the ambiguous attitude toward language of the "Oxen of the Sun" chapter, the locus classicus of Joyce's experiments with style. The chapter makes a powerfully egalitarian and emancipatory gesture by putting all of the prose styles in the history of the English language on the same plane and thereby demonstrating that none is inherently privileged. All are potentially available resources for new expression and exploration. Despite the chapter's setting in a maternity hospital and its many references to childbirth, Joyce's juxtaposition of styles shows that language is not like a fetus whose different phases are transitional stages in a progress toward a final maturity. As is also often the case with the notorious Homeric parallels, the allusion operates ironically, with the discrepancies more significant than the similarities. The various styles of "Oxen of the Sun" suggest that the history of a language is not a hierarchical sequence of stages in a teleological development but a series of equal but different language games.

By dramatizing the relativity of language games, Joyce doubly challenges the power that any set of codes exercises over its users. First, those powers are not as absolute as they may seem to those within the boundaries of a language because the existence of other codes, fully equal in their authority and similarly restrictive in their effects, contests the hegemony of any particular code. Second, the ability to make new meanings out of old materials—like antiquated, superseded prose styles—suggests the emancipatory capacity of linguistic play. Although the users of any particular language may be confined within its historically specific limits, its horizons are unstable inasmuch as codes change. As linguistic beings whose perceptions are shaped and limited by the codes available to us, we may be trapped in contingent cultural modes of saying and seeing; but language changes for the very reason that those codes are artificial constructs, and this means in turn that innovation is always possible by doing what Joyce does on a grand scale in this chapter—by reworking existing conventions in unprecedented ways.

Pragmatically considered, though, is this experiment emancipatory or evasive? Can others benefit from Joyce's example here, or is it a vain act of self-display? The answer, once again, is "Both." "Oxen of the Sun" does not offer itself as a model for others to copy. Now that Joyce has done it, emulating the history of English prose styles is not something most readers would probably want to do. It is a strategy he exhausts as he uses it. On the one hand, Joyce thereby avoids making hegemonic demands on the reader—he does not want to act as a model who, in being copied, becomes an authority like the languages whose hegemony he invokes and contests.[12] On the other hand, the peculiar, nonrepeatable quality of the experiment suggests its vanity and presumption. Oddly, although playful and emancipatory, it is a closed option, a dead end. "Oxen of the Sun" is both an insightful demonstration of the epistemological relativity and contingency of language games and a self-aggrandizing display of powers no one can emulate. Joyce claims the transcendent status of being beyond imitation by copying everyone else but refusing to allow himself to be copied in return. His linguistic play is simultaneously an egalitarian, emancipatory denial of the priority of models over our capacity for semantic innovation and an egotistical assertion of powers that are so great that they cannot be imitated.

Ulysses is a particularly useful and interesting book because it exhibits more than its author's private aspirations for ascendancy. It counteracts such assertions of privilege with guidance about how to do justice to others in a world of competing values with no fixed norms. The first step is to show respect and concern for other forms of life with incommensurable beliefs and to recognize their potential vitality and validity. The most radical "Other" to Joyce's limitless drive for linguistic innovation is perhaps the cliché-ridden discourse of "Eumaeus" and "Nausicaa." What is remarkable about both chapters is that, although Joyce, like Flaubert, treats stock, stereotyped language with great irony, his criticism is unmixed with contempt. Because no position for making meaning exists outside of conventions, Joyce suggests that being conventional is not a fault. To rule other conventions inadmissible in advance without giving them a hearing is, rather, an act of tyranny and terror. Such listening requires imagining that interesting games might be playable within rules or with materials that might seem exhausted.

---

[12] Stephen Heath makes a related point: "It is impossible to parody Joyce. . . . Where is Joyce's style? in which of the sections of *Ulysses?* . . . In place of style we have *plagiarism*" (33). Because his style consists of copying others, it cannot be copied in turn. Paradoxically, then, although he is a plagiarist, he is profoundly original—not in spite of copying others, but through the very act of imitation.

In "Eumaeus," typically regarded as a tired chapter appropriate to the lateness of the hour, language falls into repeated clichés, and even the sentiments can seem lazy. Remarkably, however, the clichés still manage to convey meaning—even new, distinctive meaning worth attending to with more energy than Bloom or Stephen can muster at this point. The following typical passage suggests the peculiar combination of stock phrases and semantic creation that saves the chapter from being devoid of meaning:

> —Of course, Mr. B. proceeded to stipulate, you must look at both sides of the question. It is hard to lay down any hard and fast rules as to right and wrong but room for improvement all round there certainly is though every country, they say, our own distressful included, has the government it deserves. But with a little goodwill all round. It's all very fine to boast of mutual superiority but what about mutual equality. I resent violence and intolerance in any shape or form. It never reaches anything or stops anything. A revolution must come on the due instalments plan. It's a patent absurdity on the face of it to hate people because they live round the corner and speak another vernacular, in the next house so to speak. (16:1094–1103)

Highlighting all of the clichés in this passage would leave very little unmarked, and its guiding sentiment of "love your neighbor" seems trite as well. The validity of Bloom's appeal for "mutual equality" beyond violence is still visible, however, through the dead language in which it is enunciated. In ways Bloom may not fully understand, his history suggests the need for creating conditions of mutual respect and concern to replace the scapegoating and demonization that threaten in a culturally heterogeneous world where people in "the next house" may "speak another vernacular." The nontrivial implication of Bloom's sermon is that we should not dismiss in advance the claims on us of another language simply because it seems nonsensical or repulsive—an insight we would miss if, with the violence and intolerance he warns against, we rejected his perspective out of hand because we are repelled by the stock phrases he uses.

Joyce's original use of unoriginal language here is testimony to his egalitarian respect for the capacities of world-making of seemingly marginal, unexalted, discarded linguistic materials. Margot Norris oversimplifies the two-sidedness of Joyce's attitude toward the clichés of everyday speech when she identifies his position with Heidegger's condemnation of *Gerede* (idle talk) as inauthentic, fallen language (81; see *Being and Time* 211–14). Precisely because Joyce doubts that any language in this finite, contingent world can be truly authentic, he suggests that unoriginal conventions that repeat previous speech acts are our only resource for making new meaning—and that there is no reason to believe that any newly created language (like the stylistic games the late Heidegger plays to let Being speak) will be any more authentic than the conventions it replaces. Hence Joyce's refusal to allow his linguistic innovations to develop into a style others might emulate in the belief it has an authority other languages lack. In this respect he is more like Derrida than Heidegger. The plethora of clichés in "Eumaeus" asks us to recognize that, in a world where only copies exist, entropic exhaustion of the power to mean by the repetition of semantic structures is a risk built into the very structure of signification. The chapter encourages the reader to enact Bloom's call for justice by taking stock language seriously. In deciphering Bloom's message by separating its wisdom from its triviality, we stage his ethic of "mutual equality" by granting respect to a perspective we might at first dismiss.

"Nausicaa" conveys a similar lesson in the nonreified recognition of another world by asking the reader not only to acknowledge the integrity of meanings coded in clichés but also to see beyond them to the uniqueness of a personal experience that transcends the stereotypes that offer our only access to it. Gerty MacDowell both is and is not defined by the language of romantic novels and women's magazines in which her perspective is rendered. By copying their stock phrases and conventional categories, Joyce allows her own memorable world to emerge. Gerty, an Irish adolescent Madame Bovary, resembles Emma in that her very typicality—her identification with the romantic clichés of her discourse—paradoxically grants her a distinctive identity. But we also imagine Gerty as not reducible to her discourse, in part because of the distancing effect of the persistent, intrusive narrative voice in her section of the chapter, a voice that affirms her perspective in an annoying way: "But who was Gerty? . . . as fair a specimen of winsome Irish girlhood as one could wish to see" (13:78, 80–81). Even before her limp is revealed and the chapter switches to Bloom's point of view, there is ample evidence that the narrator's categories are not all there is to Gerty. The cloying inadequacy of the narrator's stereotypes, which both constitute Gerty's experience and fail to encompass it, has the effect of distancing Gerty from the language with which she is identified.

We recognize Gerty's uniqueness both by discounting the mediating materials through which it is rendered and by acknowledging that they are its very substance. One effect of this contradiction is to criticize but at the same time to recuperate the discourse of sentimentality against which other high modern writers rebelled. Joyce's depiction of Gerty's linguistic self-fashioning confirms that sentimental discourse is gendered feminine but denies that it is any less legitimate or semantically powerful for that, and he thereby questions the superiority of the modernist discourse of impersonality and detachment (typically considered masculine) with which, thanks to T. S. Eliot, he is often associated.[13] Like all language in a world of endless copying and repetition, the discourse of sentimental magazines and romance novels is necessarily inadequate to the particular limitations, annoyances, hopes, rivalries, and desires of Gerty's world, but it is the only language available to her, and the doubleness with which it both expresses and fails to capture her identity is a commentary on the general dilemma faced by all language users of creating original meanings with borrowed, conventional materials. Joyce thereby demonstrates the equality of sentimental discourse with other modes of language that might claim superiority, even as he calls for suspicion about the discrepancy between what it says and what it means, not because this difference is peculiar to sentimentality but because it is a general feature of language.

"Nausicaa" consequently requires a doubled mode of attention from the reader. The likely readers of "Nausicaa" (my "we"), schooled to suspect trite language, at first invoke the authority of a position beyond sentimentality only to question the superiority of its skepticism as they recognize the equal authenticity of a sentimental world. This doubling sets in motion a to-and-fro between incommensurable worlds that reveals a hitherto unsuspected potential for interaction between perspectives. Boundaries of class, intellectual background, interpretive orientation, and (for some readers) gender are crossed as the reader's skepticism of emotion-laden clichés enters into a dialogue with the language of sentimentality. What results is not a merger of Gerty's horizons and our own but an experience in nonconsensual reciprocity. We are never asked to agree with Gerty's perspective despite the respect and recognition we accord her, but the unexpected capacities of sentimental discourse to generate a meaningful world may question the smug self-sufficiency of skeptical sophistication, and the resulting back-and-forth creates conditions of exchange on the assumption of "mutual equality" instead of "mutual superiority."

By asking us to credit Gerty's perspective without merging with it or forgetting its distance from our world, Joyce models the doubling that recognizing another's world entails. An oscillation between detachment and involvement is inherent in doing others justice because we can hear their claims only from our own position, which is necessarily not theirs. Hearing a

[13] Suzanne Clark and Marianne DeKoven discuss the sexual politics of modernism. David Hayman misses these complications when he dismisses Gerty's sense of self as "a figment of the male imagination, even in her own eyes" (99). By contrast, see Gibson's wonderfully detailed exposition of Joyce's use of popular magazines to construct Gerty's perspective: "Joyce was clearly aware of the imperial, English discursive formation in the women's magazines, and treated it critically. But he also recognized that the magazines were an important and even enabling feature of Gerty's development as a young Irishwoman at the turn of the century. . . . The laughter in the chapter is not principally at the expense of a supposedly pathetic, dim-witted Gerty" (145, 146).

plea for justice entails construing the assumptions and interests motivating it through interpretive acts premised on our own perhaps very different presuppositions and values (a clash at this deep level of commitment and perspective makes conflicts about justice particularly difficult to resolve). Doing justice to the claims of another perspective requires us to be both inside and outside of it in that we must interpret its demands by employing categories and values whose authority is contested by the otherness they seek to make sense of. By simultaneously criticizing and recuperating the legitimacy of sentimental discourse in his portrait of Gerty, Joyce sets in motion a mutual critique of the assumptions and interpretive practices we might use to judge her and the assumptions and interpretive practices through which she understands the world, and this back-and-forth movement demonstrates the doubleness of doing another justice.

A similar doubleness characterizes the process of reading the "Penelope" chapter. Like "Nausicaa," this chapter can be seen as an attempt by a male author to do justice to feminine discourse. Its fluidity, plurality, and openness have been judged so successful in enacting the preoedipal rhythms of feminine desire that some feminist critics have elevated it into an exemplar of antipatriarchal writing.[14] It would be wrong, however, to privilege Molly's discourse as an authentic language. For one thing, it is neither purely fluid (it could not be and still make sense) nor unique as a subversive discourse of disorder. Although the punctuation and paragraph structure of the chapter are unusually sparse, Molly's actual syntax can be sorted out into coherent sentences most

[14] See Hélène Cixous's famous claim in "The Laugh of the Medusa" that Molly's monologue "carr[ies] *Ulysses* off beyond any book and toward the new writing," which she characterizes as an unpredictable, subversive language of presence and plenitude: "It will always surpass the discourse that regulates the phallocentric system; it does and will take place in areas other than those subordinated to philosophico-theoretical domination. It will be conceived of only by subjects who are breakers of automatisms, by peripheral figures that no authority can ever subjugate" (314, 313). It is hard not to think that she has Molly in mind as she writes this. Also see Cixous, "Joyce: The (R)use of Writing." Suzette Henke echoes Cixous in calling Molly's "sinuous prose-poetry" a "linguistic paradigm of *écriture féminine*" and in connecting it with Kristeva's notion of the "semiotic": "a threatening and subversive discourse associated with pre-Oedipal attachment to the body, voice, and pulsions of an imaginary maternal figure," "a subversive feminine discourse that defies logocentric boundaries," "an epic articulation of the repressed female story embedded in a male master-narrative" (127, 161, 139). Henke's interpretation of Molly's narcissism is insightfully contradictory, however, inasmuch as she sees it not only as subversive of phallic domination but also as symptomatic of Molly's lasting sense of deprivation because of her childhood abandonment by her mother: "Searching for the patriarchal signifier that will heal the gap of maternal absence, Molly reverts to a pre-Oedipal model of emotional satisfaction in her conjugal relationship with Leopold Bloom" (132). Molly's narcissism is thus both a personal symptom and a subversion of gender hierarchies and is therefore both lamentable and laudable. See Attridge, "Molly's Flow."

of the time, and restoring the missing punctuation would with a few exceptions be easy to do. Her discourse has the feel of fluidity but is still structured, then, and this paradox suggests that it is a way of figuring the world, with its own peculiar combination of organization and mutability, pattern and openness to variation. There are other, differently figured kinds of incoherence in *Ulysses:* the gibberish at the end of "Oxen in the Sun," the solipsistic confusions of "Proteus," the exhausted ramblings of "Eumaeus," and so on. These many forms of disorder in Joyce's text suggest both that fluidity is not a fundamental, invariable essence and that no particular mode of incoherence can claim authenticity. Its (always only relative) lack of hierarchy and structure is not a priori grounds for entitlement. As a kind of language, Molly's discourse makes particular claims that contest the rights of other discourses (like her husband's), and the problem the chapter poses for the reader is not how to rank other claims against the norm of authenticity provided, at last, by her language but how to adjudicate contesting claims in a world without norms, where even a language that might seem the bedrock of discourse turns out to be contingent.

These linguistic complications suggest that gender is not an essence but, rather, an arena of differences and contingent categories in which justice is contested. Replacing patriarchal with matriarchal values is not the solution to the problem of justice because how to understand gender is a problem for justice. Molly suggests as much by invoking and questioning the authority of women as rulers: "itd be much better for the world to be governed by the women in it you wouldnt see women going and killing one another and slaughtering when do you ever see women rolling around drunk like they do or gambling every penny they have and losing it on horses" (18:1434–38). In the next breath, however, she takes this away: "its [always] some woman ready to stick her knife in you I hate that in women no wonder they treat us the way they do we are a dreadful lot of bitches" (18:1457–59). The authority of women as dispensers of justice is no more privileged than that of men. Women are not inherently figures of community, nurture, and peace any more than men are essentially combative, competitive, and violent (indeed, both Molly and Bloom can be all of these). Instead, the meanings of "feminine" and "masculine" are unstable and open to dispute, as are all contingent categories in a world where justice is established not by fixed norms but by negotiation.

The doubleness of the back-and-forth in such debates is suggested by Molly's ambiguous pronoun references. The bewildering experience of trying to figure out who Molly means by "he" and keeping track of her shifting references as one "he" merges into another not only dramatizes her promiscuity; it also recreates the doubled sense of being inside and outside of her world, a doubleness that is integral to doing justice to others. Dorrit Cohn comments suggestively about how Molly's pronouns render an effect of alternating solipsism and intersubjectivity: "Even as Joyce creates [an] impression of cryptic privacy he plants just enough signposts to guard against total incomprehensibility" (229). The impression of private self-communion conveyed by the unclarified pronoun references gives us a powerful sense of intimacy with Molly, but their mystery simultaneously reminds us of our distance from her. The opacity of different worlds that this confusion dramatizes prevents simple sympathetic identification of one world with another from providing an adequate answer to the question of how to recognize another's claims. The difference between my world and another's creates the possibility of a to-and-fro between perspectives even as it necessitates such exchange to ward off solipsism and mediate conflicts. This opacity may prevent another's claims for justice from ever coinciding completely with mine, however, and that difference can make justice an elusive, unstable value that defies any final consensus.

It is not clear where justice lies as *Ulysses* ends. When the novel closes, Molly and Bloom have claims on each other that are mutually exclusive and still open to negotiation. That need for further exchange is represented by Bloom's much-discussed request that Molly make him breakfast and her bemused uncertainty over what to make of this unprecedented demand. Critics cannot decide what Bloom's request portends because his demand and the uncertainty of Molly's response figure the sort of open-ended negotiation through which rights and claims get recognized or refused.[15] By forestalling a decision at the end about who is in the right and instead dramatizing an ongoing process of adjudication, the novel suggests that justice is never finally delivered but ever deferred, as it must be if it is not a fixed norm but a necessarily unstable process of call and response between different forms of life. Molly's claim for justice is no more privileged than Bloom's, and vice versa. Similarly, Joyce's claim on us is no more privileged than either of theirs. By ending *Ulysses* with a powerful, demanding voice whose sense of entitlement is both legitimate and highly questionable, and by having Bloom counter with a demand that this voice has not yet decided how to answer, Joyce models the problem of justice as a conundrum that his novel cannot resolve but only stage. In the process, he asks us to do justice to his own demand for recognition even as we rightly question and resist its will to power.

[15] McMichael's notion of justice can be unfortunately rigid and monolithic, as when he labels Bloom guilty of injustice for not meeting his wife's sexual demands (see 21). But it is equally unjust to regard Molly as a complaining, vulgar narcissist, which is the image of her offered by many traditional male critics. Neither view sees Bloom and Molly as partners in a negotiation about claims that, necessarily, are partial and one-sided and open to dispute.

Reading and the Politics of Modernism

The conventional wisdom once held that the novel lost its political conscience in the early twentieth century when, turning inward, it became more concerned with psychological exploration and formal experimentation than with representing the manners, morals, and conflicts of the contemporary social scene.[16] From Balzac to Proust, it was thought, the novel shifted from representing the relation between individual and society to analyzing how the self knows itself and its world, and as a result the personal displaced the public. The now widely accepted view that the very process of knowing is social and political has prompted a rethinking of the politics of modernism, but this has not yet included the full-scale reconsideration that the problem of reading deserves. As I have tried to demonstrate in the preceding chapters, the experiments in form through which many modern writers explore the vicissitudes of consciousness and the constitution of the self are not self-referential aesthetic exercises. To understand this, we need a theory of the politics of fiction that is not limited to representation and that sees reading itself as a political act.

The politics of modernism is determined not exclusively or even primarily by the themes of a work but rather by the way in which problems of power and authority are staged for the recipient. The very experience of responding to the narrative experiments characteristic of modern fiction confronts the reader with issues about the reconcilability of perspectives, the authority of ways of seeing, or the contingency of commitments—issues that may have wide-ranging social implications even when the explicit subject matter of the story itself does not. If, as I have tried to show, the interpretive challenges of reading modern fiction can be an occasion for reflecting about the conflict of

---

[16] The classic and still influential statement of this position is Lukács in "The Ideology of Modernism" (for more recent formulations see Larsen and Pecora). Lukács's argument was importantly contested within the Marxist tradition by Benjamin, Brecht, and Adorno, but the identification of realism with political engagement has long been a commonplace of leftist aesthetics. Interestingly, however, although Jameson criticizes postmodernism on grounds similar to his precursor's indictment of modernism, he has voiced doubts about Lukács's claims:

> One of the more commonly held stereotypes about the modern has of course in general been that of its apolitical character, its turn inward and away from the social materials associated with realism, its increased subjectification and introspective psychologization, and, not least, its aestheticism and its ideological commitment to the supreme value of a now autonomous Art as such. None of these characterizations strikes me as adequate or persuasive any longer; they are part of the baggage of an older modernist ideology which any contemporary theory of the modern will wish to scrutinize and to dismantle. ("Modernism" 45)

The notion that modern fiction makes an "inward turn" is not confined to Marxist critics. Among many examples, see Cohn; Genette; and Edel.

interpretations, the negotiation of differences, and the vicissitudes of justice, then the modern novel's turn away from representing the social world should be seen not as a flight from politics but as a redefinition of the politics of fiction.

As we have seen repeatedly in previous chapters, one place where form meets politics in modern fiction is in the question of the aesthetic and social uses of "irony." It is not at all obvious, however, that "irony" is a politically productive attitude. An ironic consciousness can inspire resistance and opposition, or it can encourage adaptation and resignation. Ross Chambers calls irony "the trope of opposition" because its negations can promote a liberating criticism of existing constraints and thereby open up "room for maneuver" (235, 18). Ironic questioning of oppressive conditions need not lead to an attempt to change them, however, but can be a strategy of accommodation. Vincent Pecora complains of Joyce, for example, that "in learning to read him one learns all the more effectively how to adjust one's own ironic self-detachment . . . to a social order for which a pervasive sense of irony and self-detachment is the first requirement of compliance" (215). Cultivating an ironic distance from the inadequacies of one's world may be indistinguishable in practical terms from resigning oneself to them.

Irony is an inherently double attitude—taking a position while simultaneously calling that position into question—and its doubleness means that its effects can go in different, even contrary directions. But this doubleness also makes irony useful as a means of staging paradoxical dilemmas that defy any single, unified resolution. The situation of politics disclosed by modern fiction is full of contradictions that require a doubled response of the sort that irony makes possible, but the uses of such acts of staging are not foreordained.

Even though the outcome of an ironic politics cannot be decided in advance, there is, I think, an emancipatory telos implicit in the doubled staging of differences characteristic of much modern fiction. This is a different dynamic from the much-discussed conservatism of Eliot, Pound, and Yeats that is often thought to constitute the dominant politics of modernism. Despite differences in approach and concern, a common goal projected by the narrative experiments of the writers I have considered is a noncoercive, irreducibly heterogeneous community where opposing positions engage one another with reciprocal recognition of their worthiness of respect and concern. This telos may be nowhere explicitly stated (usually it is not), but it is implied as the condition without which a productive staging of differences is impossible. How there might be what James Clifford calls "human connectedness" without "any stable or essential grounds of human similarity" (145) is a problem and a challenge pondered by writers as different as Joyce and Conrad, Beckett and Forster, Lawrence and Woolf.

Hence the abiding concern of Woolf with the mystery of intersubjectivity and the danger of solipsism. As Clarissa Dalloway wonders: "here was one room; there another. Did religion solve that, or love?" (193). Even Lawrence, whose susceptibility to preaching is well known, famously reminds his reader to "trust the tale, not the teller," because he recognizes that the irony with which he questions his own deepest convictions is what keeps them vibrant and engaging—energized by the to-and-fro of exchange and opposition that distinguishes life, relationship, and creativity from rigidity, tyranny, and death (hence the difference between the failure of *The Plumed Serpent* and the triumph of *Women in Love*). The hardest case might seem Beckett, whose reduction of fiction to its barest elements of differentiation and opposition ("I can't go on, I'll go on" [179]) may seem to purge narrative of any social content, but the power of this exercise in radical simplification is that it exposes starkly the contrasting alternatives of violence and play to which negation can lead (will his experiment kill off meaning, narrative, and character or liberate their very conditions of possibility?). The question for all of these writers, as for many other great moderns, is what to make of the irreducibility of the linguistic, epistemological, and cultural differences that constitute their world and ours.

I say "theirs" and "ours" because the problems and challenges I have identified are defining concerns of modern fiction even as they are also, early in this new century, prominent contemporary issues. This is partly a reflection of the continuities between modernism and postmodernism that suggest that, despite our differences, we are still living in the modern period. It is also, however, partly a reflection of how the horizons of interpretation join past and present as we see these writers speaking to us across several generations about concerns that mattered then and also matter now. The sense I have, as an early-twenty-first-century reader, theorist, and citizen, of the ideal of community and the problematic of difference informs my understanding of what is going on in these novels, and they seem interesting and compelling texts to me because their experiments with the reading process make them important instruments for thinking about issues such as the politics of irony and the mutability of justice that matter to contemporary liberalism.

For my own politics, then, as for the politics of modern fiction as I read it, the ideal community would not be an "I'm OK—You're OK" pact of mutual coexistence that leaves both parties unengaged with each other in a pretense of tolerance that is indistinguishable from indifference (the noncommittal eclecticism Joyce mocks). What is needed instead is the ability to communicate *about* differences *across* differences in order to test and explore opposing, incompatible visions of freedom and fulfillment. When "Reason" cannot guarantee a single version of liberation, the process of emancipation requires the imaginative generation and the rigorous comparison of differing conceptions of human possibility. Narrative is an important vehicle for such acts of creation and criticism. A community that fosters such imagination and critical exchange would have inclusiveness as its principle of justice in recognition that opposing notions of the "good life" are worthy of equal respect and concern. As *A Passage to India* and *Ulysses* in particular suggest, however, an adequately ironic sense of inclusiveness must realize that it can never do justice to the demand of others to be acknowledged on their own terms. Inclusiveness can be unsettling rather than reassuring because, instead of defusing the threat of the Other, it may call attention to irreducible conflicts that divide us and thereby demonstrate that doing justice to difference is an ideal that recedes as we approach it.

The dangers that an ironically chastened pursuit of inclusiveness seeks to avoid are violence, scapegoating, and solipsism, and the benefits it hopes to accrue are a testing of its own beliefs and values and a widening of its imagination of human possibility. These are dangers worth avoiding and benefits worth pursuing precisely because differences cannot be overcome in a grand, harmonious, totalizing synthesis. Reading modern fiction can be both maddening and exhilarating as it oscillates between these extremes—demonstrating through its challenges to our customary categories how closed and narrow our everyday worlds may be, while opening us up to dizzying new possibilities of meaning. From experiences of this kind, a reader may learn resiliency and humility, virtues appropriate to an ironic ethos of inclusiveness that has abandoned dreams of harmony and totality.

Reading is an important political activity because it can be a staging ground for exploring and enacting many of these problems. Reading is not the solitary, private, purely psychological activity it is often taken to be. It is social through and through—from the learned, collectively shared assumptions about interpretation through which readers approach texts, to the socially significant changes in a reader's attitudes and habitual practices that a transformative experience with a work can bring about. My analysis of the politics of modern fiction from James through Joyce has emphasized two aspects of the reading process that can have especially significant social uses: how the element of play in reading can stage reciprocal relations with difference and how the resulting doubleness in the reader's attitudes toward temporarily adopted beliefs and values can provide an occasion for learning about the challenges of irony. Reading may offer the opportunity not only to learn about otherness but also to practice the paradoxical epistemological play that engaging heterogeneity requires. The inherent doubleness of reading—its paradoxical conjoining of "me" and "not-me"—may allow it to become a testing ground for experimenting with the sorts of contradictory behaviors needed to make connections between disjunctive epistemological and cultural fields.

The doubleness of reading also makes it an ideal arena for staging the contradictions of irony. There is already something intrinsically ironic in the contradiction, basic to reading, of deploying one's own habits of understanding in order to disclose divergent ways of seeing. The doubling of one's own and another's habits of mind while reading can expose the contingency of both in much the same way as would an ironic unmasking of their claims to univocal authority. This doubling also suggests a further paradox of irony—the necessity of preserving beliefs and values even after accepting their lack of inevitability because without them one could not continue to work or play (or read).

By focusing on reading itself as a political problematic, modern fiction foregrounds an epistemological process with a variety of uses. Reading can stage paradoxical, contradictory states of affairs that defy unitary resolution in life, and these acts of staging can be useful in enhancing the reader's self-consciousness about baffling, intractable dilemmas of the sort that abound in a world of limitless hermeneutic and semantic heterogeneity. Enacting contradictions for the reader can be a way of educating us about paradoxical habits of understanding and behaving that are needed in a world characterized by disjunction and disagreement. In these and other ways, the experience of reading modern fiction may educate us about an ethical ideal that is also a pressing political need—an emancipatory reciprocity where difference gives rise to mutual transformation, not through coercion and violence, but through play.

PEDAGOGICAL POSTSCRIPT

Liberal Education, the English Major, and Pluralistic Literacy

A model of reading that addresses problems of justice, democracy, and intercultural relations has a variety of pedagogical implications. Reading for nonconsensual reciprocity should, I think, be a defining aim of liberal education and language arts instruction because of its potential value in forming citizens of a democracy. Classrooms and curricula should be structured to foster the playful interaction that can teach students how to negotiate social and political differences in an emancipatory, noncoercive manner. Language arts instruction has a particularly vital role to play in such an education because, as I have argued throughout this book, learning to negotiate differences in reading can provide crucial preparation for transforming ideological and cultural conflicts into mutually beneficial and enlightening exchanges. The humanities have an important political mission in our educational institutions today, not because of the moral or ideological content of what we teach, but because of the way in which reading can and should model various democratic processes. Teaching reading as a playful exercise of reciprocity with otherness can help prepare students for a democracy understood as a community of communities.

Recent battles about language, culture, and the curriculum have been heated, even strident, because of the implicit connections between the educational goals of the humanities and beliefs about democracy, justice, and community. The relation between educational and social models has a long history, however. At least in this country, the seminal figure in this tradition is Ralph

Waldo Emerson, whose classic address "The American Scholar" in 1837 challenged his generation to embrace his vision of the civic responsibility of education to provide the cultural leadership needed by the still new nation. Emerson felt that defining the role of "the American scholar" mattered politically because fundamental principles of citizenship, nationhood, and culture were embedded in the way that teaching and learning were conceived. In his view, the responsibility of students and teachers was to cease deferring to European traditions and, instead, to read experience and nature as primary texts. "Our day of dependence, our long apprenticeship to the learning of other lands, draws to a close," Emerson said in words that connect political emancipation to educational independence (64). "Colleges . . . can only highly serve us," he said, "when they aim not to drill, but to create; when they gather from far every ray of various genius to their hospitable halls, and by the concentrated fires, set the hearts of their youth on flame" (69). Emerson distrusted inherited conventions but valued inspiration not only because traditions were foreign imports but also because he felt that universal truths could be found in our innermost thoughts and feelings.[1] Central to Emerson's vision is his belief that students should not imitate the lifeless learning of European books but should look into their unspoiled American souls because there they could read the true spirit of nature. This is not simply a private duty but a civic responsibility, Emerson felt, because the scholar, by diving into his innermost thoughts and feelings, would find insights and inspiration that the wider public would recognize.

This romantic credo would inspire Thoreau and Whitman, but already by the end of the century Henry James and other realists would object that the social bond is constructed not out of private emotions or universal spirit but from conventions, beliefs, and values that can vary widely and even be irreconcilably at odds. James's international novels consequently depict Americans misunderstanding and running afoul of Europeans not because one continent is "nature" and the other is "culture" but because the two worlds operate according to different, sometimes incommensurable assumptions. These worlds are governed by manners of behaving and norms of conduct that vary widely and at times differ as to what counts as right or wrong, true or false. James's vision of a heterogeneous global world teeming with cultural variety rings

[1] As Kenneth S. Sacks points out in his interesting study of the historical contexts of this famous address, Emerson intended to challenge not only European conventions but also the materialist assumptions and deference to authority of his "Harvard-Utilitarian culture" that "found spiritual and intellectual confirmation in empirical proof, scientific progress, and material success. Emerson acknowledged understanding derived from observation of external phenomena, but believed that the more important truths are eternal and intuitive, emerging from within" (16).

truer to our sense of things today than does Emerson's romantic spiritual monism. Indeed, anticipating the internal diversity that would increasingly characterize America, James sensed that immigration patterns were already redefining the land of the New England Puritans as something quite other— and something, he felt, potentially powerful and exciting because of its vital, unpredictable multiplicity.[2]

What, then, is the civic responsibility of the American scholar today, in a country defined by its irreducible diversity? The answers to this question offered by the cultural conservatives have been framed variously by William Bennett, Lynne Cheney, E. D. Hirsch, Allan Bloom, and others, but they are united in the conviction that the nation will split apart into anarchy and cultural solipsism unless all citizens share a common tradition—a canon of texts, a vocabulary of references that everyone can take for granted, a shared set of beliefs and values, a unified narrative of American history. In their view, the role of general education is to teach these common values, to impart the stories that unite us by constituting our shared culture. The citizen is defined by the public knowledge and virtues he or she shares with others, without which common ground there would not be a community (or so this argument goes). Like Emerson, these cultural conservatives seek a oneness that unites all citizens; they find it not in our souls, however, but in the texts, traditions, and values that the "core curriculum" should teach. Like James, the cultural conservatives understand the power of conventions to define a culture, and that is why they advocate a pedagogy that they believe will unite citizens by giving them a single shared tradition to combat the centrifugal force of opposing values.

The problem with this pedagogical philosophy is not only that the traditional canon excludes valuable texts by women, African Americans, Asian Americans, Hispanic Americans, and others and should be expanded to include them (a concession some conservatives are willing to make). The more fundamental question is whether a society can have multiple canons, a variety of traditions that may not perfectly synthesize, and still constitute a civil community (a community of communities). Although these are old battles—the culture wars of the 1980s and 1990s—they still rage. Consider, for example, the State University of New York, where I was for a time dean of arts and sciences at the Stony Brook campus. A group of conservative trustees voted in 1999 to impose a core curriculum on all sixty-four campuses in the system, including the stipulation that everyone must take a course in American history

---

[2] See James's late work *The American Scene*, which reports his reactions to the changes he observed upon returning to his country in 1904 after a twenty-year absence, and Beverly Haviland's insightful commentary.

that would provide a unified narrative ("from Columbus to Clinton," as one SUNY official put it) of America's cultural experience. The faculty at Stony Brook had required students to take courses introducing them to "American pluralism," but they were instructed by the trustees that these courses had to be replaced by a "single coherent narrative" of American history.

My colleagues in the history department were aghast because they view American history as a complicated, multifaceted network of narratives with different beginnings, middles, and ends (depending on whether you start, say, with Columbus, or with the migration across the Bering Straits of what became the Native American peoples, or with the slave traffic from Africa through the Caribbean to the American South, or with the Spanish missionaries and conquistadors who sought in their different ways to establish their regime in the Southwest and California, or with the Puritans seeking religious freedom in New England, or . . .). The heterogeneity of American identity today is a product of the crossings and collisions of these different stories of America, and it is not reducible to one unified narrative without denying vital differences that define who "we" are—or so the faculty vainly protested to the system's administration in Albany.

An alternative to a pedagogy that would suppress such differences by unifying them into a "single coherent narrative" is provided by the kind of "open curriculum" that can be found at a small number of pedagogically progressive institutions (usually private, and therefore better able to resist the public pressures of the conservative educational activists). These institutions have found values in such a curriculum that go beyond its origins in the rebellious counterculture of the 1960s.[3] That at least has been my experience at Brown, the institution I was lucky enough to move to just as the SUNY culture wars were escalating. Brown's curriculum is defined not by an absence of requirements but by a conception of "liberal learning" that values difference not only because intellectual diversity is an important end in itself but also because a pedagogy focused on difference can foster a cosmopolitan kind of citizenship.

Instead of prescribing a set of courses or texts, Brown encourages students to construct a liberal education for themselves, not by assimilating a common tradition or acquiring shared values and beliefs, but by exploring the relations between different ways of making meaning, constructing knowledge, and

[3] In addition to Brown, which I know best and will discuss in some detail, I have in mind places like Amherst, Smith, Wesleyan, Hampshire, Evergreen, Eugene Lang, Sarah Lawrence, Antioch, the University of California at Santa Cruz, and the Gallatin School at New York University. This is a diverse list, including schools with distinctively different educational philosophies and programs, but by and large these institutions regard general education as a matter of thinking about epistemological and cultural difference rather than acquiring a shared tradition, and they view active, self-directed learning by students as a primary value.

understanding the world (what students and faculty often refer to here as "modes of thought").[4] According to this pedagogical model, the liberal arts entail learning to value and negotiate differences while discovering (and creating) one's own path through the "multiverse" of knowledge, meaning, and value, to borrow a term from the inveterate pluralist William James. Hence the emphasis such a curriculum places on learning to think about how different disciplines and conventions work as well as on the possibility for creation and discovery that our differences from one another make possible. This is a pedagogy of generative pluralism that envisages difference as an occasion for innovation and productive exchange and that imagines community as a heterogeneous conversation of individuals who may not and need not all share common ground.

At Brown and elsewhere, proponents of this kind of liberal curriculum have not been good at making their case. The cultural conservatives have succeeded in making it seem that a curriculum that does not require a core of common texts lacks rigor and standards. That is of course a logical fallacy. One can be rigorous in the demands one makes on students and have high standards for measuring their accomplishments while giving them the freedom to design a course of study that aims to explore the complementarities and conflicts that characterize different ways of thinking and acting. It is not unusual, however, to encounter scoffers who imagine that institutions with an "open curriculum" are throwbacks to the laxities of the 1960s. Where the "open curricula" that were instituted in the 1960s have survived (and many have fallen by the wayside), however, they have typically been modified to serve different purposes and uses than their originators envisioned.

For example, one impetus for abandoning core requirements in the 1960s was a romantic rejection of disciplinary traditions in favor of students' self-discovery. This led early on at Brown to encouragement of interdisciplinary exploration and undergraduate research, two ways of questioning conventional epistemological boundaries and promoting individual exploration. Interdisciplinary study seems critically important in many areas of inquiry today, but not primarily because it rejects the conventional wisdom as stifling to individual creativity. Rather, there has been a growing recognition that disciplines, although valuable communities of knowledge, are not ends in themselves but at most provide instruments for inquiry that have limits to their uses. The most innovative researchers in a wide spectrum of fields now recognize that disciplines have fuzzy, permeable boundaries. Hence the increasing importance of multidisciplinary research programs as disciplines seek to

---

[4] See the *Guide to Liberal Learning* that is distributed to newly matriculating students and that explains and explores this philosophy through essays by students, faculty, and deans.

complement one another or to extend their defining limits. In this climate of cross-disciplinary exploration, undergraduate research seems like a good thing to encourage, not only because it makes students active learners but also because it introduces them firsthand to the instrumentality of disciplinary and interdisciplinary knowledge. And this in turn helps them as citizens to negotiate epistemological differences they encounter in their social and cultural worlds.

This is, of course, how all traditions survive—by reinterpreting their originating values in light of new challenges and discoveries, so that the old is renewed by being both conserved and altered. The idea of a community of differences is not a notion that was much in circulation in the 1960s, but it is the sort of community that the increasingly heterogeneous country we live in must become if it is to be genuinely democratic. Although not a purpose that was (or could have been) envisioned by its earliest advocates, an "open curriculum" that foregrounds the problem of epistemological and cultural difference holds greater promise for fostering such a community than does the consensus model of the core curriculum.

Similar issues are at stake in ongoing debates about the structure and content of the English major. "Coverage" could act as the organizing principle of English studies only as long as students and teachers could assume unity in the canon of works to be studied and in the methods by which mastery of them could be attained. Such unity meant that students could be given the simple injunction "Read everything," and teachers could expect that coherent knowledge would result. This expectation has come to seem strange and unreasonable. The field of English studies expanded extraordinarily over the last several decades because of challenges to the canon and a multiplication of interpretive methods, and this amazing growth has exposed a diversity that had already existed but had been largely repressed or ignored.[5] The expansion of

---

[5] See J. Hillis Miller's reflections on his fifty years in the teaching profession, during which the disciplinary unity he took for granted at the beginning of his career was disrupted in a number of (to his mind) beneficial ways, as well as Jonathan Culler's analysis of what was gained as well as lost when the "coherence" that Northrop Frye assumed to characterize the study of literature could no longer be taken for granted. Wendy Moffat, Lawrence Schwartz, and Alan Shepard also offer thoughtful reports about how different English departments have revised their majors in response to these changes. In the introduction to the 2003 volume of the *ADE Bulletin* in which these essays appear, David Laurence notes the relation of such curricular revisions to changes in contemporary social life: "Even if we allow that the prior formation of the field that Miller recollects really could boast a significantly greater measure of programmatic clarity than curricula will typically afford today, it does not follow that today's undergraduates are served less well than their grandparents were. Surely the increased range and diversity of the materials available for study, and also our altered sense of what makes study in English worthwhile, have some connection, however indirectly, to the increasing range and diversity of the undergraduate student population itself—ethnic, racial, economic, demographic" (3).

the canon has lengthened the list of texts students must know to the point where the demand for complete knowledge seems impossible (cover "Beowulf to Virginia Woolf" plus women's literature, minority literature, English literature outside the Anglo-American sphere, . . .). By insisting that a broad range of truths and values be granted cultural authority, these challenges have helped call attention to the internal diversity of the previously existing canon that the myth of a unified tradition had obscured.

This destabilization of the subject matter of literary study has been accompanied by a denaturalization of the act of understanding. The notion that "covering" a group of works would result in coherent knowledge seemed reasonable when reading was viewed as an unproblematic activity. But understanding could seem like a natural act only as long as consensus reigned about its goals and procedures. No new consensus has emerged in the wake of the New Criticism that provided such paradigmatic agreement in the 1950s and 60s (and it should be obvious that I think this is a good thing). Neither term in the injunction "Read everything" is stable and uniform.

Diversity need not be debilitating, however. In greater or lesser degrees, theory has come to replace coverage as the guiding principle of the English curriculum at many colleges and universities because theory—defined broadly as reflection about textuality, language, and interpretation—can help students find their way in the multifarious world of literary studies. This curricular transformation (still not complete or universally accepted) reflects the fact that our discipline is a heterogeneous field, a diverse but bounded enterprise characterized by fundamental disagreements about what to study and how, as well as by many complex convergences and resemblances in our goals, assumptions, and procedures that resist reduction to a core of common principles.

The need to move from coverage to theory in the face of the challenges of difference informed the proposals put forward by the so-called English Coalition in the late 1980s for a fundamentally revised English major. The English Coalition was a group of eight professional associations concerned with the teaching of English from the elementary grades through graduate school, organized by the Modern Language Association and the National Council of Teachers of English. I was among the sixty representatives of these groups who met for three weeks in the summer of 1987 at the Aspen Institute in Wye Plantation, Maryland. The purpose of the conference was to assess the state of language-arts instruction at the elementary, high school, and college levels and "to chart directions for the study of English into the twenty-first century" (Lloyd-Jones and Lunsford xvii). The Coalition thought of itself, perhaps vainly, as a gathering of historical importance akin to the well-known 1966 Dartmouth conference that was influential in setting the agenda for the teaching of literature in secondary school and college (see Elbow, *What Is English?* 3–9).

The English Coalition was indeed a remarkable moment during which a consensus was formed about a new model of English studies in a conversation across rarely breached institutional boundaries from kindergarten to the university. This model was based on the conviction that the assumption of (or desire for) homogeneity in reading, textuality, or culture does not work, is even pernicious, and needs to be replaced. The paradox, of course, is that this was a consensus opposing the value of consensus—that is, an agreement among a group of practitioners that building the language arts curriculum on the assumption of heterogeneity made more sense and would have better effects than postulating unity as the basis and goal of our work. This is only an apparent self-contradiction, however, not only because the opposition of the Coalition members to the cultural conservatives is itself evidence of the epistemological diversity of the languages arts but also because the participants in the conference were productively in disagreement among themselves about fundamental issues concerning language, literature, and interpretation.[6]

The English Coalition responded to the disappearance of a unified canon and the proliferation of interpretive methods by proposing that the heterogeneity of literature and the conflict among ways of reading be thematized as central problems around which the English major (and indeed all of the language arts curriculum, even in elementary and high school) should be organized. Instead of regarding the diversity of the canon or the competition among interpretive approaches as obstacles to the coherence of the major, the Coalition proposed that the major take the causes and implications of this literary and hermeneutic multiplicity as its focus. The college teachers at the Coalition meeting came from a wide variety of educational settings, including urban community colleges, elite private institutions, historically black colleges, and large public universities, but they nevertheless reached agreement about "a general itinerary for all English majors" (Lloyd-Jones and Lunsford 35): not a list of "core texts" or required courses but a set of five goals that different departments could pursue in the ways most appropriate to local needs, interests, and resources.

The first goal explicitly addresses the question of epistemological differences: "All English majors should know several methodologies of reading and interpretation, be acquainted with the premises and the modes of arguing that each pursues, and be aware of issues connected with a choice of one

[6] It is, however, a fair criticism of some Coalition documents that a felt need for solidarity against a powerful enemy allowed it to succumb to the temptation of rhetorical oversimplification that may at times have blunted the intellectual subtlety and power of its arguments. The conversations at Wye were heated and full of opposition and disagreement, but the political nature of the Coalition's pronouncements (sometimes reading like a manifesto) perhaps wrongly suppressed this diversity and its accompanying energy and richness.

perspective versus another" (35). Teachers should not present a preferred way of reading as "natural," "self-evident," or unproblematically authoritative but instead should make their own presuppositions a subject for debate by self-consciously staging its conflicts with potential alternatives. By the same token, departments should not simply add faculty members with new perspectives and then let these differences sit inertly side by side. Curricular structures should be developed that will encourage differences to engage one another.[7] The goal of these structures would be to help students make sense of the heterogeneous ways of reading that they encounter so that they can choose their own interpretive allegiances deliberately and intelligently, with an appreciation of what is gained and lost by any such choice.

The second goal recognizes and attempts to address some of the historical dimensions of these problems: "All English majors should know something of the critical and historical principles behind the construction of literary and cultural histories. They should know the terminology of literary periods, be aware of controversies concerning the establishment of distinctions between periods, and understand the general significances attached to various views taken of the transitions between periods" (35). The members of the Coalition felt that majors should not only study literary history but also acquire a historical sense, which should include among other things an understanding that history is a variable, contestable construct. Coverage alone is not the same as genuine historical understanding, and it is indeed an undesirable goal if it takes the place of serious inquiry into the problem of history.

The third goal sets these issues in a linguistic context: "All English majors should know something about the study of language and discursive practices. Avenues to such knowledge include study in the history of the language, formal grammar and rhetoric, psycholinguistics and sociolinguistics, and semiotics" (35). The purpose of this proposal is not to make all majors into theoretical linguists but to give them a conceptual understanding of language that, the Coalition hoped, would enhance their practical power to make and decipher meaning. According to the Coalition report, "an important reason for epistemological and cultural heterogeneity is that knowledge is language-bound and that language is extremely malleable" (30). Some theoretical knowledge about how language works would therefore be useful in accounting for the diversity of literature, the ways in which literature changes, and the disagreements

---

[7] This is a matter not just of curricular design but also of the culture of departmental conversation. See my essay "Deprivatizing the Classroom" for a discussion of how reciprocal classroom visitation can encourage dialogue about conflicting pedagogical, hermeneutic, and professional assumptions that students often find bewildering. The structure of the requirements for an English major often assumes an epistemological coherence among a faculty's courses that simply does not exist.

among interpretations. Such inquiry can be concrete and practical and relevant to students' lives in a society where signs of all kinds compete for attention and where seductive images often ask to be taken for "nature."

The fourth goal proposes that textual differences be a structural principle of the curriculum: "All English majors should have the experience of reading texts drawn from the full diversity of literary periods and genres, written by authors representing the full range of social, ethnic, and national origins that have contributed to the corpus of literature in English. They should also have experience with critical texts and with expository prose and other types of writings that have frequently not been made use of in the curriculum of the major, including writing by their fellow students" (35). This proposal responds to the breakdown of the coverage model and to the expansion of the canon by advocating a broadening of the notion of textuality that is the proper subject of the English major. To say that the coverage model is unworkable is not to deny the importance of reading widely. Quite to the contrary, students need to be exposed to a broad, diverse range of texts precisely because the unity and coherence of what counts as "literature" can no longer be assumed.

The fifth and final goal recognizes that difference is a matter not only of the interpretation of texts but also of their production: "All English majors should practice writing in several modes and for different audiences and purposes, with an awareness of the social implications and theoretical issues these shifts raise. Classroom practice should bring teachers and students to experience writing, reading, listening, and speaking as integrated, mutually supporting exercises" (35). This proposal advocates "a new balance" in the relation between reading and writing in the English major (26). Instead of privileging reading over writing, as the coverage model implicitly does, English courses of all kinds should make prominent use of writing as a means of inquiry and as a way of producing and negotiating differences.

The Coalition's report emphasizes the social and ethical uses of the English major and of all language-arts instruction, and it contends, finally, that literary studies can contribute importantly "to educating students for participation in democracy" (85). Since "citizens of a democracy must be able to appreciate diversity even as they advocate their own beliefs about what is good and true," then "teaching students how and why different ways of reading can find different meanings in the same text can provide important experience in understanding and appreciating opposing perspectives." Similarly, "learning about the many different kinds of writing and ways of thinking which are the subject matter of the language arts curriculum can expand the capacity of students to imagine and value worlds other than their own" (86).

This is a more pluralistic conception of literacy and linguistic competence than the notion of "cultural literacy" that conservatives often propose as necessary equipment for citizenship. The term "cultural literacy" gained wide currency so quickly because it seemed to offer a simple solution to urgent problems. As with all quick fixes, this promise is deceptive. The title (especially the subtitle) of the book by E. D. Hirsch Jr. in which he coined the phrase is boldly ambitious: *Cultural Literacy: What Every American Needs to Know.* "Cultural literacy" is single and definable; Hirsch has discovered what it is, and he is going to tell us. This book, first published in 1987 (the same year as the English Coalition meeting), has been one of the central texts of the so-called "culture wars," which have quieted down since the 1980s and 1990s but have not ended and show signs of escalating again. Its arguments are worth considering because the issues of cultural difference and educational policy that it addresses have not gone away but, rather, have become even more pressing with the ever-increasing ethnic, racial, and linguistic diversity of our nation. A sign of the book's continuing relevance is the extraordinary publishing industry it has spawned under the title "The Core Knowledge Series." This series includes texts for every primary grade level, starting with *What Your Kindergartner Needs to Know*, and culminating in *The New Dictionary of Cultural Literacy: What Every American Needs to Know* (a revised edition was published as recently as October 2002), prescribing in 672 pages what counts as indispensable "core knowledge."

The original *Cultural Literacy* is a classic text in the conservative pedagogical program to create cultural unity through a consensus model of citizenship and community. Students who memorize Hirsch's list of key terms in the hope of acquiring "cultural literacy" will not be equipped to read and communicate effectively in the heterogeneous world they are entering, however, because "culture" and "literacy" are more diverse and changeable than Hirsch's educational program assumes. Cultural heterogeneity demands a pluralistic conception of "literacy" because different communities practice different ways of reading, and competence in one mode of understanding is no guarantee of facility in another. What students need is "pluralistic literacy"—the ability to deal effectively with cultural differences and to negotiate the competing claims of multiple ways of reading.

One of Hirsch's fundamental mistakes is to equate linguistic competence with vocabulary. He argues that students need a large stock of "specific, communally shared information" in order to read efficiently and "to participate in complex cooperative activities with other members of their community" (*Literacy* xv). He defines "cultural literacy" as "the national vocabulary"—"a vocabulary that we are able to use throughout the land because we share associations with others in our society" (29, 26). No one would deny that learning vocabulary is necessary to acquiring facility with a language. But knowledge of vocabulary is at most only half of linguistic competence—command of the paradigmatic axis (which elements substitute for each other, as synonyms, antonyms, or otherwise equivalent parts of speech). Equally important is the syntagmatic axis (rules, patterns, and conventions governing how to combine elements in meaningful, grammatical units).

Someone cannot read a newspaper or communicate to a stranger (two of Hirsch's favorite examples of literacy) if he or she knows only the vocabulary of a language and not its grammar and syntax. Words alone are of limited use without an understanding of how to combine them. Hirsch's omission is crucial, because inventing new patterns for fitting together old linguistic materials is an important way of creating semantic novelty and multiplicity. Different interpretive communities can use the same language but understand the world differently not only because they define the same terms differently but also because they combine them according to different conventions.

Hirsch does not forget combination entirely but tries to fit it into his definition of vocabulary. The result is a contradiction in the function he attributes to the elements in his list—a contradiction that suggests a different pedagogy than the memorization of content he advocates. Hirsch's primary definition of cultural literacy is "the network of information that all competent readers possess" (*Literacy* 2). The purpose of acquiring this information is to be able to supply the facts and associations that are assumed but not explicitly mentioned in any communication. Hirsch recognizes, however, that we read not only by filling in gaps but also by fitting elements together in consistent patterns. In fact, Hirsch's early book *Validity in Interpretation* is still one of the best explanations of the necessary circularity of understanding—the classic hermeneutic circle whereby one can make sense of the parts of any text only by seeing their relation to the whole, even as one can only grasp the whole by working through its parts.

This model of understanding governs the most useful and illuminating section of *Cultural Literacy*—chapter 2, "The Discovery of the Schema"— but it changes the function of the vocabulary of literacy. No longer just implicit background "information," the elements on the list are seen in this chapter as patterns for understanding, models for building consistency. "To make sense of what we read," Hirsch argues, "we must use relevant prior knowledge to form a model of how sentence meanings hang together" (*Literacy* 39–40). The items on his vocabulary list represent not just missing facts or implicit context but "categories" or "schemata" that aid interpretation by providing patterns for fitting parts into wholes.

This shift in definition calls into question Hirsch's entire educational program. If the essential elements of literacy are interpretive schemata rather than factual information, then the way to develop competence in reading and communicating is not by memorizing vocabulary but by learning how to control and generate synthesizing patterns. Reading is not a mechanical process of filling in from memory what is missing in the text but an imaginative, potentially variable activity of building consistency. Learning the categories that other interpreters in one's community have found useful is still a valuable enterprise. But the reason is not only that one will therefore know what everyone else assumes when they write and talk but also that one will have a collection of previously tested guidelines for experimenting with hypotheses of one's own about how elements fit into patterns. Competence in making elements cohere can be acquired only by practice, by repeated trial and error. It is not simply a matter of how to use the dictionary, and it cannot be provided by the dictionary alone.

The status of Hirsch's vocabulary as "schemata" rather than as information calls into question his claim that cultural literacy is politically neutral. Here again his argument is contradictory. On the one hand, he claims that "the central issues of literacy are more technical than ideological" ("Talk" 7)—a matter of acquiring the tools necessary to prosper in our society, regardless of political convictions. On the other hand, he traces the foundations of cultural literacy back to "a civil religion that underlies our civil ethos" and that provides "a central source of coherence in American public culture" (*Literacy* 98, 99). The story of George Washington and the cherry tree (an example frequently cited by Hirsch) is not just a piece of information competent readers need to know but a parable that conveys a complex set of moral attitudes.

As ways of seeing and models for configuring the world, the "schemata" that make up cultural literacy are based on presuppositions about human being, society, right conduct, and like matters, which cultures with different beliefs and ways of reading may contest. A language or a mode of understanding can seem "natural" and self-evident unless it is juxtaposed against an opposing set of terms and conventions, which organizes the world according to different principles that seem equally obvious to its adherents. As Robert Scholes notes, "the way to see one discourse is to see more than one" (144). Juxtaposing ways of seeing against one another makes it possible for students to understand and criticize the various interpretive conventions that compete for ideological control in our culture and that offer different opportunities for creativity, discovery, and expression.

Defining cultural literacy as mastery of vocabulary, Hirsch imagines a test of the student's stock of information analogous to the multiple-choice sections of the verbal SAT. The alternative definition I am proposing—literacy as the ability to understand and generate different kinds of coherence— conceives of it as less mechanically calculable but still recognizable and perhaps even measurable (but the measure would have to include multiple scales appropriate to

different ways of reading). Rather than a machine-scored test of word recognition, the assessment instrument I would prefer would ask students to write
in response to different texts. Such an instrument would test three indicators
of "pluralistic literacy": (1) the ability to construe and create new sentences;
(2) the capacity to extend prior knowledge to make sense of something unfamiliar, and (3) the power to translate a different use of language into one's own
vocabulary and conventions (and to recognize the limits of translatability).
These are all abilities that students may have developed to a greater or lesser
degree and in varying ways, and tests can be developed to measure and evaluate their competence.

On the first point, students do not have adequate facility with a language if
all they can do is recite its vocabulary or even its grammatical rules. A better
gauge of linguistic competence is the ability to generate recognizable, correct
sentences and to make sense of new, previously unknown texts. These capacities require training in consistency building, in using vocabulary and grammatical rules, and in experimenting with the semantic combinations they
make possible. Hirsch himself argues against narrow training for specific jobs
and urges instead "education for change," which equips students to "deal
with new ideas, events, and challenges" (*Literacy* 126, 11). Instruction in
reading and writing is excellent "education for change" precisely because the
ability to deal with novelty—to generate new meanings and to understand
new texts—is central to facility with a language. A primary goal of language
arts instruction is (or should be) to teach students how, within the limits of existing conventions, to make meanings that are their own, as well as how to
bend, stretch, or alter those rules (through innovative uses of language such as
metaphor) when their constraints are unsatisfactory. Developing these abilities requires experimentation with a variety of semantic possibilities, not the
rote learning of information.

Semantic facility with generating and comprehending new sentences is
closely related to epistemological competence in extending prior knowledge to
assimilate something surprising, unprecedented, and for that reason perhaps
bewildering. What is at stake here, with the second indicator of literacy, is the
ability to transfer what we know and how we understand from familiar to unfamiliar situations. Again this is something students do more or less well, and
it can be tested. Hirsch is adamant that skills do not transfer: "People do not
develop general, transferable skills in problem solving, critical thinking, or in
any other field" (*Literacy* 62). Hirsch advocates teaching students facts rather
than forms of thinking because only a broad stock of information, not abstract
problem-solving skills, will allow them to make sense of the unknown. The
ability to use what one knows to understand something unfamiliar does not depend on content alone, however, but goes back once again to the hermeneutic

circle. As Hirsch himself recognizes, understanding the unknown is inherently circular because "we learn something new only by attaching it to something we already know" ("Talk" 10). As he notes, "our minds have a remarkable ability to change initial schemata according to the situations in which we find ourselves," and they do this by discovering analogies (*Literacy* 52; see 122).

Altering and extending interpretive categories to adapt to new challenges cannot be accomplished without a large supply of schemata to experiment with, but once again memorized content is not sufficient. The indispensable component of this dimension of literacy is what Peter Elbow calls "metaphorical thinking"—"the capacity for inventing new concepts" by the imaginative discovery of similarities and by "good guessing" about possible patterns (*Embracing Contraries* 29–30). To be prepared for the unknown, students need to develop an ability to invent new ways of fitting things together by recognizing and creating new analogies, new patterns of similarity and difference. This is something students can learn to do better—not by memorizing lists, but by practice, experimentation, trial and error, guided and inspired and corrected by experienced practitioners (their teachers, who should not be reduced to rote recitation or teaching to a test). New combinations cannot be created without old materials, a stock of existing categories to alter and extend, but mastery of content alone will not give students confidence in their capacity to generate good guesses about how best to configure unforeseen situations.

A crucial capacity in dealing with the unknown is the power to translate an unfamiliar language, the third indicator of literacy. Part of teaching students a language is teaching them how to learn a language—how to develop new vocabulary, how to recognize and understand new syntactical patterns, and how to ask questions about puzzling irregularities. Again this is a matter of practice, trial and error under expert guidance, and not the rote learning of lists. Hirsch claims that "we will be able to achieve a just and prosperous society only when our schools ensure that everyone commands enough shared background knowledge to be able to communicate effectively with everyone else" (*Literacy* 32). Communication depends not only on what we share but, perhaps even more importantly, on our knowing what to do when we find an absence of commonality. Hirsch's insistence that common ground is necessary for exchange makes a goal of conversation its precondition. The discovery of convergences of attitude, interest, or knowledge is often what we're after in a conversation, and where we begin is frequently with a breakdown in understanding or a vague, baffled sense that divergent backgrounds and perspectives are somehow hampering our interactions. Students cannot be given formulas for moving from bewilderment to mutual understanding and productive exchange. But teachers know that students do this more or less well, and they can learn to get better at it.

Users of a language typically share much and differ much as well, and their convergences and divergences are equally necessary parts of conversations. Shared background information is not sufficient to adjudicate disagreements or overcome differences, because what is *not* shared is the issue. In such instances a language user needs the power to translate between different systems of meaning in order to discover how much common ground exists, as well as the ability to recognize when differences are so insurmountable that translation is not possible (or not desirable, if translation means giving up one's own perspective). The final test of "pluralistic literacy" is one's ability to translate from one code to another in order to participate in conflicts productively, with understanding and respect but without sacrificing one's own meanings. Negotiating different perspectives when one discovers that common ground is lacking is essential to using language effectively. It is also a requirement for participating in a democracy. "Pluralistic literacy" is what every American needs to know.

WORKS CITED

Achebe, Chinua. "An Image of Africa." *Massachusetts Review* 18 (1977): 782–94.

Adams, Robert Martin. *Surface and Symbol: The Consistency of James Joyce's* Ulysses. New York: Oxford UP, 1962.

Ahmed Ali. "E. M. Forster and India." *E. M. Forster: Centenary Revaluations.* Ed. Judith Scherer Herz and Robert K. Martin. Toronto: U of Toronto P, 1982. 278–87.

Alcalay, Ammiel. "Stop-Time in the Levant," *Nation* 20 Dec. 1999.

Althusser, Louis. *Lenin and Philosophy and Other Essays.* Trans. Ben Brewster. London: New Left Books, 1971.

Anderson, Benedict. *Imagined Communities: Reflections on the Origin and Spread of Nationalism.* London: Verso, 1983.

Armstrong, Paul B. *The Challenge of Bewilderment: Understanding and Representation in James, Conrad, and Ford.* Ithaca: Cornell UP, 1987.

——. *Conflicting Readings: Variety and Validity in Interpretation.* Chapel Hill: U of North Carolina P, 1990.

——. "Deprivatizing the Classroom." *ADE Bulletin* 107 (spring 1994): 13–19.

——. "E. M. Forster's *Howards End:* The Existential Crisis of the Liberal Imagination." *Mosaic* 8 (fall 1974): 183–99.

——. "Reading James's Prefaces and Reading James." *Henry James's New York Edition: The Construction of Authorship.* Ed. David McWhirter. Stanford: Stanford UP, 1995. 125–37.

Attridge, Derek. "Molly's Flow: The Writing of 'Penelope' and the Question of Women's Language." *Modern Fiction Studies* 35 (1989): 543–65.

Attridge, Derek, and Daniel Ferrer, eds. *Post-structuralist Joyce: Essays from the French.* Cambridge: Cambridge UP, 1984.

Baines, Jocelyn. *Joseph Conrad: A Critical Biography.* London: Weidenfeld and Nicolson, 1960.

Barthes, Roland. *S/Z.* Trans. R. Miller. New York: Hill and Wang, 1974.

Beckett, Samuel. *The Unnamable.* New York: Grove, 1958.

Beer, Gillian. "Negation in *A Passage to India.*" *A Passage to India: Essays in Interpretation.* Ed. John Beer. London: Macmillan, 1985. 44–58.

Benstock, Bernard, ed. *Critical Essays on James Joyce's* Ulysses. Boston: G. K. Hall, 1989.

———. *James Joyce: The Augmented Ninth.* Syracuse: Syracuse UP, 1988.

Bercovitch, Sacvan. "The Problem of Ideology in American Literary History." *Critical Inquiry* 12 (1986): 631–53.

Bergman, David, ed. *Camp Grounds: Style and Homosexuality.* Amherst: U of Massachusetts P, 1993.

Bernstein, Richard J., ed. *Habermas and Modernity.* Oxford: Basil Blackwell, 1985.

Berthoud, Jacques. "Anxiety in *Under Western Eyes.*" *Conradian* 18.1 (autumn 1993): 1–13.

Bhabha, Homi K. "DissemiNation: Time, Narrative, and the Margins of the Modern Nation." *Nation and Narration.* Ed. Bhabha. London: Routledge, 1990. 291–322.

Bharucha, Rustom. "Forster's Friends." *E. M. Forster: Modern Critical Views.* Ed. Harold Bloom. New York: Chelsea, 1987. 153–68.

Bhaskar, Roy. *Philosophy and the Idea of Freedom.* Oxford: Basil Blackwell, 1991.

Billson, Anne. "Our Kind of People." Forster, *Howards End* 467–68.

Bonney, William. *Thorns and Arabesques: Contexts for Conrad's Fiction.* Baltimore: Johns Hopkins UP, 1980.

Booth, Wayne. *The Company We Keep: An Ethics of Fiction.* Chicago: U of Chicago P, 1988.

Born, Daniel. "Private Gardens, Public Swamps: *Howards End* and the Revaluation of Liberal Guilt." *Novel* 25 (1992): 141–59.

Bourdieu, Pierre. *Distinction: A Social Critique of the Judgment of Taste.* Trans. Richard Nice. Cambridge: Harvard UP, 1984.

Bové, Paul A., ed. *Edward Said and the Work of the Critic: Speaking Truth to Power.* Durham, NC: Duke UP, 2000.

Brannon, Julie Sloan. *Who Reads* Ulysses? *The Rhetoric of the Joyce Wars and the Common Reader.* New York: Routledge, 2003.

Brantlinger, Patrick. *Rule of Darkness: British Literature and Imperialism, 1830–1914.* Ithaca: Cornell UP, 1988.

Brennan, Timothy. "The Illusion of a Future: Orientalism as Traveling Theory." *Critical Inquiry* 26.3 (winter 2000), 558–83.

Buruma, Ian. "Misplaced Person," *New York Times Book Review* 3 October 1999.

Butler, Judith. *Gender Trouble: Feminism and the Subversion of Identity.* New York: Routledge, 1990.

Caillois, Roger. *Man, Play, and Games.* Trans. Meyer Barash. Glencoe, IL.: Free Press, 1958.

Chambers, Ross. *Room for Maneuver: Reading (the) Oppositional (in) Narrative.* Chicago: U of Chicago P, 1991.

Chaudhuri, Nirad C. "Passage to and from India." *Encounter* 2.6 (1954): 20–22.

Cheney, Lynne V. *50 Hours: A Core Curriculum for College Students.* Washington, DC: National Endowment for the Humanities, 1989.

Cheng, Vincent. *Joyce, Race, and Empire*. Cambridge: Cambridge UP, 1995.

Cixous, Hélène. "Joyce: The (R)use of Writing." Attridge and Ferrer 15–30.

———. "The Laugh of the Medusa." *Critical Theory since 1965*. Ed. Hazard Adams and Leroy Searle. Tallahassee: Florida State UP, 1986. 309–20.

Clark, Suzanne. *Sentimental Modernism*. Bloomington: Indiana UP, 1992.

Clifford, James. *The Predicament of Culture: Twentieth-Century Ethnography, Literature, and Art*. Cambridge: Harvard UP, 1988.

Cohn, Dorrit. *Transparent Minds: Narrative Modes for Presenting Consciousness in Fiction*. Princeton: Princeton UP, 1978.

Conrad, Joseph. *Chance*. 1913. New York: W. W. Norton, 1968.

———. *Collected Letters*. Ed. Frederick R. Karl and Laurence Davies. 5 vols. Cambridge: Cambridge UP, 1983.

———. *Heart of Darkness*. 1899. Ed. Robert Kimbrough. New York: W. W. Norton, 1988.

———. *Lord Jim*. 1900. Garden City, NY: Doubleday, Page, 1924.

———. *The Secret Agent*. 1907. Garden City, NY: Doubleday, Page, 1924.

———. *Under Western Eyes*. 1911. New York: Penguin, 1989.

Cooper, Michael A. "Discipl(in)ing the Master, Mastering the Discipl(in)e: Erotonomies in James' Tales of Literary Life." *Engendering Men: The Question of Male Feminist Criticism*. Ed. Joseph A. Boone and Michael Cadden. New York: Routledge, 1990. 66–83.

Culler, Jonathan. "Imagining the Coherence of the English Major." *ADE Bulletin* 133 (2003): 6–10.

Dangerfield, George. *The Strange Death of Liberal England*. 1935. London: Paladin, 1970.

Das, G. K. *E. M. Forster's India*. Totowa, NJ: Rowman and Littlefield, 1977.

DeKoven, Marianne. *Rich and Strange: Gender, History, Modernism*. Princeton: Princeton UP, 1991.

Derrida, Jacques. *Specters of Marx: The State of Debt, the Work of Mourning, and the New International*. Trans. Peggy Kamuf. New York: Routledge, 1994.

———. "Two Words for Joyce." Attridge and Ferrer 145–59.

———. "Ulysses Gramophone: Hear Say Yes in Joyce." Benstock, *Augmented Ninth* 27–75.

Dworkin, Ronald. *Taking Rights Seriously*. Cambridge: Harvard UP, 1977.

Eagleton, Terry. "Evelyn Waugh and the Upper-Class Novel." *Exiles and Émigrés: Studies in Modern Literature*. New York: Schocken, 1970. 33–70.

———. *Literary Theory: An Introduction*. Minneapolis: U of Minnesota P, 1983.

Eakin, Emily. "Look Homeward, Edward," *New York Magazine* 27 September 1999.

Eakin, Paul John. *How Our Lives Become Stories: Making Selves*. Ithaca: Cornell UP, 1999.

Edel, Leon. *The Psychological Novel: 1900–1950*. London: Hart-Davis, 1955.

Elbow, Peter. *Embracing Contraries: Explorations in Learning and Teaching*. New York: Oxford UP, 1986.

———. *What Is English?* New York: Modern Language Association, 1990.

Ellmann, Richard. *The Consciousness of Joyce*. New York: Oxford UP, 1977.

Emerson, Ralph Waldo. "The American Scholar." 1837. *Selections from Ralph Waldo Emerson*. Ed. Stephen E. Whicher. Boston: Houghton Mifflin, 1957. 63–80.

Erdinast-Vulcan, Daphne. *Joseph Conrad and the Modern Temper*. Oxford: Clarendon, 1991.

Fetterley, Judith. *The Resisting Reader: A Feminist Approach to American Fiction.* Bloomington: Indiana UP, 1978.

Fish, Stanley. *Doing What Comes Naturally: Change, Rhetoric, and the Practice of Theory in Literary and Legal Studies.* Durham, NC: Duke UP, 1989.

Fleishman, Avrom. "The Landscape of Hysteria in *The Secret Agent*." *Conrad Revisited: Essays for the Eighties.* Ed. Ross C. Murfin. Tuscaloosa: U of Alabama P, 1985. 89–105.

Fluck, Winfried. "The Search for Distance: Negation and Negativity in Wolfgang Iser's Literary Theory." *New Literary History* 31 (2000): 175–210.

Fogel, Aaron. *Coercion to Speak: Conrad's Poetics of Dialogue.* Cambridge: Harvard UP, 1985.

Forster, E. M. *Howards End.* 1910. A Norton Critical Edition. Ed. Paul B. Armstrong. New York: W. W. Norton, 1998.

——. "India Again." 1946. Forster, *Two Cheers* 319–28.

——. *The Notebook Journal.* 1903–07. King's College Library, Cambridge. Excerpted in Norton *Howards End.* 269–71.

——. "Notes on the English Character." 1926. *Abinger Harvest.* New York: Harcourt Brace, 1936. 3–15.

——. *A Passage to India.* 1924. Ed. Oliver Stallybrass. New York: Holmes and Meier, 1979.

——. *Two Cheers for Democracy.* New York: Harcourt Brace, 1951.

——. "What I Believe." 1938. Forster, *Two Cheers* 67–76.

Foucault, Michel. "Truth and Power." *Power/Knowledge: Selected Interviews and Other Writings.* Ed. Colin Gordon. New York: Pantheon, 1977. 109–33.

Fraser, Nancy. "Singularity and Solidarity: Richard Rorty between Romanticism and Technocracy." *Reading Rorty.* Ed. Alan Malachowski. Oxford: Basil Blackwell, 1990. 303–21.

Furbank, P. N. *E. M. Forster: A Life.* 2 vols. London: Secker, 1977–1978.

Gadamer, Hans-Georg. *Truth and Method.* Trans. Joel Weinsheimer and Donald G. Marshall. 2nd ed. New York: Continuum, 1993.

Garnett, Edward. Unsigned review of *Chance* (1914). Sherry 277–80.

Geddes, Gary. *Conrad's Later Novels.* Montreal: McGill-Queen's UP, 1980.

Genette, Gérard. *Narrative Discourse: An Essay in Method.* Trans. Jane E. Lewin. Ithaca: Cornell UP, 1980.

Gibson, Andrew. *Joyce's Revenge: History, Politics, and Aesthetics in* Ulysses. Oxford: Oxford UP, 2002.

Gifford, Don, and Robert J. Seidman. Ulysses *Annotated: Notes for Joyce's* Ulysses. Rev. ed. Berkeley: U of California P, 1988.

Gilbert, Sandra. M., and Susan Gubar. *No Man's Land: The Place of the Woman Writer in the 20th Century.* New Haven: Yale UP, 1988.

Gilbert, Stuart. *James Joyce's* Ulysses: *A Study.* Rev. ed. New York: Vintage, 1950.

Girard, René. *Violence and the Sacred.* Trans. Patrick Gregory. Baltimore: Johns Hopkins UP, 1977.

Goldthorpe, Rhiannon. *Sartre: Literature and Theory.* Cambridge: Cambridge UP, 1984.

Graham, Kenneth. *Indirections of the Novel: James, Conrad, and Forster.* Cambridge: Cambridge UP, 1988.

A Guide to Liberal Learning. Office of the Dean of the College, Brown University, Providence, RI: 2003.

Habermas, Jürgen. "Modernity—an Incomplete Project." *The Anti-Aesthetic.* Ed. Hal Foster. Port Townsend, WA: Bay, 1985. 3–15.

——. *The Philosophical Discourse of Modernity.* Trans. Frederick Lawrence. Cambridge: MIT P, 1987.

——. *The Theory of Communicative Action.* Trans. Thomas McCarthy. Vol. 1. Boston: Beacon, 1984.

Hall, David L., and Roger T. Ames. *Thinking through Confucius.* Albany: State U of New York P, 1987.

Haviland, Beverly. *Henry James's Last Romance: Making Sense of the Past and the American Scene.* Cambridge: Cambridge UP, 1997.

Hawkins, Hunt. "Conrad's Critique of Imperialism in *Heart of Darkness.*" *PMLA* 94 (1979): 286–99.

——. "Forster's Critique of Imperialism in *A Passage to India.*" *South Atlantic Review* 48 (1983): 54–65.

——. "The Issue of Racism in *Heart of Darkness.*" *Conradiana* 14 (1982): 163–71.

Hawthorn, Jeremy. *Joseph Conrad: Narrative Technique and Ideological Commitment.* London: Edward Arnold, 1990.

——. "*Ulysses,* Modernism, and Marxist Criticism." Benstock, *Critical Essays* 264–77.

Hayman, David. Ulysses: *The Mechanics of Meaning.* Rev. ed. Madison: U of Wisconsin P, 1982.

Heath, Stephen. "Ambiviolences: Notes for Reading Joyce." Attridge and Ferrer 31–68.

Heidegger, Martin. *Being and Time.* 1927. Trans. John Macquarrie and Edward Robinson. New York: Harper and Row, 1962.

Henke, Suzette A. *James Joyce and the Politics of Desire.* New York: Routledge, 1990.

Herr, Cheryl. *Joyce's Anatomy of Culture.* Urbana: U of Illinois P, 1986.

Hirsch, E. D., Jr. *Cultural Literacy: What Every American Needs to Know.* Boston: Houghton, 1987.

——. "November Talk on Cultural Literacy." Lecture. Sacramento, 1987.

——. *Validity in Interpretation.* New Haven: Yale UP, 1967.

Hollier, Denis. *The Politics of Prose: Essay on Sartre.* Trans. Jeffrey Mehlman. Minneapolis: U of Minnesota P, 1986.

Howe, Irving. *Politics and the Novel.* New York: Horizon, 1957.

Howells, Christina. *Sartre: The Necessity of Freedom.* Cambridge: Cambridge UP, 1988.

Iser, Wolfgang. *The Fictive and the Imaginary: Charting Literary Anthropology.* Baltimore: Johns Hopkins UP, 1993.

——. *The Implied Reader.* Baltimore: Johns Hopkins UP, 1974.

——. *Prospecting: From Reader Response to Literary Anthropology.* Baltimore: Johns Hopkins UP, 1989.

——. *The Range of Interpretation.* New York: Columbia UP, 2000.

Iser, Wolfgang, and Sanford Budick, eds. *The Translatability of Cultures: Figurations of the Space Between.* Stanford: Stanford UP, 1996.

James, Henry. *The American Scene.* 1907. Bloomington: Indiana UP, 1969.

——. "The Death of the Lion." 1894. *The Novels and Tales of Henry James.* New York: Scribner's, 1907–1909. 15:99–154.

Jameson, Fredric. Foreword. *The Postmodern Condition.* By Lyotard. vii–xxi.

——. "Modernism and Imperialism." *Nationalism, Colonialism, and Literature.* Essays by Terry Eagleton, Fredric Jameson, and Edward Said. Minneapolis: U of Minnesota P, 1990. 43–66.

Jay, K., and J. Glasgow, eds. *Lesbian Texts and Contexts.* New York: New York UP, 1990.

Jay, Martin. "Habermas and Modernism." Bernstein 125–39.

Joyce, James. *Ulysses.* 1922. Ed. Hans Walter Gabler. New York: Garland, 1984.

Karatani, Kojin. "Uses of Aesthetics: After Orientalism." Bové 139–51.

Karl, Frederick R. *Joseph Conrad: The Three Lives.* New York: Farrar, Straus and Giroux, 1979.

Khare, R. S. "The Other's Double—the Anthropologist's Bracketed Self: Notes on Cultural Representation and Privileged Discourse." *New Literary History* 23 (1992): 1–23.

King, Kristin. " 'Lost among the Genders': Male Narrators and Female Writers in James's Literary Tales, 1892–1896." *Henry James Review* 16 (1995): 18–35.

Langland, Elizabeth. "Gesturing toward an Open Space: Gender, Form, and Language in E. M. Forster's *Howards End.*" *Out of Bounds: Male Writers and Gender(ed) Criticism.* Ed. Laura Claridge and Elizabeth Langland. Amherst: U of Massachusetts P, 1990. 252–67.

Larsen, Neil. *Modernism and Hegemony: A Materialist Critique of Aesthetic Agencies.* Minneapolis: U of Minnesota P, 1990.

Laurence, David. "Notes on the English Major." *ADE Bulletin* 133 (2003): 3–5.

Lawrence, Karen. " 'Beggaring Description': Politics and Style in Joyce's 'Eumaeus.' " *Modern Fiction Studies* 38 (1992): 355–76.

——. *The Odyssey of Style in* Ulysses. Princeton: Princeton UP, 1981.

Leavis, F. R. *The Great Tradition.* New York: New York UP, 1970.

Lernout, Geert. "Joyce or Lacan." Benstock, *Augmented Ninth* 195–201.

Levenson, Michael. *Modernism and the Fate of Individuality: Character and Novelistic Form from Conrad to Woolf.* Cambridge: Cambridge UP, 1991. 78–93.

Lloyd-Jones, Richard, and Andrea A. Lunsford, eds. *The English Coalition Conference: Democracy through Language.* Urbana: NCTE; New York: MLA, 1989.

Lothe, Jakob. *Conrad's Narrative Method.* Oxford: Clarendon, 1989.

Lukács, Georg. "The Ideology of Modernism." *Realism in Our Time.* Trans. John Mander and Necke Mander. New York: Harper and Row, 1964. 17–46.

Lyotard, Jean-François. *The Differend: Phrases in Dispute.* Trans. Georges Van Den Abbeele. Minneapolis: U of Minnesota P, 1988.

——. "Notes on Legitimation." *Oxford Literary Review* 9.1–2 (1987): 106–18.

——. *The Postmodern Condition: A Report on Knowledge.* Trans. Geoff Bennington and Brian Massumi. Minneapolis: U of Minnesota P, 1984.

——. "What Is Postmodernism?" *The Postmodern Condition.* 71–82.

MacCabe, Colin. *James Joyce and the Revolution of the Word.* London: Macmillan, 1979.

Malachowski, Alan, ed. *Reading Rorty.* Oxford: Basil Blackwell, 1990.

Manganiello, Dominic. *Joyce's Politics.* London: Routledge and Kegan Paul, 1980.

Martin, Robert K., and George Piggford, eds. *Queer Forster.* Chicago: U of Chicago P, 1997.

Marx, Karl, and Friedrich Engels. *The German Ideology.* 1846. Ed. C. J. Arthur. New York: International Publishers, 1970.

May, Brian. *The Modernist as Pragmatist: E. M. Forster and the Fate of Liberalism.* Columbia: U of Missouri P, 1997.

McCarthy, Thomas. "Ironist Theory as Vocation: A Response to Rorty's Reply." *Critical Inquiry* 16 (1990): 644–55.

——. "Private Irony and Public Decency: Richard Rorty's New Pragmatism." *Critical Inquiry* 16 (1990): 355–70.

McClure, John A. *Kipling and Conrad: The Colonial Fiction.* Cambridge: Harvard UP, 1981.

McGee, Patrick. *Joyce beyond Marx: History and Desire in* Ulysses *and* Finnegans Wake. Gainesville: U of Florida P, 2001.

——. *Paperspace: Style as Ideology in Joyce's* Ulysses. Lincoln: U of Nebraska P, 1988.

McGowan, John. *Postmodernism and Its Critics.* Ithaca: Cornell UP, 1991.

McMichael, James. Ulysses *and Justice.* Princeton: Princeton UP, 1991.

Merod, Jim. "The Sublime Lyrical Abstractions of Edward W. Said." Bové 114–38.

Meyer, B. C. *Joseph Conrad: A Psychoanalytic Biography.* Princeton: Princeton UP, 1967.

Meyers, Jeffrey. *Joseph Conrad: A Biography.* New York: Charles Scribner's Sons, 1991.

Mill, John Stuart. *On Liberty.* 1859. Ed. Alburey Castell. New York: Appleton-Century-Crofts, 1947.

Miller, J. Hillis. *The Ethics of Reading.* New York: Columbia UP, 1987.

——. "My Fifty Years in the Profession." *ADE Bulletin* 133 (2003): 63–66.

Moffat, Wendy. "Figure and Ground: The Transformation of the Dickinson College English Department's Faculty and Curriculum." *ADE Bulletin* 133 (2003): 11–15.

Moser, Thomas. *Joseph Conrad: Achievement and Decline.* Cambridge: Harvard UP, 1957.

Najder, Zdzislaw, ed. *Conrad's Polish Background: Letters to and from Polish Friends.* Trans. Halina Carroll. London: Oxford UP, 1964.

Newman, Robert D., and Weldon Thornton, eds. *Joyce's* Ulysses: *The Larger Perspective.* Newark: U of Delaware P, 1987.

Nietzsche, Friedrich. *On the Genealogy of Morals.* 1887. Trans. Walter Kaufmann. New York: Vintage, 1967.

Norris, Margot. *The Decentered Universe of* Finnegans Wake. Baltimore: Johns Hopkins UP, 1976.

O'Hara, Daniel T. *Lionel Trilling: The Work of Liberation.* Madison: U of Wisconsin P, 1988.

Page, Norman. *E. M. Forster.* New York: St. Martin's, 1988.

Palmer, John A. *Joseph Conrad's Fiction: A Study in Literary Growth.* Ithaca: Cornell UP, 1968.

Parry, Benita. *Conrad and Imperialism: Ideological Boundaries and Visionary Frontiers.* London: Macmillan, 1983.

——. "The Politics of Representation in *A Passage to India.*" *A Passage to India: Essays in Interpretation.* Ed. John Beer. London: Macmillan, 1985. 27–43.

——. "Problems in Current Theories of Colonial Discourse." *Oxford Literary Review* 9.1–2 (1987): 27–58.

Pecora, Vincent P. *Self and Form in Modern Narrative.* Baltimore: Johns Hopkins UP, 1989.

Person, Leland S., Jr. "James's Homo-Aesthetics: Deploying Desire in the Tales of Writers and Artists." *Henry James Review* 14 (1993): 188–203.

Piggford, George. "Camp Sites: Forster and the Biographies of Queer Bloomsbury." Martin and Piggford 89–12.

Plessner, Helmuth. "Soziale Rolle und menschliche Natur." *Gesammelte Schriften.* Ed. Günter Dux et al. Frankfurt am Main: Suhrkamp, 1985. 10:235.

Poirier, Richard. *The Performing Self.* London: Chatto and Windus, 1971.

Porter, Dennis. "*Orientalism* and Its Problems." *Colonial Discourse and Post-Colonial Theory: A Reader.* Ed. Patrick Williams and Laura Chrisman. New York: Columbia UP, 1994, 150–61.

Posnock, Ross. *The Trial of Curiosity: Henry James, William James, and the Challenge of Modernity.* New York: Oxford UP, 1991.

Poster, Mark. "Postmodernity and the Politics of Multiculturalism: The Lyotard-Habermas Debate over Social Theory." *Modern Fiction Studies* 38 (1992): 567–80.

Pratt, Mary Louise. *Toward a Speech-Act Theory of Literary Discourse.* Bloomington: Indiana UP, 1977.

Rajchman, John, and Cornel West, eds. *Post-Analytic Philosophy.* New York: Columbia UP, 1985.

Rawls, John. *Political Liberalism.* New York: Columbia UP, 1993.

Rich, Adrienne. "Compulsory Heterosexuality and Lesbian Existence." *Women, Sex, and Sexuality.* Ed. C. R. Stimpson and E. Spector Person. Chicago: U of Chicago P, 1980. 62–91.

Rimmon, Shlomith. *The Concept of Ambiguity: The Example of James.* Chicago: U of Chicago P, 1977.

Riquelme, John Paul. *Teller and Tale in Joyce's Fiction: Oscillating Perspectives.* Baltimore: Johns Hopkins UP, 1983.

Robertson, Pamela. *Guilty Pleasures: Feminist Camp from Mae West to Madonna.* Durham, NC: Duke UP, 1996.

Rooney, Ellen. *Seductive Reasoning: Pluralism as the Problematic of Contemporary Literary Theory.* Ithaca: Cornell UP, 1989.

Rorty, Richard. *Contingency, Irony, and Solidarity.* Cambridge: Cambridge UP, 1989.

——. "Habermas and Lyotard on Postmodernity." *Philosophical Papers.* Cambridge: Cambridge UP, 1991. 2:164–76.

——. "The Priority of Democracy to Philosophy." *Philosophical Papers.* Cambridge: Cambridge UP, 1991. 1:175–96.

——. "Solidarity or Objectivity?" Rajchman and West 3–19.

——. "Truth and Freedom: A Reply to Thomas McCarthy." *Critical Inquiry* 16 (1990): 633–43.

Rosecrance, Barbara. *Forster's Narrative Vision.* Ithaca: Cornell UP, 1982.

Rowe, John Carlos. *The Theoretical Dimensions of Henry James.* Madison: U of Wisconsin P, 1984.

Sacks, Kenneth S. *Understanding Emerson: "The American Scholar" and His Struggle for Self-Reliance.* Princeton: Princeton UP, 2003.

Said, Edward W. Afterword. *Orientalism.* By Said. 2nd ed. New York: Vintage, 1994. 329–52.

——. *Culture and Imperialism.* New York: Alfred A. Knopf, 1993.

——. *Joseph Conrad and the Fiction of Autobiography.* Cambridge: Harvard UP, 1966.

——. *Orientalism.* New York: Pantheon, 1978.

——. "Orientalism Reconsidered." *Cultural Critique* 1 (fall 1985): 89–107.

——. *Out of Place: A Memoir.* New York: Alfred A. Knopf, 1999.

——. "Representing the Colonized: Anthropology's Interlocutors." *Critical Inquiry* 15 (1989): 205–25.

——. *The World, the Text, and the Critic.* Cambridge: Harvard UP, 1983.

Sartre, Jean-Paul. *Being and Nothingness.* 1943. Trans. Hazel E. Barnes. New York: Washington Square, 1966.

——. *Saint Genet: Actor and Martyr.* 1952. Trans. anon. New York: New American Library, 1971.

——. *What Is Literature?* 1947. Trans. Bernard Frechtman. New York: Harper and Row, 1965.

Schleifer, Ronald. *Rhetoric and Death: The Language of Modernism and Postmodern Discourse Theory.* Urbana: U of Illinois P, 1990.

Scholes, Robert. *Textual Power: Literary Theory and the Teaching of English.* New Haven: Yale UP, 1985.

Schwab, Gabriele. " 'If Only I Were Not Obliged to Manifest': Iser's Aesthetics of Negativity." *New Literary History* 31 (2000): 73–89.

Schwartz, Lawrence. "The Postmodern English Major: A Case Study." *ADE Bulletin* 133 (2003): 16–24.

Schwarz, Daniel R. *Conrad: The Later Fiction.* London: Macmillan, 1982.

Sedgwick, Eve Kosofsky. *Between Men: English Literature and Male Homosocial Desire.* New York: Columbia UP, 1985.

——. *Epistemology of the Closet.* Berkeley: U of California P, 1990.

Seltzer, Mark. *Henry James and the Art of Power.* Ithaca: Cornell UP, 1984.

Shahane, Vasant A. "Forster's Inner Passage to India." *E. M. Forster: Centenary Revaluations.* Ed. Judith Scherer Herz and Robert K. Martin. Toronto: U of Toronto P, 1982. 267–77.

Shepard, Alan. "Gumbo? On the Logic of Undergraduate Curricula in English Studies." *ADE Bulletin* 133 (2003): 25–28.

Sherry, Norman, ed. *Conrad: The Critical Heritage.* London: Routledge and Kegan Paul, 1973.

Shklar, Judith N. *The Faces of Injustice.* New Haven: Yale UP, 1990.

——. *Ordinary Vices.* Cambridge: Harvard UP, 1984.

Siebers, Tobin. *The Ethics of Criticism.* Ithaca: Cornell UP, 1988.

Siegle, Robert. *The Politics of Reflexivity: Narrative and the Constitutive Poetics of Culture.* Baltimore: Johns Hopkins UP, 1986.

Singh, Frances B. "*Passage to India,* the National Movement, and Independence." *Twentieth Century Literature* 31.2–3 (1985): 265–78.

Sontag, Susan. "Notes on 'Camp.' " 1964. *Against Interpretation and Other Essays.* New York: Delta, 1966.

Spariosu, Mihai. *Dionysus Reborn: Play and the Aesthetic Dimension in Modern Philosophy and Science.* Ithaca: Cornell UP, 1990.

Spitzer, Leo. *Linguistics and Literary History.* Princeton: Princeton UP, 1948.

Spivak, Gayatri Chakravorty. "Can the Subaltern Speak?" *Marxism and the Interpretation of Culture.* Ed. Cary Nelson and Lawrence Grossberg. Urbana: U of Illinois P, 1988, 271–313.

——. *In Other Worlds.* New York: Methuen, 1987.

Stimpson, Catherine R. *Where the Meanings Are.* New York: Methuen, 1988.

Stone, Wilfred. "E. M. Forster's Subversive Individualism." *E. M. Forster: Centenary Revaluations.* Ed. Judith Scherer Herz and Robert K. Martin. Toronto: U of Toronto P, 1982. 15–29.

——. *The Cave and the Mountain: A Study of E. M. Forster.* Stanford: Stanford UP, 1966.

Suleri, Sara. "The Geography of *A Passage to India.*" *E. M. Forster: Modern Critical Views.* Ed. Harold Bloom. New York: Chelsea, 1987. 169–75.

Taylor, Charles. *Multiculturalism and "The Politics of Recognition."* Ed. Amy Gutman. Princeton: Princeton UP, 1992.

Thomas, Brook. "Restaging the Reception of Iser's Early Work, or Sides Not Taken in Discussions of the Aesthetic." *New Literary History* 31 (2000): 13–43.

Thornton, Weldon. "Discovering *Ulysses:* The 'Immersive' Experience." In *Approaches to Teaching Joyce's* Ulysses. Ed. Kathleen McCormick and Erwin R. Steinberg. New York: MLA, 1993. 122–28.

Tomlinson, John. *Cultural Imperialism: A Critical Introduction.* Baltimore: Johns Hopkins UP, 1991.

Torgovnick, Marianna. *Gone Primitive: Savage Intellects, Modern Lives.* Chicago: U of Chicago P, 1990.

Trilling, Lionel. *E. M. Forster.* Norfolk, CT: New Directions, 1943.

——. "James Joyce in His Letters." *James Joyce: A Collection of Critical Essays.* Ed. William Chace. Englewood Cliffs, NJ: Prentice-Hall, 1974. 143–65.

Valente, Joseph. *James Joyce and the Problem of Justice: Negotiating Sexual and Cultural Difference.* Cambridge: Cambridge UP, 1995.

Walzer, Michael. *Spheres of Justice: A Defense of Pluralism and Equality.* New York: Basic Books, 1983.

Wang, Ning. "Orientalism versus Occidentalism?" *New Literary History* 28.1 (winter 1997), 57–67.

Watson, G. J. "The Politics of *Ulysses.*" Newman and Thornton 39–58.

Watts, Cedric. " 'A Bloody Racist': About Achebe's View of Conrad." *The Yearbook of English Studies* 13 (1983): 196–209.

——. *Joseph Conrad: A Literary Life.* New York: St. Martin's, 1989.

Weber, Samuel. *Institution and Interpretation.* Minneapolis: U of Minnesota P, 1987.

Weiner, Justus Reid. " 'My Beautiful Old House' and Other Fabrications by Edward Said," *Commentary* Sep. 1999.

Wellek, René, and Austin Warren. *Theory of Literature.* 1948. 3rd ed. New York: Harcourt, Brace, and World, 1962.

Wellmer, Albrecht. *Zur Dialektik von Moderne und Postmoderne: Vernunftkritik nach Adorno.* Frankfurt am Main: Suhrkamp, 1985.

West, Cornel. "The Politics of American Neo-Pragmatism." Rajchman and West 259–75.

Wilde, Alan. *Art and Order: A Study of E. M. Forster.* New York: New York UP, 1964.

——. *Horizons of Assent: Modernism, Postmodernism, and the Ironic Imagination.* Baltimore: Johns Hopkins UP, 1981.

Wills, Garry. *Nixon Agonistes: The Crisis of the Self-Made Man.* New York: Signet, 1971.

Wilson, Edmund. *Axel's Castle: A Study of Imaginative Literature of 1870–1930.* New York: Scribner's, 1948.

Windschuttle, Keith. "Edward Said's *Orientalism* Revisited." *New Criterion* 17.5 (1999): 30–38.

Woolf, Virginia. *Mrs. Dalloway.* 1925. New York: Harcourt, Brace and World, 1953.

INDEX

Achebe, Chinua, 76–77
Adams, Robert Martin, 147
affiliation. *See* filiation and affiliation
Althusser, Louis, 81
Ames, Roger, 32
Arnold, Matthew, 35
author: construction of, 63–69; intention, 71–72. *See also* narration; reading
authority, 8–9, 12, 25–26, 132, 161, 164–65, 170. *See* also narrator: as authority; power

Baines, Jocelyn, 106n8
Balzac, Honoré de, 172
Beckett, Samuel, 173–74
belief, 4, 13, 16, 124, 143, 158–60; communities of, 31, 37–38, 72; contingency of, 10, 17, 85, 146, 149–50; and conventions, ix–x, 2, 178; in interpretation, 3, 27, 97; in reading, 11, 12, 94, 103, 116–17. *See also* commitment; conflict of interpretations; irony
Bennett, William, 179
Benstock, Bernard, 155n8
Bhabha, Homi, 46
Bharucha, Rustom, 130
Billson, Anne, 119n5
Bloom, Allan, 179
Bonney, William W., 93n1
Booth, Wayne, 6, 95–96

Born, Daniel, 129n2
Brown University, 180–81
Butler, Judith, 65n3

Caillois, Roger, 33n6
camp, 115–16
Casement, Roger, 108n10
Chambers, Ross, 71n8, 173
Chaudhuri, Nirad, 131n5
Cheney, Lynne, 179
Cixous, Hélène, 169n14
Clifford, James, 76–77, 173
Cohn, Dorrit, 170
Colvin, Sir Sidney, 95
commitment, 10–11, 14, 85–86, 90, 149–50, 160
community. *See* belief: communities of; consensus; heterogeneity of community
conflict of interpretations, 4, 104, 147, 183–85, 188; and cultural differences, 32, 101, 127, 136n6, 140, 178, 192. *See also* differences; hermeneutic circle; pluralism
Confucius, 32
Conrad, Joseph, xii, 18, 140, 142–43, 146, 173; double identity, 45–46, 48; irony, 78, 90–92, 140; politics, 74–75; skepticism, 20–21, 160–61; "Amy Foster," 46; *Chance,* 93–108; *Heart of Darkness,* 75–80, 89,